Project Adventure, In

QuickSilver

Adventure Games,
Initiative Problems,
Trust Activities
and a Guide to
Effective Leadership

Karl Rohnke

Steve Butler

 This edition has been printed on recycled paper.

 KENDALL/HUNT PUBLISHING COMPANY
4050 Westmark Drive   Dubuque, Iowa 52002

QuickSilver?

While at Project Adventure in Brattleboro, VT, for a photo shoot for this book, Steve Butler acknowledged a proposed title: *Son of Silver.* OK, but all I could think about was the Lone Ranger, horses, etc.

Having been a science teacher for many years, "Quicksilver" — the common name for mercury (Hg) — popped into my mind.

Quicksilver is a metal at room temperature; if dropped, it scatters in all directions. Its movements are quite unpredictable. This unpredictable nature, its ability to change, its intriguing characteristics seem to mirror the creative spirit I've encountered with these authors and at PA. And yes, there may be a hint of instability as well.

Don't dwell on the fact that mercury is environmentally unfriendly. Grasp the elements of fun, unpredictability and creativity that you'll discover inside this book.

— *Bob Henry*

CAUTION

Adventure activities by their very nature are highly active and participatory. Improper use of the activities described herein may result in injury. The activities should not be attempted without the supervision of trained and properly qualified leaders.

Neither the author, publisher, seller or any distributor of this publication assumes any liability for loss or damage, direct or consequential to the readers or others resulting from the use of the materials contained herein, whether such loss or damage results from errors, omissions, ambiguities or inaccuracies in the materials contained herein or otherwise. No warranties, express or implied, as to merchantability or as to fitness for any particular use or purpose are intended to arise out of the sale or distribution of this publication and this publication is sold "as is" "with all faults." The liability of the author, publisher, seller, or any distributor of this publication on account of any such errors, omission or ambiguities shall, in any event, be limited to the purchase price of this publication.

Printed in the United States of America
20   19   18   17   16   15   14   13   12   11

Dedication

This, my first book, is dedicated to my parents, who always emphasized the value to be found in books, and to my son, who I hope grows up with the same appreciation.

— *Steve Butler*

I was recently reading through the *Acknowledgments* on page 181 of *Silver Bullets.* In there I wrote: "…and particular thanks to my wife, Gloree, for putting up with and encouraging an inveterate 47-year-old Peter Pan." I'd like to repeat that acknowledgment (It's not easy living with an ersatz Peter Pan), so read as above, but change the 4 to a 5.

— *Karl Rohnke*

A Note From Steve

A number of people deserve thanks for assisting this project to completion:

Karl — for being willing to take on a rookie as a co-author and for spending numerous hours talking and brainstorming the ideas that led to this book;

Nicki Hall — for reading the first draft and providing some wonderful feedback and photos;

Jim Grout — for reading, commenting and always trying to move it forward, and for being patient when it seemed to go on and on;

Mark Murray — for discussions and suggestions on the leadership section and providing ideas for several activities;

Tom Zierk — for never getting too angry about the passing of deadlines;

Ken Demas — for being interested and sharing what he could;

Bob Henry — for sharing the idea that led to the title;

The Brattleboro Photo Gang — for showing up on a cloudy, raw New England day to play and be photographed;

and,

My wife and son — for giving up many hours of togetherness in the interest of this book.

A Note From Karl

The names that appear on this page represent individuals who accepted and implemented Project Adventure as part of their physical education programs in the early to mid-70's, and are *still* doing it. These people have taught thousands of Adventure education classes and have positively effected the lives of untold students.

This is not a dedication, rather a listing of dedicated teachers who were open to a unique curriculum before it was fashionable to be "adventurous", and stuck with it for 20 years.

I apologize if I have inadvertently left anyone off this list who should have been included. The names are listed alphabetically.

Sally Woodsum-Anderson — Hamilton-Wenham Regional High School

Mary Dugranier — Newburyport High School

Mike Dymon — Quabbin Regional High School

Jim Madore — Dunn Middle School

Steve McBride — Lynnfield High School

Cliff Mello — Hamilton-Wenham Regional High School

Pat Metcalf — McCarthy-Towne Elementary School

John Mulvaney — Newburyport High School

Tom Steele — SUNY-Cortland

Bob Welch — Newburyport High School

Jack Welch — Ipswich High School

Editor's Note: On Sexist Language

Those who use the English language to communicate, especially when their work dictates they pay close attention to proper grammar, are in a dilemma. The universal use of the singular male pronoun in all instances, which has been standard in past usage, is now precluded due to awareness of sexist language. The dilemma lies in the fact that there is no non-gender, singular pronoun to replace the now maligned "he/him." Current convention calls for she/he, him her, his/hers, she or he, him or her, his or hers, that person (when it works), and the alternating of either gender so as to give equal weight.

The expectation of proper grammar being clear, concise and unambiguous communication, this specifying of a gendered pronoun when the referred to person unambiguously has no gender seems, well, ambiguous. Is more confusion introduced by assigning gender to a specifically non-specified (therefor genderless) person?

In struggling with this dilemma as an editor, I have listened to what others do and say, especially those persons who by necessity or desire (commentators, for instance) adhere to strict rules of grammar. (Note the pointed avoidance of the singular pronoun in the last sentence.) Editing this book has presented enough instances of this problem to tax the most patient booksmith. Readers are therefore forewarned that this book contains likely every currently correct usage of non-sexist, singular pronouns. We have even occasionally lapsed into incorrect grammatical constructs by using a plural pronoun to refer back to a singular antecedent: "Give each participant a fleece ball and have them…"

If any reader takes offense at this inconsistent style, we sincerely apologize in advance to her/him, him or her, you. If you have any better ideas, please let us know.

— *Tom Zierk*
Project Adventure, Inc.

Contents

Initiatives   **145**

Why Write About Adventure Leadership?

By Steve Butler

Why should you read this book? Here you are, page one, what could we possibly write that would be valuable and worthwhile?

You folks ask tough questions.

Off the top of my head, here's a half dozen reasons to keep turning these pages:

- To learn over one hundred innovative new activities for your program, *cost effective training — good choice;*

- To look at all the pictures and see if your face is in any of them, *a bit self-gratifying, but people do enjoy seeing themselves in print;*

- To add another book to your shelf so that your colleagues and supervisors will think that you are incredibly knowledgeable in your field, *smart thinking — provided you don't try to lead any games when someone is watching; you;*

- To familiarize yourself with our hints and techniques of Adventure facilitation, *appropriate recognition that this is a serious, scholarly work;*

- To laugh and giggle when no one else is around at work, *pat yourself on the back, adding some play and fun to work is always a worthy rationale;*

- To examine our ideas and then write us telling us that we're off-the-wall, *thanks for the thought, but no need to write, we already know.*

Do any of those ideas sound sufficiently valuable to arouse your curiosity and intellect? If not, here's why we wrote the book.

In most bookstores you will find shelves of books covering just about every facet of leadership imaginable. You may find some or most of them thought provoking and temptingly buyable. You can probably uncover some eminently successful techniques and strategies in those books that will help enhance your skills as an Adventure facilitator.

Nonetheless, we are convinced that the art of Adventure leadership is subtly different from the topics usually covered by these premium-priced tomes. If you've ever attended a workshop led by one or both of us, perhaps this stated difference will be obvious. We tend to do things in a whimsically unique way, where charisma and fun count more than coercion and structure: that's what *QuickSilver* is about.

We hope that as you read this book you will reflect upon your own past leadership experiences and compare those experiences with our nitty-gritty recommendations. Evaluate the differences, smile within — including a deep breath, then take a chance or two with your future programming efforts. Congratulate yourself for being an innovative risk taker.

We want you to recognize yourself as being successful and effective in your leadership efforts. More importantly, we want you to have fun making Adventure programs more exciting for yourself and for those with whom you work; to be capable, creative, enthusiastic and effective.

You, the readers, are the reason for this book. We want to pass along the laughter, the fun and the joy that lie within every activity. Grab it! We can't give you anything more valuable. Then share it.

With this in mind, we hope our spontaneous and often zany approach to Adventure leadership proves acceptable enough so that you will challenge yourself to try something new, just try...

Have fun first!

Yeah, Why?

By Karl Rohnke

When Steve Butler and I began talking about collaborating on this book we both agreed to turn up the volume on fun and also try to keep things as simple as possible. God knows, you can buy a raft of books that detail how to be an effective leader, but it seems inevitable that to understand the heavy rhetoric you need to take a course in jargon in order to understand what the author(s) are trying to say. Why do we do that to each other? Someone gave me an article recently on Initiative problem implementation, and as part of the text, three entire pages were devoted to a jargon glossary: That's just not necessary.

Most of the writing I have done for Project Adventure in the past has been expository how-to text, so perhaps I'm better able to recognize what needs to be said and, more importantly, what needs *to remain unsaid* to make a topic understandable.

Communication, in part, involves understanding what someone is trying to tell you, and if you can't understand what we are trying to write because of an ostentatious show of in-the-know vocabulary, or because of a sanguine sense of what sounds sentient, then what's the use? Tongue-in-cheek? Alliterative? Irreverent? Fun? Correct.

You also have to accept that Steve and I enjoy playing. This devotion to play occasionally spills over, slides between the lines, and could be interpreted as an irreverent pedagogic attitude, but it's a benign facetiousness at play helping to keep phrases like "...a draconian presumptive application" at bay.

Plato was quoted as saying, *"You can learn more about an individual during an hour of play than in a year of conversation."* Martin Buber said that, *"Play is exultation of the possible."* Nietzche indicated that, *"Inside of every man is a child wanting to play."* If these very famous philosophers are so high on play and its by products, how come we relegate playful people to a lesser status than the individuals involved in a consuming work ethic? Tradition, I suppose, and perhaps ignorance of alternatives. But we continue this slavish attendance to the ten-hour work day notwithstanding overwhelming evidence that a playful, creative attitude produces a happier more productive worker.

It's also been proven beyond doubt that a half-hour nap or meditative session during mid-afternoon of a work day will cause a worker to be more rested, creative, happier and productive than by attempting to work through the PM blahs, or by trying to combat this diurnal lethargic time by dousing the circulatory system with caffeine in its various forms. After reading this last sentence, did you (answer honestly) think to yourself, "Yeah, but..." See why we continue this ultimately destructive work quest?

The ludicrousness of the situation is further manifested by management ignoring all the research which indicates that play, rest and meditation produce a happier more productive worker, then exacerbating the situation by applying not-so-subtle occupational pressures to "fake it" by looking busy all the time, producing "work" notwithstanding the quality, and putting in additional hours to make up for the reduced efficiency of a tired and bored individual.

Play and a playful attitude may not be the panacea, but it sure beats extra hours and too much coffee.

Play gets some people riled up. They don't know how to play, or even how to recognize its usefulness in others, so any situation that is not tied directly *and* seriously to a bottom line result is dismissed as frivolous and counterproductive. If reading this is upsetting you, perhaps you are a candidate for some play revival. Now you're really riled up, eh? Time to stop reading and take a nap or perhaps take a few minutes to play.

Introduction

"Do you have any *new* activities for my program?"

"Are all these activities written down somewhere?"

The answer is YES! At least for the moment, before anything newer appears in a workshop anyway.

QuickSilver includes ten year's worth of new ideas: Icebreakers, Warm-ups, Games, Stunts, Initiatives, Trust Activities, Closures and more. There's a plethora of programmatic play in these pages, enough to delight even the most avid game collector.

But hold on for a moment; there are other questions begging for answers.

"What are the important skills I need to learn to present Adventure activities effectively?"

"What are the basic concepts of Adventure programming?"

"What qualities are important in an Adventure leader?"

"How do I respond if a game I lead bombs, if there's no enthusiasm for an activity?"

"What does it take to debrief effectively?"

These questions are all important. The opening section of *QuickSilver* addresses leadership issues. The intent is to provide you with an understanding of the concepts of leadership, share a model of leading Adventure programs, and pass along practical tips to make your leadership more effective.

Reading the leadership chapters you will be asked to think about and evaluate what you know and do as a leader or teacher. If you're a novice to Adventure, you'll discover information that will help you understand what Adventure leadership is, how it works, and why it is different from other types of leadership. If you're an experienced practitioner, you'll gain insights into what you do and gather specific suggestions on how to address a variety of leadership issues.

QuickSilver isn't magic. Reading these pages won't automatically make you or your Adventure program successful. What this book will do is give you practical and useful information, ideas to evaluate and ponder, and most importantly, an opportunity for you to develop your own personal skills and understanding. Read, have fun, and share the Adventure!

Section One

Adventure Leadership

Introduction to Section One

"It's what you learn after you know it all that's important."

— *Earl Weaver, ex-manager of the Baltimore Orioles*

Since Project Adventure started in 1971, thousands of teachers, health care professionals, PE instructors, corporate trainers, recreation specialists and others have attended Project Adventure workshops.

Most of the participants enjoy the fast-paced action, the trust and bonding between people, the intriguing challenges, and the atmosphere of risk-taking set within a safe environment. However, when these people return to their jobs and sites to begin leading their own Adventure activities, they realize that there's more to being a good leader and facilitator than simply completing a workshop.

The essence of Adventure programming is pretty simple. You're teaching the basics of communication, cooperation and trust in a milieu of FUN. This isn't hard to understand. The program isn't complicated. Nor does leading a program utilizing Adventure experiences have to be confounding. The essential ingredients of a successful leader are easily

understood. It's the art and practice of leadership that's subtle and a bit more difficult to grasp.

You probably already have much of what it takes to get started. The same qualities of leadership that make anyone a good teacher, a good trainer, a good recreation specialist, a good counselor will help you become a good, if not excellent, Adventure facilitator. But if you're a game aficionado, simply eager to expand your personal bag of tricks, recognize that your leadership expertise is equally valuable as a burgeoning bag of Adventure activities.

We co-authored this book to share our varied experiences and insights. Our aim is to provide you with some simple, hands-on techniques. Use them, and we feel they will help differentiate *you* as an effective Adventure facilitator from someone who does an *OK* job.

Between us we have 43 years of experience, much of which has been OJT — On the Job Training, or learning to be accurate shooting from the hip. After all these years, we both agree that there is not one right way to lead a specific activity, but there is also no shortage of ill-conceived words, actions and behaviors that can short circuit even the best prepared and planned Adventure experience.

Our goal is threefold:

1. To offer hints and suggestions from our experiences on ways to improve your facilitation of Adventure programs;

2. To stimulate your thinking and creativity about your own leadership style and behavior;

3. To advocate strongly for the heart of the Adventure spirit — FUN.

So here's how, without a lot of baloney (you need a *little* baloney to grease the skids of humor). Our recipe for success includes a hearty and healthy desire to play, a large measure of creativity, a brimming cup of confidence, a heaping handful of humor, a spoonful of silliness, a pinch of experience, all spiced with a pungent dose of fun.

Now that you looked over the menu, select a tempting morsel and enjoy.

Chapter One

The Basics

To paraphrase an old saying: "It's not *what* you play that's important; it's *how* you play it." The field of Adventure is different from traditional physical education activities, from traditional methods of counseling, from traditional styles of teaching, and from the "old school" of training and professional development.

What's the difference? Two things:

1) The leader/facilitator doesn't provide all the answers to the group; primarily the participants learn from each other.

2) Adventure experiences intentionally contain a certain amount of spontaneous unpredictability. Spell that F–U–N.

In more traditional models of teaching and leading, the instructor is seen as the definitive source of all pertinent information. The teacher passes knowledge on, and the participants learn it. The participants, in this sense, are generally viewed as receivers rather than learners. As Adventure *facilitators*, leadership is different. Adventure leaders present activities in a way that allows the group to develop its own abilities, with guidance from the leader when appropriate.

Adventure leaders take people out of their standard frame of reference and ask them to engage in things new and different. You're not playing volleyball, basketball or football. Adventure programming involves people hitting a beach ball as many times as possible without allowing it to touch the ground. Adventure activities ask people to *create* an animal using their bodies. Adventure leaders encourage

utilization of the same skills — cooperation, teamwork, communication, trust, decision-making, creative problem-solving — that are taught more didactically in schools, seminars and training programs. The educational outcomes may be similar, but the approach is purposefully different.

The Leader's Role

Do not try to satisfy your vanity by teaching a great many things. Awaken people's curiosity. It is enough to open minds; do not overload them. Put there just a spark. If there is some good inflammable stuff, it will catch fire.

— *Anatole France*

In Adventure, what is the optimal role for a leader in a group? Are you the center — with everything revolving around you? Are you in front directing everyone to follow you — like a flock of geese? Are you the focus of attention? Are you, in fact, the *leader*?

This topic has raised many questions over the years. The strict definition of a leader is one who is in front guiding or directing those following behind. To some extent, an Adventure leader is conforming to this definition. When and how?

In the Beginning

In the first 15–30 minutes of a program, put yourself front-and-center to show people you know what's going on and to help put them at ease by providing a comfortable and confident persona that they can easily relate to.

Any analysis of group dynamics indicates that when a group first comes together it looks to the *leader* for direction and support. At the outset of an Adventure experience, you, as the leader, will be maintaining a high level of visibility and modeling the types of behavior you want in the group.

Your directions need to be clear and concise; your attention is focused on getting the group involved in activities as quickly and easily as possible. You would most likely be the focus of the group's attention — if they're focusing on you they are less likely to be worrying about how others are perceiving them. Your presence provides stability, security and purpose.

You might begin by telling them something about your background and training — provide them with a reason(s) to trust. The Experiential Learning Cycle, The Full Value Contract, Challenge By Choice — are all pieces of information that may allow people to understand and feel comfortable about what they are going to do together. In many instances, giving people background information can be a wonderful lead-in. It's easy to assume that this information is boring and dull compared with the activities you want to present, and thus to ignore it. But just because it's low energy stuff doesn't mean it is ineffective.

When might this type of information *not* be useful?

How about with a group of elementary school students? At a conference where you

only have 90 minutes to present? To a gym full of teachers (50 or more) for a half day of team building?

Even in these situations, while you might not use a lengthy verbal presentation, a case could be made for including one. For the elementary students, it could give them some understanding of the behaviors appropriate for the day. At the conference, it might give the activities more meaning and put them in a context where the participants see more value in the Adventure approach beyond just the "fun and games" aspect. For the 50+ teachers, it may create some mental "buy-in" if they are at all resistant to the idea of Adventure programming.

More often than not, we start our programs with this type of introduction.

> When not starting with a verbal introduction, get people actively involved as quickly as possible. Physical activity usually captures people's attention, so movement is a good starting point. *Pairs Tag, Birthday Line Up,* any name games (*Name By Name, Toss-a-name, Wompum,* etc.), *Circle the Circle* are common choices to kick off a program.

> What these games tend to have in common are: Simple rules, little or no equipment, no skills required and fun. They also allow you, as the leader, to join in. Being part of the group at this stage is a great way of opening the door for everyone to participate. When people see that you are involved, they are more likely to feel comfortable participating.

Over the years, I think I have started programs with almost every conceivable activity — from *Quick Name (a.k.a. Hustle Handle)* to *Lap Sit,* from *Human Knots* to *Porcupine Progression,* from *Pairs Tag* to *Moonball.* Each choice reflected my interpretation of what was going to start that group's experience with the appropriate level of energy and involvement. These ideas of how to start and with what activity is not a guaranteed recipe for success. You must be able to discern for yourself what will work best for you. If you don't like all of the activities mentioned above, then using them as an introduction would in all likelihood be a poor choice. Consider them as examples as models, of what work well.

Moving On

As a group progresses in its development, your role changes. By presenting trust activities, you begin to establish a comfortable and secure feeling among group members. They will not need to rely solely on your influence and presence to be safe, and the group can begin to be responsible for itself.

Progressing to Initiatives and low ropes course elements focuses the group on communication, cooperation and decision-making. Again, your role lessens if you want the group members to be able to develop their own abilities. Your presence becomes one of a supporter, an encourager, a coach.

The level at which you verbalize and demonstrate this support is determined by certain variables:

- The age and maturity of the group — the more responsible people can be for themselves, the more space you can provide for them to develop on their own. A group of elementary students generally needs more coaching than a group of adults.

- The readiness of the group — some individuals and groups are more able to process their own experience. If group members are able to manage safety issues, conflict and other issues as they arise, then a facilitator provides little more than guidance, because people are developing insights and generating questions on their own.

- The length of the program — usually, a group develops better skills over time. You need to be more directive and visible in a shorter program. But if the group has time to establish its own process, your role is more of facilitation than leadership.

- The goals of the program — a day of fun and activities for an orientation requires one level of involvement; a day of team

building with a staff that is at odds with each other dictates a different approach. It's essential to understand the goals of the group so that your actions can be focused on the outcome desired.

A question to ask yourself: "From what I say and do, am I *leading* the group — helping them to learn — or *facilitating* — helping them to learn from each other?"

My (Steve) initial training and experience had been leading New Games trainings, where the leadership style was more attuned to creating and maintaining a high level of involvement for and with the participants. It was difficult to change that pattern of facilitation. In particular, presenting Initiative activities was an uncomfortable role at first — having to stand back and allow the group to work on its own with little or no input. I sometimes felt that I wasn't doing my job as the leader of the group.

As was often the case in my own personal development as a leader, new ideas and ways of doing things dawned slowly. I wanted the group to succeed so they (and I) could feel successful. I wanted them to try it "my way" — either how I had learned it or how I perceived it to be easier for them — so that they could perhaps accomplish the task but also so that I could provide some direction and support to the group. I didn't want to sit still and observe because I didn't like the silence. I felt that I knew something — the answer, a technique, a strategy — and I wanted to share it. Sometimes I would intervene to offer a suggestion, a thought, an idea. Now I try not to.

I came to learn over the years that my interventions were not always appropriate or helpful. I would insist that my motives were nothing but the best (to help the group), but was I really working toward that goal? Did the group really need (or want) *my* help to complete their task? I came to realize that the answer was oftentimes *no*.

It took some careful observation of other leaders to recognize that my help might not be the best resource for the group. I saw other leaders "help" by not offering suggestions and hints, but by sitting back and then, during a debrief, asking insightful questions that allowed the group to understand what had just happened. While my input might lead to a successful solution and lessen or eliminate some conflict, at the same time my input might also diminish the accomplishment of the group. Would I become a crutch, an aid, that they would come to rely on? Was I setting myself up as a leader, without whom the group could not succeed? Was my leadership and direction masking issues and opportunities for the group to learn about itself, to develop and improve its own skills?

These questions are not easy ones to answer. What may work for one group in one situation may be inappropriate for another group in the same situation. What works for one group once may not be effective at a later time because the group dynamics have changed. The central question is: Are you helping the group to learn its own lessons or are you trying to teach them your lessons? In some cases they may be the same and your input may provide important insights. The answer should be (as much as possible) that the group learns best from itself with the minimal amount of help and input from you.

You might think this point refers only to Initiatives. Not so: The same ideas apply to the entire range of Adventure programming. Even simple warm-ups and icebreakers can be presented in a way that limits rather than enhances the group's ability to make the experience its own. As leaders, your goal is to create an atmosphere of fun and learning where people have a wide range of opportunities available to them. If they like some aspect of a game that is different from what you like, their choice is more important. So long as safety issues and concerns aren't being compromised, give the group as much flexibility as you can to define the experience for itself.

You can interpret this style of leadership as being limiting. It limits your ability to influence the group's decisions and your response to problems that emerge within the group. Challenge that idea. By limiting your direct input to the group during an activity, your facilitation can enhance the group's growth and ability to improve itself more than if you had *led* them to success.

Elements of a Successful Program

There are four basic elements of an Adventure experience. It is the goal of the Adventure facilitator to see that they all happen.

- Trust
- Communication
- Cooperation
- Fun

Trust

Trust is the safety key that opens the experiential door. It allows people to share pieces of themselves without fearing that they'll be laughed at or ignored. It creates opportunities for people to meet new challenges, knowing that others are there to support them. It means giving something a try, perhaps not succeeding, but knowing that the group will support additional attempts without ridicule.

Trust starts with you as the leader. From the start, if you model openness, encouragement, sensitivity and competence people will feel safe with you. They will also feel safe with and may open up to others in the group. Your role is to create an encouraging blanket of trust so that group members can learn to rely on each other. As the leader you also continuously monitor the trust to ensure that no one is hurt by the experience.

A sure-fire method to begin developing trust is to start your activity sequence by having people learn each other's names. Most people we know, ourselves included, feel somewhat intimidated by groups of people we don't know. *Toss-a-Name, Wompum, Peek-a-Who* and *Name By Name* are almost certainly to appear in the first hour of any session we lead. Name recognition develops trust.

There's no doubt that participants often look askance when we explain *Speed Rabbit*, do the *Dog Shake*, or embody the spirit of a *Gelfling*. People may feel embarrassed and uncomfortable for a while. But they participate. If you demonstrate by example that it's OK to look silly, people will feel more willing to take an emotional or physical risk. Demonstrate that you know what you're doing. Let them see your competence yet don't be afraid to look silly. Let them know you too are willing to take some risks.

Remember, people need to trust *you* first.

Communication

Communication is linked closely with trust. People working closely together need to communicate to prevent problems from arising. Communication allows people to share their viewpoints, to learn from the experiences of others, and fosters an environment where people can talk openly about their feelings.

Like trust, communication begins with you, the leader. Set a tone, help establish goals, and provide a framework for the participants. Your ability to communicate what to expect of the experience and how it works is a crucial element in making people feel included and safe.

Your *style* of communicating can be as influential as *what* you communicate. (More on *style* later.) Humor and personal warmth are invariably more effective than a strict and belabored approach. Invite people to join; don't force them to participate. This freedom results in a greater sense of involvement and usually allows people to feel more comfortable taking on new challenges.

Use mixer-type games early in the program to establish bonds between people. *Categories, Nonsense Numbers, Invisible Partners* are examples of some fun ways to encourage people to share a little about themselves. Hearing about others, recognizing there are similarities and differences, finding something in common with someone else — all these factors can contribute to a sense of belonging. Don't underestimate the value of allowing people to get to know each other. And remember, it can (and should) be fun.

As the leader, you want to open the lines of communication. How? Listen to what people are saying. Show that you value their comments and suggestions. Ask if they have any questions before starting a game. Be open to changing a rule or adapting the action if it will allow more involvement. Try not to restrict what people do — provide opportunities for them to decide for themselves what they want to do.

Embody the behaviors you want to see in others. People "understand" as much or more about you by watching what you do and don't do as they gather from listening to what you say.

Strive for simplicity. Keep things moving. Participate in the games. Have fun.

Cooperation

Adventure activities focus on people working and playing together. The goal is to increase each participant's ability to work as part of a group, and to develop in each person a better appreciation of what she or he can contribute.

People sometimes have the impression that because Project Adventure activities focus on cooperation, there is no competition in our programs. Competition isn't inherently bad, but we do feel that designating individuals as winners and losers isn't necessary. The

win-at-all-costs mentality causes many students to feel that they are not skilled enough to compete with their more talented peers and that physical activity is something to be avoided.

Cooperation doesn't have to replace competition. But since there are so many opportunities for people to compete and lose, why not offer some opportunities where everyone can compete and win? Competition can be structured so that everyone can feel good about their involvement. After hitting a moonball 77 consecutive times, it doesn't matter if everyone in the group hit the ball an equal number of times. The whole group takes credit for achieving the score, and even someone on the periphery of the action feels included in the group's success. Early in a program, this sense of accomplishment and success can influence profoundly the ability of the group to work together later in the program doing more challenging Initiative tasks like the *Spider's Web*.

Activities like *Moonball, Group Juggling* and *Warp Speed, Quick Line Up*, *Earthwinds* and *Birthday Line Up* provide attainable challenges for most groups. People feel good about their success. They work together, share in the accomplishment, and learn techniques that allow them to attempt more difficult problems and overcome greater risks.

Remember, though, that working together takes effort and is not always easy. It takes practice. Some people don't like to do it. Give the group time and expect some rough spots. Be there to support them when necessary, but don't give away the solutions.

Successful teams, performers and artists spend countless hours developing their skills before they can use them proficiently. Create opportunities. Provide challenges. Encourage creativity and praise effort, even when it may not produce a successful solution.

Fun

Leading Adventure programs is serious business. Don't let anyone tell you otherwise. If it wasn't serious, we wouldn't be in business. What's serious about it is that you're trying to help people learn and grow. Learning and developing new skills are serious endeavors.

The unusual thing about Adventure is that it's also fun. Fun, and play, are not supposed to be serious. To most adults, fun is considered frivolous — something with little long-term value. Fun is associated with amusement, recreation and merriment, not usually with education, at least not in the traditional sense.

Fun is central to the Adventure experience. Fun is important because people are involved when they're enjoying themselves. People are motivated, their attention is more focused, their energies are higher. Fun can be an end in itself, as well as a powerful tool in an educational program.

What are some of our most favorite *fun* activities? What do we go to if the group seems sluggish, nervous, uninterested or unenthusiastic? Anything that creates action, laughter and energy. *Pairs Tag, Pairs Squared, FFEACH, Peek-a-Who, Asteroids* and *Anklebiters, Pitfall* and *Wizards & Gelflings*. These are certifiable sparklers, games that produce intensity, gaggles of giggles and that flush of satisfaction that says, "Let's do that again!"

Whether you work in a school, hospital, camp, service agency or corporation, the fun component will be necessary if your Adventure program is to succeed. Fun is intertwined in everything that we do to the extent that some might say we have too much fun. For us, however, always keeping the fun quotient high is our way of ensuring that the quality of the program is also at its highest. You can have an Adventure program without fun, but we don't think you can have a very good one.

What is Fun?

By Steve Butler

To me, fun is a feeling and therefore somewhat hard to describe. Fun is laughter, energy, imagination, sharing, risking, challenge. It's spontaneous, focused, delightful, unpredictable. Fun is hard to manufacture, but easy to recognize when happening. Fun tends to be the kind of experience that you recognize being part of, but you may have a difficult time initiating.

Fun is contagious. People want to be part of it. You may risk looking silly to be a *Speed Rabbit*; you may feel nervous wearing a blindfold in the *Pitfall*; you may feel awkward jumping in *Hop Box*, but you'll try it if it looks like fun. Remember that fact. If you can present activities so people can see the fun inherent in what's happening, their fears, anxieties and concerns will most likely seem less inhibiting.

Fun is the invitation toward active involvement. It's the welcome sign that indicates it's OK to relax. Fun creates an immediate sense of togetherness and camaraderie that is essential to the group process. Even with the name games we play to start a workshop, the emphasis is on fun. Adding a rubber chicken or a weird ball to *Toss-a-Name* injects levity. The hilarity of guessing an opponent's name in *Peek-a-Who* establishes that there can be competition without fear of losing. Fun is essential to beginning a program, class or workshop. If you want to get folks enthusiastic about Adventure, start your course with a series of activities that have a high fun quotient.

Fun in Adventure is all this and more. It's a new experience with unpredictable outcomes — it's the uncertainty of finding your partner in *Hog Call,* the anxiety of a *Trust Fall*, the abject fear of stepping off the *Zip Wire* platform. Yet the experience is sequenced so as to produce trust and encourage involvement. You, as the leader, need to carefully prepare the group, physically, mentally and emotionally.

Fun can sometimes be hidden or seem to disappear. When a group has been working hard on an Initiative and is about to give up, fun may feel like an illusion. But fun is your tool to bring people back, to focus them again on what is happening within the group. Even in a serious debrief, highlighting some of the fun that occurred or asking people to draw a picture of what happened are ways to have participants put their struggles in perspective. With a serious set of program goals to achieve and a short time-frame, it can be easy to forget the enjoyment and focus only on the didactic learnings. Remember, when the fun disappears, people's energy and enthusiasm are often next.

It may seem difficult to justify fun during times of tight budgets, when people want value for their program dollar. But if one thing has been consistent for us over the years, it is that if the Adventure program is fun-filled, people always seem to want more. If they want more and participate more actively, the result is that they benefit more from the experience.

In all the successful programs we know, and for all the accomplished leaders we see, the one factor that remains constant is fun. It's what makes the experience come alive. It keeps people focused, engaged and connected to each other and the activities. That is why fun is not only important; *it is absolutely essential.*

Chapter Two

Functional Leadership

Even if you're on the right track, you'll get run over if you just sit there.

— *Will Rogers*

Can anyone be a good Adventure facilitator?

The answer depends on who you talk to. Anyone can improve his or her skills. Working at developing and improving skills should produce a good facilitator.

But how? What steps can you take towards enhancing your abilities? The sequence below may give you some ideas. It's a continuum and a process. Depending on your present skill level, you can fit into the pattern at any point.

Think of your growth as a leader as a process, not a result. No matter what your present skill level, there is always room for growth.

Training

Select your training carefully. When you want to develop skills, find someone who can teach you well. Good teaching should enhance your skills smoothly and effectively; poor training will need to be corrected and repeated.

Training assumes that you are dealing with knowledgeable instructors who can teach you what you need to know. They can transfer to you knowledge that will enable you to continue to grow professionally. Training provides information, and it is information that you need to get started.

Practice

Knowledge without practice is like a book without a reader. There's lots of potential inside, but nothing happens until it's used. Knowledge can help you develop skills, but skills need to be practiced or they fade and disappear. The best way to integrate knowledge and learn skills is to practice.

Lead groups. Volunteer to assist others who are leading. Practice on your job. Practice with your co-workers. Practice with any group that is interested. The more you put into use the knowledge you've gained, the better you can judge how to use that knowledge effectively. Practicing essentially is self-instruction; you teach yourself how to best use the knowledge and skills you learn. After all, this is *Experiential* Education.

Coaching

The essence of good coaching should be support, encouragement and feedback. If your coach does all the leading for you, you won't have the chance to experience the situation for yourself. What would *you* do in that situation? A coach works with you as a kind of safety net — someone who helps you out if you get in over your head.

If you can co-lead with someone who acts as a coach or mentor, your leadership development will progress considerably faster. If you cannot find someone more skilled than you,

Training ➡ Practice ➡ Coaching ➡ Experience ➡ Mastery

lead with a co-worker. You can then provide each other with practical insights, alternative ways of dealing with situations, and helpful advice intended to broaden your critical thinking process. Two perspectives are better than one and generally produce more insights.

If you work with someone more experienced than you are, perhaps she can give you better feedback. But remember that each leader has her own style. So what one person tells you, if that's your only source of information and feedback, may not give you a complete picture.

Experience

Experience is the *Catch-22* of leadership. You need it to be effective, but you can't acquire it without first practicing, without the benefit of experience.

Experience is valuable because it brings wisdom. Wisdom is practiced knowledge. A wise leader is someone who can anticipate what needs to be done, can effectively decide how

to do it, and can react appropriately when the situation changes unexpectedly.

If you are not an experienced leader, prepare to take some risks. You will need to lead before you become an experienced leader. You will have some great times; you will make some mistakes. Some days you'll feel great about what you do; some days you will wonder why you ever decided to lead Adventure activities.

Experience offers opportunities for reflection and analysis. The value of experience is greatly diminished if you don't take the time to evaluate what you've done. Learn from your efforts all that is available.

Mastery

Mastery is acquiring a skill, using it effectively and knowing that it is a reliable tool for future use. Remember to maintain your tools and constantly keep them serviceable. As a leader, maintaining your skills at peak performance means constantly seeking new knowl-

overconfident and assume that you have nothing more to learn. The best course of action for experienced leaders is to make constant journeys through all the stages of skill development.

As Max DePree states in *Leadership Is An Art*, "In the end it is important to remember that we cannot become what we need to be by remaining what we are."

A Leadership Profile — or How Would You Recognize a Good Leader if You Met One?

This part of the book is something that you can have fun with. Rather than the usual read-the-book approach, try something different — a little interactive, experiential reading. Participation is good for you.

As we were thinking about this book and the essence of leadership, we had lots of questions. Such as:

- Can anyone be a good Adventure facilitator?
- What skills and abilities do you really need to be a great leader?
- Is charisma necessary?
- How much expertise is needed to be effective?
- Do you participate with your groups and is this important for success?
- How can you be a good leader and not be the center of attention?
- Are there times when you need to be more visible, more the focus of the group? How do you know when it's appropriate?
- How can you change a bad play experience into a good one?
- What type of personal qualities or skills are needed to be effective? Can these abilities be learned? Do some people have what it takes and some don't?
- Are leadership skills used in one setting (physical education, for example) applicable in another type of program (corpo-

edge, new techniques and new practices. New knowledge allows you to evaluate and improve upon your existing abilities.

The price of mastery is practice and experience. Don't be afraid to take some calculated risks. Look for opportunities to continuously challenge your presentation skills.

Perhaps mastery is like personal computer technology. If you bought a computer 10 years ago, it may still work, but it will be woefully inefficient compared to today's machines. Even if you buy the best computer today, probably within six months there will be something new to make it obsolete.

Leadership skills don't become obsolete, but they do require maintenance. They benefit from use and new insights and ideas. Remember, mastery is not a final destination, it's more of a stop along the way. You can say that you've been there, enjoyed the experience, and can make use of that knowledge again when it's useful to you.

If you're a novice, don't feel overwhelmed wondering how you'll ever become a good facilitator. There is a progression that occurs; if you work at it, your skills will improve. When you're an experienced leader, don't feel rate training, let's say)? Are all leadership skills transferable between Adventure disciplines? Are certain skills client and/or program specific?

- Can a good leader make a bad game good? Can a bad leader make a good game bad?

- Is there, really, a "right" way to be an Adventure facilitator?

Have you ever asked yourself these or other questions? If you're reading this book, it's assumed that you're interested in improving your own leadership style and effectiveness, or at least interested in learning more about what you are doing well and what you might be able to do better. Recognizing that everyone has their own preferences about leadership, let's examine what you, the reader, respect and admire in a leader.

Step One — A Leadership Profile

The first step in this leadership odyssey is for you to do some thinking and evaluating. If there is some blank paper nearby or a blank space in the book here, grab yourself a suitable writing implement and get ready to sit back and contemplate for a few moments — BUT NOT QUITE YET!

First you need to know what to think about during your cerebral ruminations.

Bring to your mind at least one Adventure leader with whom you have had an experience. (Identifying a second or third leader who you respect and creating a separate list for each person can be helpful. But focus on one person at a time, and choose no more than three to start. Whomever you select, this person should be someone you think does an above-average job as a leader.

Identify an experience where this person was leading. Reflect, in as much detail as you can, on what that individual did. How did she create a successful Adventure experience? What did she do/say? How did she act/interact? What personal qualities did she exhibit? What professional skills and abilities did she demonstrate? Why do *you* feel she did a good job?

After thinking about the leader and the experience, list as specifically as possible all of the qualities or skills that you feel make *that person* a good Adventure facilitator.

Spend as much time thinking as you want or need. Close the book and really concentrate. Write down all the qualities that immediately come to mind, and then perhaps consider what subtle techniques are evident that make this person successful.

Leader #1

Space For Reflection

Was it easy? Did you generate a long/short list? Whatever you have, it's OK.

Step Two — An Ideal Profile

In creating your lists, did you think of any qualities or attributes that, in addition to those demonstrated by that individual, would be desirable? Make a new list and include any other skills, qualities, behaviors that you think an excellent Adventure leader *should* possess.

Make this list as comprehensive as possible. Include any qualities you value from Step One.

This new list can represent, for you, an ideal leader — someone who has all the skills, qualities and abilities of the *perfect* facilitator.

Leader #2

Space For Reflection

Step Three — A Personal Profile

This next step is more difficult for most people. (If you didn't do the previous steps, this next profile may not have as much meaning for you.)

Consider yourself as a leader. Think about experiences where you were leading. Think about what you do, what you say, what techniques allow you to be effective. Create another list. Again, focus on specifics, enumerating the qualities, skills, actions, behaviors and abilities that *you* feel help *you* to be the best Adventure facilitator that you can be.

A few words of advice on this step:

- Be as specific as possible.
- Think hard about yourself. Then think again. Don't miss anything.
- Don't be overly modest — give yourself credit where credit is due.

- Be honest — accept your strengths along with the areas where you can improve.
- No matter what you come up with, it's OK.

If you are a novice leader, with little or no practical experience, don't despair. Create a list of qualities based on what you *think* you can do well. Use the same advice above, and identify everything about yourself that will be helpful as a facilitator.

Put the book down again and create your personal leadership profile.

An Ideal Leader

More Space For Reflection

Step Four — Self-Evaluation

Look at all the profiles. How do you compare — your personal skills and abilities versus those of someone you respect or those of your *ideal* leader? What are the similarities? What are the differences?

Make note of the similarities and give yourself a pat on the back for what you are doing well. Remember the differences because these qualities offer you opportunities for improvement. And notice, too, any qualities that you admire but where you don't feel you have much skill. These may be specific ones to develop through training and/or working with people who can help you.

A Personal Leadship Profile

More Personal Space For Reflection

For most of us, it's safe to assume that the profile lists of others and of an ideal leader may outnumber your personal profile in terms of skills and abilities. That's as it should be. As facilitators, there will always be room for improvement. The comparison isn't intended to grade you. Its intent is to provide you with information that can help you assess your leadership qualities.

An Unscientific Study — Additional Comparisons

Conducted by Steve Butler

As is appropriate, I tried this leadership profile on myself and others before including it here in writing. It proved to be most interesting.

I discovered that some qualities I see in myself, others didn't. Some qualities I felt were weak, others identified as strengths. But mostly there was consistency between the lists. I enjoyed the comparison and analysis, so I started sharing the idea with other leaders inside and outside of Project Adventure.

Everyone who tried this exercise felt it was informative. Comparing and discussing the profiles allowed people to gain a glimpse of themselves and to conduct a more honest evaluation of their own skills. Some people discovered that they did not appreciate all the skills they possess. Others wondered if they should work on skills that they admire in others yet which they do not use themselves.

The other part of the profile that was exciting were the lists of qualities that people generated about themselves and others. As we reviewed what people said about leadership, the idea surfaced of conducting a *scientific* study and passing along the results.

They may not be scientific, but the profile lists that follow are a random sampling of what leaders at Project Adventure think are important leadership qualities. We don't make any claims for this summary of leadership qualities; like anything else, it's subjective and open to interpretation. They are included as another source of information. Remember that the profiles are guidelines, not necessarily step-by-step formulas for making an effective facilitator. You can't create a leader from a list of qualities.

In no particular order or ranking, here's a sampling of leadership qualities respected and admired by PA staff, trainers and workshop participants.

Profile A	Profile B
knowledgeable	creative
competent	laid back
experienced	innovative
enthusiastic	ability to shift quickly on the run
humorous	fun
creative	non-judgmental
charismatic	open, receptive
irreverent	willing to learn from others
keen sense of challenge	inspirational
willingness to experiment	grounded
willingness to let go of control	relaxed demeanor
puts people at ease	
physically and technically adept	*(Continued next page)*

(Continued from previous page)

Profile C	**Profile D**	**Profile E**	**Profile F**
open to ideas	personable	gently persuasive	friendliness
pursues creative moments	caring of group	team p≠layer	intelligence
knows his stuff	experienced	experienced	charisma
distinct speaking voice	playful	competent	patience
good sense of timing	witty	personable	insight
knows when to lead and when to keep quiet	models leadership	approachable	size
people listen to him easily	approachable	humorous	judgment
can be delightfully off-the-wall	sensitive	focused on group's needs	risk taking
experience	joins in with group	takes personal risks	empathy
imagination	casually competent	casually professional	
	focused	seasoned	
	relaxed	confident	
	spontaneous humor		
	empathy		
	casually professional		
	teacher		
	facilitates		

What's interesting about the profiles is that they are different. No one person embodies everything on all the lists. Each person has certain qualities that make them unique. Where some qualities appear more than once, it suggests that that specific quality may be more significant than some of the others.

The key message in these lists is to see the qualities as a package. There needs to be balance, there needs to be a combination of different abilities, there needs to be both personal and professional skills, and there needs to be an awareness and valuing of the fact that each person develops a unique set of leadership qualities.

What's Next?

Using this profile can help you gain a better awareness of your own leadership style. That was its original intent. Here are some suggestions for other ways to use this profile and learn from it.

- **Do the profile with your peers.** Make lists for yourself and for each other. Share the lists with each other as a way of assessing individual skills. Then, set some leadership goals and provide feedback to each other to help yourselves develop better skills.

- **Do the profile with your students or clients.** Ask them to create lists of leadership qualities to help you get in touch with what they need and value in a leader and to help them learn more about what leadership means to them.

- **Do it with yourself regularly.** See if you improve your skills, develop new ones, enhance old ones, change your ideas and ways of doing things.

- **Change the perspective of the profiles.** When doing it with your colleagues, develop two profiles of each other: 1) Those qualities and techniques you do well; and 2) those qualities and skills that you lack. Work with each other to develop yourself in the skill areas that need improvement.

(Continued from previous page)

Profile G

compassionate

humorous

grounded

experienced

skilled

flexible

sensitive

lack of pretentiousness

willing to learn from others

personal

excellent counseling skills

sets safe boundaries

ability to listen

committed

Profile H

humility

flexibility

challenging

sincere

concise

caring

supports group actions

makes everyone feel special

safety conscious

makes participant feel she/he is one of them

knows when to encourage, when to support

sense of humor

makes it fun

creative

Profile I

sees both sides of an issue

can make a decision

speaks clearly

consistently demonstrates his/her values

sense of humor

credits others

is honest

values opinions of others

flexible and adaptable

The purpose of this profile is to allow you a chance to think and reflect. It's an opportunity to learn something about yourself. The point is not to say your skills are less than or better than someone else's. It's about constantly looking for ways to improve. By improving your leadership abilities, you can make Adventure experiences more meaningful for those you lead.

Lastly, share with us your insights into how it works for you. What would make it better, more helpful?

Chapter Three

Core Leadership Functions

Before describing how to lead, perhaps it's best to define what a leader does. Listed below are what we consider to be core functions of Adventure leadership.

Boundaries

A good leader sets parameters that are safe, yet flexible; challenging, not overwhelming; thought provoking and fun; focused yet allowing diversity; planned but not rigid.

A leader has responsibility for moving things along at a pace that allows issues to surface and be dealt with meaningfully. Too slow may mean the group doesn't make any progress; too fast and issues may remain unspoken and unattended. The leader needs to provide a time structure that provides enough freedom for the group to do its work yet ensures that the program ends within its prescribed time.

A leader monitors issues and concerns to maintain an integrity to the process. The leader holds the focus when activities and discussions are supporting the goals of the group; intervenes and shifts the focus if the group or an individual is pushing an agenda that is distracting the group.

A leader establishes ground rules about safety. The leader should understand the physical safety guidelines for planned activities and should be comfortable managing any emotional issues that can and does commonly arise from group-based activities. Leaders need to know their own limits and structure the program to stay within those issues they have skill to manage.

Lastly, a leader should develop a plan for dealing with the goals and agenda of the group, while always recognizing that these goals may not include every issue that may be important to the group. A good leader can adapt the plan to accommodate unanticipated outcomes.

Trust

Like we said in Chapter One, a leader must establish and demonstrate trust, openness and honesty. Adventure activities require communication and a sharing of ideas and opinions. A group cannot function at peak performance without a commitment to each other.

Trust assumes a high level of caring for one another. The leader must attend to the needs of all the participants, modeling how they can become responsible for each other. People need to know that they can be themselves, can express their opinions, can give an honest attempt at an activity and be valued for that contribution. A leader's acknowledgment of an individual's efforts sets a tone of respectful interactions and full commitment.

Energy

A leader provides a spark to the potential of a group and then feeds the fire as needed. A leader seeks to maintain momentum, to keep the atmosphere fun and enjoyable. Strike a balance between action and discussion, between experience and learning. Gear your attention towards maximum involvement and participation to keep everyone engaged at a high level of interest.

In the words of Pam Kelly (a workshop participant), "A leader doesn't just give energy to the group; a leader takes the group's energy and gives it back." The leader works with whatever energy the group has at the moment, attempting to keep it flowing in a positive direction, and working with the group whenever the energy becomes stuck. Sometimes the leader is the focus for shifting the energy; at other times, the leader merely points out a path that allows the group to change its own direction. A good leader knows the difference between these two situations and acts accordingly.

Meaning

A leader helps the group to understand the lessons emerging from its experiences. The leader's role is to assist individuals seeking to transfer insights from an activity back to the real world.

A leader starts by assisting people to set goals and understand the significance of their actions and behaviors. A leader can help bring clarity, point out alternative perspectives, raise questions. A leader's observations aren't directed at telling people what happened, but attempting to help people interpret the experience for themselves.

A leader's involvement with the group can be critical in working through the Reflection-Generalization-Application stages of the Experiential Learning Cycle. People can become so caught up in the activities that they lose sight of the learnings available to them. A good leader maintains perspective and helps the group focus on the learning opportunities that present themselves during the program.

Shared Responsibility

An Adventure leader is not solely responsible for leading the group. Adventure experiences require a commitment from the group members. The leader provides a framework and activities, but the group must contribute their energy or the activities will seem ineffectual.

A leader moves *with* the group. At times you pull them along behind you. Sometimes you stand with them and guide. Ideally, you allow the group to develop its own skills and take responsibility for itself. You strive to provide a destination and allow them to set their own course to arrive there.

In Adventure, a leader who is too strong will deprive a group of its opportunity to grow by not allowing them to fully test their abilities. A leader who is too weak will not allow a group to grow by not providing sufficient challenge to test the group's abilities. The gifted leader keeps a balance — working with the group to allow people to go beyond what they think they are capable of, but without feeling over the edge.

The authors gratefully acknowledge the contributions of Mark Murray, PA staff trainer, for his thoughtful insights on a leader's functions that helped shape these descriptions.

A Leadership Model

A leader is best

When people barely know that he exists,

Not so good when people obey and acclaim him;

Worse when they despise him.

"Fail to honor people,

They fail to honor you."

But of a good leader, who talks little,

When his work is done, his aim fulfilled,

They will all say, "We did this ourselves."

— Lao-Tzu, Chinese Philosopher

Perhaps in some ways, leadership is not even the proper word for what's described here. The role of the Adventure leader/facilitator is one of guiding, coaching, supporting, encouraging, challenging and helping. A dictionary definition describes facilitation as "increased ease of performance of any action resulting from... the continued successive application of the necessary stimulus." Adventure leadership is facilitation. Adventure leaders provide the constant "stimulus" that allows people to learn, grow and develop with "increased ease."

Knowing when to be visible, when and how to provide support and guidance without controlling the outcome are challenges to all Adventure leaders. Adventure leadership is an art, not a science. A good facilitator is someone who is present when needed but indistinguishable from the group members at other times. Ideally, the best growth for the group comes from within, not from the leader.

This image of the Adventure facilitator brings us to a simple model of leadership. There are five steps, each contributing to a leader's ability to do a good job of facilitating.

The first three steps occur before a program begins.

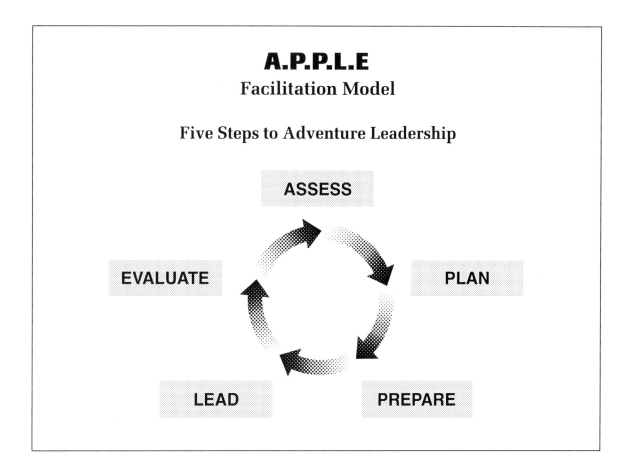

A.P.P.L.E
Facilitation Model

Five Steps to Adventure Leadership

ASSESS

PLAN

PREPARE

LEAD

EVALUATE

Assess

The first step helps you gather information about the group. The questions below are ones that may be helpful to answer in order to provide the best possible experience.

- *Who is the group?* — What age? What is the mix of age, sex, interests? Are they coming voluntarily or are they being told to go? Do they want to be there?

- *What do they want to accomplish?* — What are the goals for the program? Are the goals of the group's leader the same as those of the participants? Are the goals consistent or contradictory? Are you comfortable working to accomplish these goals? (Some program objectives may be more than you feel capable of handling.)

- *How many participants will there be?* — Is it a group of 10 or 200? Can the goals

realistically be achieved with a group of this size?

- *How long will the program last?* — Is it too short to accomplish the goals? Is it too long? Do you have enough quality material — games, Initiatives and practical applications — to fill the program?

- *Where will the program take place?* — Is it indoors or out? Do you need more space? Do you need a back-up space in the event of larger numbers or bad weather? Is the space safe for the activities planned?

- *Are there any special considerations?* — Is there anything special you need to know about this group? Have they done Adventure activities before? What do they know about what they will be doing?

There are a variety of assessment techniques. Written or oral interviews, questionnaires, attitude surveys and the like can be used prior to the start of a program.

Assessment can also occur during an Adventure experience if it proves impractical beforehand. Discussing objectives, activities such as *The Being*, and engaging people in setting personal goals can give you pertinent information about the group. The disadvantage of acquiring details in this manner is that it gives precious little time to analyze, evaluate and react.

The more you can identify what the group wants and who they are, the better you can predict what types of activities might be appropriate.

Plan

Planning allows you to select the tools you want to use. With the details gleaned from your assessment, you can begin to focus your activity selection on addressing the needs of the group. Also, you can consider designing specific scenarios for the activities that may have more relevance to the group and assist in the transfer of learnings from the activities back to the group's real world environment.

You can now answer another series of questions:

- What activities will focus the group on the issues they want to examine?

- What icebreakers will be necessary to set a tone and establish trust?

- How many activities, hence how much time, will be needed to bring the group together?

- Will you need to be ready to deal with resistance from some members of the group? How will you address this?

- Will they respond better to active games and Initiatives or will you need to moderate the activity level due to age, ability or even weather conditions?

- How much information do they need, or want, about the program and you?

- How much time can you allow per activity and ensure that you include everything you want to cover?

- What sequence of activities will produce the best results?

- How will you wrap up the experience? What activity or format will bring the program to closure?

To some degree, everyone has a plan in mind. Whether we sit down and prepare a detailed list of activities or simply rely on instinct and gut reaction, all leaders use some method to decide which activities they will use.

Decide for yourself which style works best. Novice leaders may want to spend more time planning and preparing. As you become more skilled, you still may find it comforting to develop a plan, but you may become more willing and ready to adopt a spontaneous switch from your prepared sequence.

What has worked well for us over the years is to brainstorm several activities that we think will work at each stage of a program. Select a few name games, several icebreakers and warm-ups, and some games and lead-up Initiatives before you begin a session. Try to select activities that will cover all eventualities, giving yourself several options no matter what happens.

Three thoughts to keep in mind about planning:

1) **Be prepared to alter your plan.** The surest way to derail Adventure activities is to have a set of expectations and refuse to recognize that reality is different from what you expected. Be prepared, but don't be regimented. *The best lesson plan is the one you wear on your hip.* Sometimes, giving up your plan is the best plan you can have.

2) **Have fun.** *Plan* fun into your program. If you see your planned sequence producing lackluster results, go for whatever provides action, energy and interest. Adventure comes in many forms, but all of the best experiences contain fun. Fun doesn't always mean games; discussions, creative arts, journal writing have all been successfully incorporated into Adventure programs. Remember that people are different. Varying your techniques to create an educational experience will allow you to respond more successfully to individual needs.

3) **Planning doesn't mean you have to approach everything seriously.** Have a healthy appreciation of spontaneity, flexibility, unpredictability, *joie de vivre*, *laissez-faire*, serendipity. *Rely on the spirit of Adventure, not the plan.* The spirit is more reliable.

Prepare

Preparing, different from planning, begins the implementation stage. For many leaders, this step creates some peace of mind. Don't skip it in hopes of lessening your workload, especially as a novice leader. Preparing puts into place all the elements of the planning phase so that everything is ready to go.

Preparing augments the planning phase. Some may say it's redundant. (Steve, unlike his co-author, has been accused of being a tad overly organized during his career.) Preparation means doing whatever else is necessary to be ready to go when the group arrives. By taking this step, you may find you can reduce some anxieties so that you can concentrate on the important things.

What's involved in preparation?

- Assemble whatever materials you need or want.

- Confer with your co-leaders (if there are any) to ensure that the plan is understood.

- If possible, inspect the site beforehand to determine if your activity selection is appropriate.

Why worry about finding the props you need just before leading the game? Why bother to plan at all if you don't gather the materials you'll need to implement your ideas? Who needs to be distracted by the little minutiae? Call it compulsive or whatever you want, just do what you need to do in order to feel relaxed before your program begins. If you're comfortable before the group arrives, you may find the anxiety of leading to be reduced.

Lead

Leading implements all the work done in preparation. This step is the crux. You don't really know how well you've done until you get out there and lead.

As you lead, ask yourself this question, "Why am I doing what I'm doing?" Do you have an answer? Is it a good answer? If your answer satisfies you, then what you are doing is legitimate.

If your answer pleases you, then your leadership may be effective. You have a reason and you're satisfied with the reason. Do you have results? Be careful that your satisfaction doesn't preempt the needs of the group.

If your answer is that the group is responding well to what is happening, then you will be successful. You have a reason, you have satisfaction, *and* you have results.

The key to leading is to react. Watch what is happening, ask yourself why you're doing what you're doing, then react to your observations and your answer to the question. Leading successfully relies on reacting effectively.

Practically speaking, leading involves:

- Creating appropriate scenarios to enhance the learning potential of the activities;

- Presenting the rules to the activities and monitoring any rule infractions;

- Observing the group to gauge the success of the program as it progresses;

- Determining if an intervention is needed, then deciding when and how to make the intervention so that it supports the growth of the group;

- Debriefing the activities so that people can learn from their shared experiences.

Evaluate

The last step occurs both while you lead and after the program ends.

Evaluating indicates that you always monitor what you are doing. You're observing the group to check behaviors, you're analyzing the behaviors to determine if you need to alter your

activity selection, and you're providing both appropriate challenges and discussions when needed to assist the group in examining its performance and behaviors.

Post-program evaluation gives you the opportunity to reflect on what happened. It's the final step of the leadership model, as well as the final stage of the Experiential Learning Cycle. As the leader, this step can contribute tremendously to your own growth. You can double check your planning process to see if you were on target in your preparation. You can consider if your leadership responded to the specific needs of the group during the program. You can examine both the successes and the mistakes to determine what you might do differently next time.

This final step is often overlooked. When the program ends, it can be difficult to sustain the energy needed to review what you did. Consider this suggestion: Every program you lead is as much an opportunity for you to learn as it is for the participants in the group. The experience will be more fun, more engaging and more challenging if you see yourself as a learning partner, not as the teacher or instructor.

To benefit from the lessons available, evaluate what you did. In the role of an Adventure leader, you can never know or learn too much.

A.P.P.L.E. Facilitation Model / Reference Guide

ASSESS

- who are they?
- identify program goals
- logistics:
  - time
  - location
  - number of leaders
  - number of participants

PLAN

- what will work?
- what will be fun?
- does it meet the goals?
- Sequence of Activities:
  - what do I start with
  - how much time for "icebreakers"
  - how much time per activity
  - how does it wrap-up
- what information do they need to know about you?

PREPARE

- gather props and materials
- prep co-leaders
- have a back-up plan (for bad weather)
- check the location

LEAD

- invite, don't impel
- set a tone:
  - build trust
  - make people feel comfortable
  - model appropriate behaviors
- style:
  - clear and simple
  - be enthusiastic
  - use humor and fantasy
  - communicate (listen and respond)
- provide appropriate challenges
- be creative
- experiment and model risk taking
- Ask yourself: Why am I doing what I'm doing?" – Have a good answer.
- Be prepared to change your plan
- Observe and listen
- Have fun

EVALUATE

During the Program:

- monitor the group and adjust activity selection accordingly

- debrief when appropriate
  - what is group ready for
  - is it safe to discuss
  - focus on 1–2 topics
  - ask "What / So What / Now What"
- REACT – adapt to what happens with the group

After the Program:

- what worked?
- what would have worked better?
- what would you do differently next time?

Chapter Four

Facilitate or Recreate?

Instill fun, but amidst the frivolity remember that the established enjoyment factor is your lever to further learning. If your eager and smiling group moves enthusiastically from game, to Initiative, to game, etc. without any inclination as to what they are trying to accomplish as a group, you are presenting an entertaining recreation program and not much else.

If you are working in a summer camp program or elsewhere, and full-bore recreation is all you want or need, keep up the pace, some good things are bound to happen. But if you want your audience (elementary to corporate)

to experience the benefits of problem solving, the enjoyment of positive competition, and the individual exhilaration of achieving beyond anticipation, your role as facilitator must eventually be honed and developed to anticipate, motivate and manage the various people-to-people situations that predictably occur, and which closely mirror those typical scenarios that make up our day-to-day existence.

Start off playing for the fun of it, but recognize that once you become a games person there is a plethora of useful insights and learnings that are initially secondary to the fun, but soon

become the raison d'être toward achieving your curriculum or bottom-line goals.

Facilitate or recreate? What's the distinction between the two. In a word — *Debriefing*.

Many people comment that debriefing is the most difficult leadership skill to learn to do well. Since it is a skill that doesn't come easily, many Adventure leaders avoid debriefing.

Some of the reasons why people avoid debriefing include:

- I don't do it well;

- I'm afraid I'll get in over my head (an issue will emerge that I cannot manage safely);

- I don't feel debriefing is fun;

- I can't get people to share opinions and talk freely.

All these concerns are valid; simply stated, however, *don't avoid debriefing*. Your Adventure program will be better with it than without it.

If you don't feel comfortable leading a debrief, it may mean that you're uncertain of how to do it. Fear of the unknown is predictable, and fear will interfere with your ability to debrief effectively. Get some training. Learn about debriefing — why it's important, how it's done, what makes it work. Try it. Get some feedback and observe how others do it. Try it again. Remember the cycle for a leader's development: training… practice… coaching… experience… mastery.

Elements of a Good Debrief

Understanding the components of a good debrief is a helpful place to begin feeling more comfortable about this essential skill.

Boundaries

People need to feel safe to discuss issues openly and honestly. The Full Value Contract is an effective tool for establishing guidelines for group behaviors and discussions. Setting out the parameters of acceptable behavior is a key factor early in a program.

Just identifying these boundaries isn't enough. People have to accept them and agree to adhere to them. As the leader, you need to model openness, honesty, compassion, directness. People will look to see if you uphold the established guidelines. If *you* establish the guidelines, you had better abide by them. Demonstrate by word and example that you will follow the guidelines and that you will not allow anyone to stray beyond the accepted limits.

Lastly, know your own personal boundaries. Deal only with topics and issues that you can manage comfortably. Use your common sense. If an issue arises that you cannot deal with effectively, seek out help and support from someone with more skill.

Permission

Closely related to boundaries, permission implies that people agree to discuss issues. Permission is acceptance of the debriefing process. If your group does not want to talk about its experiences, no amount of leadership skill will open their minds and mouths.

Be certain that the group and individual goals for the program include agreement to discuss relevant issues that emerge. Sometimes the leader creates permission for the group by framing the idea of the Full Value Contract. The group may give itself permission simply by showing up to participate in the Adventure experience.

Recognize that if the leader doesn't establish this permission, the result may be little or no participation in the debriefing process.

Purpose

A debrief without purpose is simply random discussion. An open-ended debrief can produce significant learnings, but the outcomes are less predictable. Identifying a purpose for the group creates focus.

Purpose often arises from group and individual goals. When participants have goals in mind, the debrief can concentrate on those goals. This purpose fuels the debrief because people are examining the experience as it relates to their goals.

Goal setting can be elaborate and formal — each individual publicly stating a personal or professional goal to the group. Goal setting can be experiential — using an activity like *The Being*, members of the group work together to define the types of behaviors and interactions they want as part of their experience. Goal setting can be simple — brainstorming ideas and thoughts to be pursued during the program.

The essential element for a successful debrief is to have a purpose. Purpose generates opportunity for learning and creates meaning from the experience.

Focus

A good debrief needs focus to ensure that the relevant learnings are brought to the surface and understood. Debriefs focus on the "here and now" — that is, they examine the direct group experience.

If group members want to drift off track to other topics, the leader needs to refocus the group's attention. If someone makes a statement or asks a question, the leader needs to hold attention on that comment if it is relevant and important. If the issue is difficult or unpleasant, people will often attempt to shift the focus to avoid confronting the issue or the feelings associated with it. Avoidance doesn't make an issue disappear.

A good leader and a good debrief holds attention on topics, difficult and easy, and doesn't allow irrelevant ideas to intrude on the process.

A good debrief also allows transference of learnings to the *real world*. While it's important for individuals to understand their actions and the consequences of their behaviors in the context of the Adventure program, the greater value in these learnings comes from connections made to real world experiences. Knowing when and how to focus on this transference, helping people understand the *application* of what they are learning, is the critical final step in any debriefing process.

Responsibility

It's important to remember that Adventure programs are *shared* experiences. The leader does not own the sole responsibility for making the experience work. Group members must take ownership and responsibility for their own learning.

A debrief works best when the participants are doing most of the talking. Sometimes the discussion needs prompting from the leader. Open-ended questions, opportunities to describe feelings, creating a visual or written symbol of an event are techniques that encourage group members to share their thoughts and opinions.

If you find yourself doing most of the talking, hear yourself pointing out all the learnings, you may want to re-examine your leadership style. Good debriefing isn't telling people what to learn, it's encouraging people to learn from themselves.

Individuals need to understand their roles and responsibilities in creating a quality debrief.

Structure

Just as you sequence activities, debriefs need a structure and format that works for the group. Initial debriefs with a group should be simple, focused and brief. Create a climate that allows and invites sharing.

As the group develops, expand on the length of the debrief and present opportunities for exploring more complex issues. Although the format may change, maintain simplicity. Focusing on one or two topics ensures clarity and understanding. If a debrief attempts to deal with all the potential issues at hand, people will feel confused, overwhelmed and lose interest in the process.

Closure

Debriefs need a good ending. Asking, "Are there any last thoughts before we move on?" is a good technique to ensure nothing is left unsaid.

Closing a debrief doesn't necessarily mean that all issues have been resolved. Sometimes a group or individuals will need several experiences to work through an issue. Effectively closing a debrief means that everyone in the group is ready to move on — that whatever topics are on the table are comfortable enough that people are willing to move forward to another experience.

It's good to remember that closure doesn't always mean resolution. Closure brings a safe and satisfactory ending, with the recognition that an issue can be re-examined at a later time if necessary and appropriate.

The Levels of a Debrief

Leaders can get confused and uncomfortable about debriefing because they don't understand the dynamics of the issues. Debriefs operate at three levels: Group, interpersonal and intrapersonal. Recognizing these levels and understanding the differences makes it easier to lead an effective debrief session.

Group

Group dynamics focus on what is happening with the entire group. It looks at the interpersonal dynamics affecting the group's cohesiveness. The group level can operate mostly on a cognitive level, that is, people can conceptualize the problems and rationally attempt to solve issues that arise.

Due to this ability to rationalize the experience, group issues can sometimes seem safer. Typical topics that emerge include: Communication, leadership, teamwork, planning, goal achievement and acceptance of ideas.

While group oriented debriefs may appear less volatile, recognize that other issues can linger just beneath the surface, such as devaluing behaviors, group trust and support, cliques, sexism, peer pressure and commitment to the group. Any of these topics can bring forward strong emotional feelings that will need attention.

In any program design, it is important to establish boundaries so that participants know what is appropriate and what is not. For a corporate team-building program, it may be overstepping the bounds to delve too deeply into emotional issues; but in a counseling setting, it may be ineffectual not to pursue those same issues.

Interpersonal

Interpersonal issues focus on dynamics between individuals. Sometimes these dynamics can profoundly affect an entire group, either holding it back or spurring it to move forward. Interpersonal issues can also be cognitive but are more likely to involve some degree of emotion and feeling.

Some examples of interpersonal issues are: Negativism, cliques, acceptance, trust and safety concerns, recognition and devaluing, peer pressure, fear of being judged and stereotypes. Interpersonal problems often involve perceptions that people have of each other and the way those perceptions affect people's behaviors and interactions.

Attending to interpersonal issues involves another level of awareness from the leader. At times, the group dynamics are tied directly to the issues between individual members of the

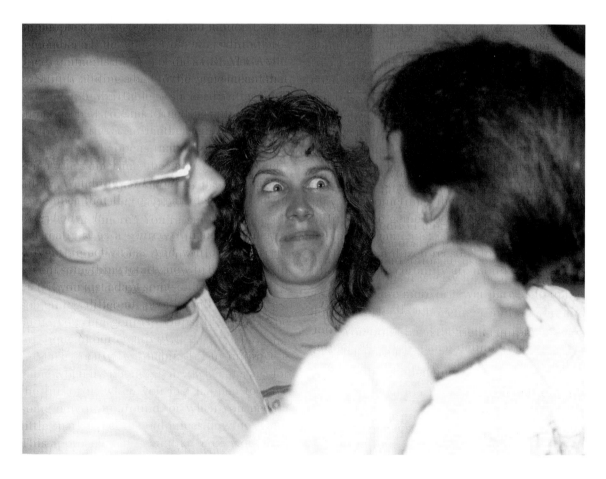

group, but the group doesn't want to, or isn't comfortable, confronting those individuals.

A good debrief can provide a framework where group members feel it is appropriate to confront and deal with such interpersonal issues. Depending upon the group, the leader may need to model effective techniques for addressing interpersonal issues so that the group can learn how to manage its own issues successfully.

Intrapersonal

Intrapersonal issues relate to a single individual. Intrapersonal issues involve personal feelings and need skill and understanding to manage effectively.

Intrapersonal issues can include: Fear, safety and trust, self-concept, acceptance, feeling devalued by self or others. These issues can surface unexpectedly, because for the individual involved, the issue is likely tied to experiences outside of the Adventure program. When the issue arises in the Adventure setting, it then becomes involved in the debriefing process.

Most leader's concerns about debriefing probably relate to fears about managing intrapersonal issues. There is a fear of the unknown, of opening up an issue that is too painful to deal with or that the leader feels incapable of managing safely and appropriately.

In the context of debriefing, it's important to recognize that these issues do exist and that they will emerge in Adventure experiences because we encourage people to share their feelings. As a leader, you need to know your own abilities and limitations. You don't need to be an expert counselor to lead safe and effective debriefs. You need only have enough common sense to know when an issue is beyond your capability and where and how you can provide additional support to help that individual.

Catching Fish

Earl Davis, PA Trainer and friend, shared this metaphor for debriefing, and it has proved helpful to many aspiring leaders.

How do you know what to focus on in a debrief? How do you know what issues to pursue? Adventure leaders constantly comment that it seems difficult to track topics in a debrief, and that it is difficult to identify topics so that a group will want to discuss them.

In Earl's metaphor, think of a debrief as a fishing trip. You're out in your boat on a lake. The lake represents the experiences of the group. As the leader, your task is to find some issues in the lake and reel them in so the group can learn from them.

Here are some hints: Start a debrief by asking some open-ended questions. How did you feel during the activity? What allowed the group to be successful? What just took place in this activity? Begin with a broad net — cast it out and see if there are any ripples on the surface. Avoid asking pointed questions: Did you succeed at this task? Was there good communication? Did anyone see examples of leadership? All these questions beg for Yes/No answers, and that is probably what you'll get.

If you see a ripple, cast your hook in that direction. For example, a subtle ripple might sound like this, "I felt frustrated during that activity." A statement such as this is an indication that for that person the group process was less than satisfactory. The issue is probably worth closer inspection. Ask follow-up questions to get additional information — throw your hook out again in the same area and you'll probably get another bite. The small fish, frustration, may lead to bigger ones, like the group not allowing some people to speak up freely.

Suppose someone says, "I felt left out in that activity because several people were talking so loudly that I couldn't share my ideas." There's a fish that's jumped right out of the water. Some leaders will hear the fish and pursue it, but others will miss it and cast out in a different direction.

The key to good debriefing is being able to read the ripples. If there are no ripples presently visible, a good leader can be patient and skilled enough to bring some to the surface. A good leader also will not overlook or bypass a fish that jumps out of the water. They usually have a lot of energy and need immediate attention. When one jumps, take that fish — it's an easy one.

Practical Stuff

"OK, all this fishin' stuff sort of makes sense, and I've got the three levels. But, how do I *do* it?"

Good debriefs come in assorted styles and formats. No one example is perfect for all situations, just like no single game will suit all your program applications. Asking questions and generating a discussion is the most common style of debrief, but there are countless variations on the theme.

Quickly, here are some techniques.

The Whip — Ask participants to state a word or phrase that sums up the experience for each of them. Ask everyone to listen to all the comments before any follow-up discussion. Oftentimes, one-word comments are easier to share and can be just as informative as longer statements.

Thumbs Up — Show people the Thumbs Up scale. A thumb straight up signifies total success, the highest level of teamwork, whatever you want to measure. A thumb straight down means nothing worked, no teamwork, the opposite end of the spectrum. The scale is a continuum — thumbs can point anywhere between up and down, so if a thumb sticks out horizontally, that means it felt OK. Ask participants to declare their personal feelings about the exercise through a Thumbs Up, and use the visual clues to begin a discussion about why people feel the way they do.

Headliners — Give people pieces of newsprint. Tell them they are the editors of a large newspaper and they need to create a front-page headline describing the most significant part of the experience for them. Give participants a separate page, or ask them to work in pairs or threes. This technique works well to summarize an entire day as well as a specific activity.

Claydough — Give people some claydough and ask them to create a symbol that represents something from the experience. Once completed, the symbols are shared and people can discuss their significance.

Last Thoughts

To be effective leading a debrief, here are some general guidelines:

- Be non-judgmental.
- Be sincere and honest.
- Show compassion and understanding.
- Be willing to listen.
- Be open to the feelings of others.
- Pay attention to what is said and not said.
- Be observant, watch for clues from body language.
- Ask questions rather than make statements.

A good debrief can transform a difficult and/or unpleasant group activity. Allowing people to examine and understand what happened and to find value in the process (despite the difficulties) is a delightful benefit of artful facilitation. Individuals and groups can completely shift their emotional, mental and physical response based upon a successful debrief. It is perhaps the most powerful tool you carry in your facilitation tool box.

If games and fun are the building blocks of Adventure, debriefing is the skill that crafts those blocks into a marvelous structure that protects and enriches all those who enter into it.

Good fishin'.

Chapter Five

How You Do It

If you tell people where to go but not how to get there, you'll be amazed at the result.

— *George Patton*

Leadership style has a tremendous effect on the success of an activity and a program. But style can be a troubling issue to discuss because everyone responds to different actions and behaviors in their own way. It is difficult, if not impossible, to have everyone agree on what the "right" style is for a leader. Most people will agree, though, that style can influence an experience to a great degree. The goal is to expand your style of delivery so that the broadest range of people will respond positively to you.

Doing It With Your Own Style

Style involves many aspects of leadership. The following elements of a leader's style are ones that work well. Consider them a basic set of skills you can use selectively or together.

Fun and Humor

Fun and humor are two great qualities that will carry you a long way. Having fun yourself is a great way to invite others to do the same.

Working with a group early in a program, you ask participants to hold hands for a circle exercise. For a group of adolescents, you might make a joke out of the Cooties (you remember those awful, deadly but mysterious "things" that other people always have but you don't want to get) that you need to watch out for by holding someone's hand. By making a joke out of something that people are perhaps anxious about, it may make it easier for people to feel comfortable. Or employ a fantasy to encourage people to link hands. ("If we all hold hands, we can prevent the alien Cooties from invading our bodies because they can only get you if your hands are empty.") Appealing to people's imagination often allows participants to do something that otherwise they would avoid or resist doing. Framing an experience in another perspective, particularly a humorous one, is a wonderful technique for reducing nervousness and anxiety.

Choose a silly game to ease the tension when people: 1) Are just getting to know each other; 2) have just completed an intense Initiative problem; 3) have just finished a lengthy debrief; 4) need to take a break from learning technical information like tying knots; 5) are tired and you want to generate some new energy within the group. What games might work well? *Speed Rabbit, Hog Call, Whiz-Bang, FFEACH* are good possibilities.

A couple of hints about silliness: As the instructor, always model the silly behavior first. Don't think that anyone will do the *Dog Shake, Speed Rabbit, Get Down* or *Return to the Earth* without seeing it done first. You too may not want to do these activities after just reading them! They want me, *ME*! to do that! Next page, please.

It's important to say that silliness, humor and fun work only if *you* are having fun, too. If the anxiety of demonstrating the *Dog Shake* causes you to shiver with fear, then it may not be a good choice (unless your shivering resembles a dog shaking, in which case shake on!). As with anything, moderation is probably the best rule. The more you become comfortable as a leader by practicing, the more you will be willing to expand your style of presentation.

Fantasy and Imagination

Remember when you were a kid, how exciting it was to make believe you were a policeman, a nurse, an astronaut, a princess, etc., etc? We don't forget that sense of excitement from fantasy as we grow older, we just forget to exercise our imaginations often enough. Look at the success of adventure movies like *Star Wars, Close Encounters* and *ET*. People of all ages were captivated by the fantasy — the possibility that something extraordinary could happen.

In Adventure activities, fantasy and imagination are the catalyst that tap into people's sense of excitement and danger. Most descriptions of play indicate that risk, danger and excitement are integral parts of the experience. Look back at the development and evolution of many Adventure activities, you'll discover a hefty dose of imagination poured into the mix.

Samurai, a simple activity requiring jumping and ducking, enters another dimension of fun when accompanied by a solemn introduction of the ancient traditions of the samurai and including appropriate gestures and vocal

incantations. The game fizzles without the fantasy.

Wizards & Gelflings involves running and yelling, but the frantic dashing around and the struggle to "be free" is intensified by the imaginary conflict between the Wizards and their fun-loving antagonists. Players love this game because of the high-pitched squealing of the distress call, the fear of getting caught, the delight in the chase. All these playful factors are created in part by the fantasy.

The Initiative problem *Toxic Waste* simply involves picking up a can and pouring some objects into another can. But the concentration and determination are magnified by the "reality" that if the toxic waste spills, that's the end for us all.

Foes & Questors, a fantasy/Adventure game we created back in 1981, is the ultimate proof of the fantasy appeal. The various roles and power objects create an incredibly confusing array of rules to remember. (Yes, Jim and Charlie, we admit it!) But the sheer delight that people experience while playing is amazing to behold. In the 80's, we played for several years at Crane's Beach, near Project Adventure's Massachusetts headquarters. Once a month, right through the winter, querulous Questors and feuding Foes would gather to enjoy the camaraderie and shared fun. People came from as far away as Rochester, NY (Hi, Nancy, Mary, et al) for the game. One participant wrote an evaluation of the game for her graduate work and it was fascinating to hear people describe their reasons for choosing specific roles and for pursuing different strategies.

We created the game to have fun. It took on a life of its own when people found so much enjoyment and fun in the role-playing. People to this day retell the stories of past games (especially the incredible Quest that occurred in the Hommocks School library one wintry afternoon — thanks Ken!).

F&Q is a bit elaborate, but the power of fantasy is real. Imagination is one of the best motivational techniques you have.

Silliness vs. Seriousness

So much of what we do in Adventure is perceived as silly and fun. Can it be overdone? You bet. How you introduce trust activities after playing games is always an intriguing question. A trust sequence usually follows a progression of icebreakers, games and de-inhibitizers — activities geared to get people laughing and having fun.

When trust activities are introduced, the laughter and nervous comments that usually arise reflect people's anxieties about touching one another, about feeling safe, about appearing afraid. These feelings are normal and predictable.

Expect the nervousness. It's OK. It's life. But it does raise the question of how you address the issue. In the context of trust activities, silliness and inappropriate comments (Let's drop Joan when she falls... Wouldn't it be funny if we pinch/tickle/push Johnny... I'll catch you with NO HANDS!) can quickly erode the feeling of trust and support necessary for people to feel comfortable. And make no mistake, adult groups, as well as young people, will do the same thing.

It's a judgment call. Do you intervene? Do you let it go? Is it interfering? In this context, it may be appropriate to remind people of the Full Value Contract, to emphasize the focus on the person who is falling or taking the risk, or to explore people's feelings and attitudes in a discussion before doing any trust activity.

It is always a fine line to walk. You spend so much time developing an environment of fun, then you interject some activities where a more serious focus is needed for safety reasons. These types of activities, because of the vulnerability of the participants, probably require a shift in style on your part as the leader. Physical safety demands close attention and supervision.

Spontaneity

Here's the Adventure facilitator's magic. Everything looks totally spontaneous, but only you know how much practice, planning and

Directed versus Empowering

Following this last thought further, what is empowering leadership? How do you know if you're providing too much direction?

This element of style goes right to the heart of Adventure facilitation. Why are you doing what you're doing? Are you trying to help the group, or are you trying to help the group succeed? "What's the difference?" you might ask. Sometimes helping the group means allowing them to struggle, to fail and to learn from the experience. If you constantly help the group succeed at every activity, they may conclude that they don't need to do anything to improve.

Another dynamic of too much direction is that the participants don't feel any responsibility for or ownership of the experience. With younger students, you may feel that they aren't capable of monitoring themselves. If you guide them in a certain direction, they may only follow your path. There may be other ways for them to get there.

The area where this self-directed philosophy is inappropriate is in regards to safety issues. As the leader, you can never give up responsibility for the safety of the group members. For this reason, the leader never completely lets the group set its own course.

How Good Can You Afford To Look?

As an Adventure practitioner, it's important to appear knowledgeable and confident. Because of the perceived risk in many of the activities, as well as the intentional use of fun and silliness, people need to know that you are in control.

There are many ways to demonstrate this experience and expertise. But can you look too good? Can you make things look so easy that people are either intimidated or put off by what they perceive to be excessive showmanship.

Demonstrating an activity, being the first to try something, participating with all your energy, all these traits are admirable ways of setting a tone with a group. You can encourage

forethought goes into your presentation. Spontaneity is important because games and activities sometimes produce reactions and responses that can't be anticipated. As a leader, you need to respond appropriately.

Another aspect of spontaneity involves responding to a group's questions and needs in an activity. When you first experience a game, you will remember that specific experience. But not every group will follow the same pattern. Most likely, some groups will not have fun playing it that way. Be open to variation. Allow groups to alter an activity if it moves them in a positive direction.

If you catch yourself saying, "No," to lots of questions, look at what you're doing. It may signal rigidity. Answering, "Yes!" is a sign of openness and flexibility.

people to try it by providing the example; you can initiate a sense of silliness and fun by looking silly yourself and giving permission to others; you can influence the energy level of the group by injecting your own exuberance and joy in playing.

These are positive displays of good leadership. But the line is a fine one between creating a fun experience and making the Adventure yours, not the group's. How can you tell where the line is? How do you know what's appropriate behavior and modeling? We suggest keeping two concepts in mind: *Casual Competence* and *Reasonable Unreasonableness*.

Casual Competence

Casual Competence means that your actions, words and behavior are aimed at making people feel comfortable. You are inviting people to join you for some fun, try to make them *want* to take part by setting an example that says, "I really enjoy this, why don't you give it a try." You're creating an atmosphere that allows people to experiment and try new things without fear of being judged, by you or by the other members of the group.

Be natural and relaxed (sometimes not an easy thing to do when you're facing some eager or apprehensive faces first thing in the day). Don't strain to make it fit for people, don't come on too strong. *Too* much competence can make people feel inadequate and incapable. You want to demonstrate your willingness to give it a go and possibly fail. No one needs to feel bad if they can't accomplish something.

Reasonable Unreasonableness

You or an activity can be new, different, foolish, even bizarre. But whatever you present has to be acceptable enough to promote participation and it cannot be done at the expense of

someone else. The freedom to attempt something that you otherwise would not do can be a wonderful outcome of an Adventure experience, but it must always be balanced by the readiness of all the individuals to attempt the activity. Fun can be a powerful tool to bond a group, to energize people, to invite participation, and to include people in a group experience. But fun can just as easily create a gulf between people and become a source of distraction and disruption if people don't feel they are voluntarily participating in an activity.

Even the level of challenge in an Initiative problem needs to be *acceptable* to a group. Project Adventure has always presented activities that have workable solutions. We don't intentionally present any activities that aren't attainable. Some may *appear* to be impossible; that's OK and intentional. It would be unreasonable to expect people to learn effective behaviors if all we presented to them were activities that were designed to cause failure.

We use, and advocate, zaniness and humor to add flavor to our presentations. In doing so, you must remain sensitive to the group's makeup and the context of the program or you run the risk of causing the group to feel uncomfortable enough to back away from the activities you present.

You will find that leading programs is risky. We support you in taking some risks. Just recognize that you are taking them. And until you have developed a clear sense of what types of risks are *reasonably unreasonable*, limit your presentation choices to fairly sure winners. The more experience you get and the more experimentation you do, the better you will be able to gauge correctly what will challenge a group but leave them clamoring for more.

The essential point about your image is that it needs to be balanced. At the beginning of a program, you may tend to be more competent and more reasonable. You will want to demonstrate your leadership in a way that will inspire and motivate the group to join the activities you present. You will most likely be right in there with them as they play. Being a good role model at this point in time can be your most effective technique.

As the program unfolds, you may start to include some de-inhibitizers and some more zany activities to broaden the scope of acceptable behaviors and to push the boundaries of people's comfort with each other. Trust and bonding don't always come just from physical activities designed for that purpose. *Hog Call, FFEACH, Commonalities* and others can influence how people feel towards each other to complement more traditional trust activities. People respond to the fun aspects of the program; they get excited and engaged and want more opportunities to work and play together.

Eventually, your role recedes and the group begins to monitor its own behaviors and efforts. All the while, your leadership is responding to and reflecting the needs of the group and its individual members. You can present more demanding activities, either physically, mentally or emotionally, only as you sense that the group is capable of handling the new level of challenge. As the group develops new skills and demonstrates more cohesiveness, you can become *more* casual and *more* unreasonable as the situation allows.

Always presenting in the same style or always following the same sequence of activities are two ways to get yourself into a rut and not effectively meet the needs of the group. The best facilitators know their strengths and draw on them, while at the same time seeking new methods and techniques to make themselves more effective.

Sequencing

We've all heard about being *in the right place at the right time*. The same principle applies when leading Adventure activities. There is an activity for any situation (and if we don't have one, we'll just have to invent it!). If you happen to know the appropriate activity for a given situation, you're half-way to a successful experience; the other half is recognizing that it fits the needs of the group and the situation.

Think of sequencing as an art — part feeling, part intuition, part analysis and part experience.

Sequencing is a key skill because the flow of the Adventure experience greatly impacts its success for the participants. Move too slowly and people lose interest due to boredom; move unexpectedly or too quickly and people become anxious and withdraw. Sequencing allows you to maintain the group in the flow state — balanced between the level of challenge presented and the participants' own abilities to meet that challenge.

Observe the group for signs of what it needs. Are they tired and needing a rest? Nervous and needing to relax and be comfortable? Anxious or bored and needing to let out some pent-up energies and emotions? Cold and wet and needing to either warm up or go inside? What your observations tell you the group needs guides your selection of the next appropriate activity. (Note: Oftentimes what *you* need at this point can give you a clue as to what the group might need.)

Your intuition combines with your observations to create a larger picture of how the group is doing. Sometimes the overt signs aren't the ones that need attention. Is the person standing alone on the side simply tired or is he feeling rejected and isolated from the group? Is a group wanting to take a break really needing a chance to refresh themselves or are they trying to avoid dealing with a thorny issue? Are they breaking the rules because they need to succeed or is it because they are trying to undermine what the group is doing? Intuition raises questions, looks beneath the surface, and identifies guideposts for selecting the next activity.

Your analysis of the group filters what you see, hear and observe. Examine the previous activities for any patterns of behavior. If people are making rude comments to each other, they're may not be ready for a *Trust Fall*. If they're struggling mightily with the *Nitro Crossing*, they're may not be ready for a difficult version of the *Mohawk Walk*. Build the group's confidence and ability by giving them appropriate challenges at appropriate times. Each time you step back to check on their performance, you're not only looking backward to examine their progress, but looking around the next corner — where you're leading them — to be sure that it's safe for them to move forward.

Remember that there are no right and wrong ways to sequence a program. You need to develop your own sequencing instincts. Your development as an Adventure leader isn't complete until you can plan, observe, react and adjust on your own.

Chapter Six

The Essence of QuickSilver

*Discovery consists of looking at the
same thing as everyone else and
thinking something different.*

— *Albert Szent-Gyorgyi*

*Imagination is more important than
knowledge.*

— *Albert Einstein*

A Leader's Best Tool —
Creativity

It's a topic that can raise some anxiety. Ask
people if they are creative and you often get a

sheepish grin and a questioning look that asks,
"Who me?" People come to workshops to learn
"new" activities. People purchase books like
this one with the expectation that they'll learn
something new.

We're no different. We read books, attend
presentations, snoop around in toy stores, explore recycling centers, and in general act like
a large suction device intent on gathering any
loose game-related material in the vicinity.
Then we dispense the reconstituted play experiences back into the world for others to enjoy.

Creativity is important to Adventure. You
want your class/program to be new, different

and unusual to arouse the curiosity of the participants. The expectation of the unknown becomes a calling card, an invitation to participate.

We have always been attracted to the creative, spontaneous side of Adventure programming. Working with anything for a combined total of 43 years could get boring. Looking for new ideas, trying to constantly improve on old ones, and being willing to try most of the whimsical notions that enter our brains has kept our internal fun furnaces stoked and belching forth new clouds of activity smoke. The pursuit of creative new ideas is one reason why Adventure programming is still fresh and attractive after all these years.

One reason people may shy away from creative thinking for their programs is because it is an unpredictable art. Trying to create something new can just as often produce something worthless as well as something valuable. Most people don't like that chance of failure. If it's not a guaranteed success, let's call the experts. Why spend time and energy when someone else is doing it and maybe doing it better.

We love to hear that. On one hand it means that we can continue to spend time pursuing endless variations and devising appealing new creations for your playful appetites. We love to create and we like knowing that our creativity enhances what other people are doing. On the other hand, it can sometimes be disappointing to feel that people don't think they can be inventive. We want to encourage *all* Adventure leaders to develop their own creative instincts so that your programs can be as fun-filled and exciting as possible.

Obviously, we're committed to this creativity consciousness. So what will it do for you? Why try to develop this skill/instinct? What is the benefit? Here is a rationale for developing your own creative potential.

1) Being creative keeps you, your participants and your programs fresh. It keeps participant interest and enthusiasm at a high level. One difference between leaders who appear successful over time and those who struggle appears to be a creative spirit, a sense that the activities in this book (and others) are a jumping off point, not the end of Adventure.

2) Injecting something new and unusual into a program or class makes it better by keeping people guessing, wondering what's next. When curiosity is aroused, people are engaged in the process and are more open to learning opportunities.

3) Creativity is a challenge. There are countless ideas and activities in the universe, why not pursue them? Take a risk, try a new approach even if it seems like a stretch for you. Tapping your own creativity is a way to keep in touch with the challenge of Adventure.

4) If you put creative energy into a program, you will do a better job. Keep yourself energized by pushing to find new opportunities for people to utilize their potential.

Here are some examples of creativity. If you understand how to be creative and why creativity works, perhaps you'll feel more confident unleashing your own creative potential.

The Evolution of Moonball

Moonball (*Silver Bullets,* pg. 31) is a simple game that people love to play. The original idea came from having a beach ball available and wanting to do something with it. No great mystery here. Creating a challenge with the ball involved hitting it as many times as possible before it touched the ground. The activity doesn't involve much — minimal equipment and minimal rules — but the fun factor averages around 7–8 on a scale of 10.

Once the game was played and proved to be a winner, we didn't stop working on its development. Here's the important lesson: Just because you have a good activity, don't assume it can't be made better. It's easy to learn a game one way and fall prey to the notion that it has to be played just like the original for it to work

again. Maybe, maybe not. A game is not like a masterpiece of artwork; a little creative addition often enhances the original product.

Here are some reasons why *Moonball* was changed and improved (not to say that *Moonball* itself isn't a great activity).

First, people quickly discovered that taller and more athletic players (jumpers in particular) could easily dominate the action if they gathered together around the ball. It was difficult and/or impossible for other players to have a hit and to feel part of the team.

This problem was addressed by adding new rules, and two new activities, *All Hit* and *Countdown Moonball* were created. *All Hit* requires that *all* players touch the ball at least once (anyone can hit it multiple times and that's okay) before it touches the ground or the total score is nullified. *Countdown* rules state that *no one* can hit the ball a second time until everyone hits it once; if all the players hit the ball before it touches the ground, one point is scored for the team and they try to repeat the process of having everyone hit the ball. For each completed rotation a point is scored.

What if *Moonball* gets too serious, if people want to achieve a certain score and they can't accomplish it? — or too boring, if people become so proficient at it that they lose interest? What to do?

Macro (or *Macho*) *Moonball*: Anytime you hit the ball, you must hit it with all your might — open-hand striking is recommended to prevent fists from potentially landing on other players. This version usually invites loud noises, grandiose swings at the ball, equally grandiose misses of the ball, and sufficient laughter at the successful and not so successful hits as to make it fun. Trying to achieve a score is possible, but it usually is secondary to the hilarity of chasing the ball as it careens aimlessly through the upper ranges of the *Moonball* stratosphere.

Here, a little creativity changes a fun game/Initiative problem into an excuse to act a bit silly, to let out your pent up energy, and to laugh while doing it. Do you need this type of game? No. Is it fun? Yes. Is it worth doing? You bet. In some circumstances, like trying to re-focus the group after several unsuccessful attempts at *All Hit* or *Countdown*, it could be a wonderful way of releasing some of the frustration and disappointment before allowing the group to make another attempt.

All these variations were created to address different aspects of how players might respond to the game. Another version of *Moonball*, *Five Aside Flatball* (*Cowstails and Cobras II,* pg. 64), came about because of the dynamics of what happens to Moonballs over time. They develop leaks. *Flatball* allowed the play to continue with a partially deflated Moonball.

As befits its continual evolution, you'll discover *Islands Moonball* — another successful adaptation of the original idea — in this book.

Group Juggling to *Eggspeediency* — A Quantum Jump

Group Juggling (*Cowstails and Cobras II,* pg. 84) is a game of laughter and silliness with balls and objects passed around a circle and often dropped. It's a great warm-up/icebreaker, oftentimes a nice transition from *Toss-a-Name*. It is also used extensively in corporate team-building programs as a metaphor for how groups simultaneously manage multiple tasks.

Group Juggling works and works well. Having played it many times, it seemed worth looking for newer challenges, because the fun factor is high but people's interest doesn't sustain itself much longer than a few minutes. By experimenting with yet another level of challenge, new ideas were born.

Warp Speed (*Cowstails and Cobras II,* pg. 83) changes the entire focus of *Group Juggling.* When you lead the activities back-to-back, the demeanor of the group is transformed. People suddenly become very intent and focused, the laughter stops, and concentration on the goal draws people together. *Warp Speed* quickly and pointedly exposes how the group works together. It produces an opportunity to extract valuable lessons about teamwork and offers techniques that may produce success in other more complex problems. Where *Group Juggling* generates laughter and fun, *Warp Speed* harnesses that fun and allows people to tap into

learnings and metaphors like a light bulb illuminating new ideas.

Warp Speed exemplifies all that is good in an activity. It's simple — few props and rules — and produces fascinating outcomes. How could you ask for anything more? The incredible success of *Warp Speed* in any program speaks loudly to the fact that good games can be transformed into better activities with some imagination. For years it seemed to be the best that it could be.

One day lightning struck. Working with a group that had just done a solid job with *Warp Speed*, I remembered that there was a box of eggs available for another activity scheduled later in the day. The group seemed ready for a higher challenge level, so a real-life consequence seemed appropriate.

"How about we include a raw egg into our pattern?" Looks of incredulity met my gaze. Then someone said, "Why not?" *Eggspeediency* was born. Now, some people reacted skittishly to this turn of events. But upon completing the

task without any mishaps, the group's enthusiasm and confidence achieved a new peak.

Eggspeediency may not be for everyone. That's beside the point. The lesson again is that a spark of imagination, a mind that asks why not instead of saying it can't be done that way leads you in new directions. That unexpected twist is what Adventure is all about.

Turnstile to *Hop Box*

"If it's worth doing, it's worth overdoing."

— *KER*

Turnstile (*Bottomless Bag Again,* pg. 116) is an old standard that has proved its worth over time. Its origins aren't certain, but you can bet that it evolved from having an old rope lying around and wanting to use it rather than throw it away. This impulse, coupled with a fanciful desire to jump rope, produced another popular activity.

Turnstile requires that all members of the group make a jump. If the rope rotates one complete turn without someone making a jump, then the group's attempt is invalid. They have to start again.

Once again, a simple idea. But in practice, this Initiative poses many challenges for a group. Some struggling and frustration often accompany this exercise. When success comes, the group is usually cheering itself on with wild enthusiasm.

Several variations emerged over the years to add new challenges. Asking people to jump in pairs, or threes, or whatever number suits your fancy adds another element of cooperation and teamwork. The ultimate challenge is to line up all the members of the group next to the rope and have everyone attempt to make a successful jump all at the same time! It is an exercise in jostling, jumping and stratagizing that produces as much laughter as it does serious effort.

When Project Adventure had its 20th Anniversary celebration in 1991, none of these versions would have worked. Why? Because we estimated that 150 people would be there! That meant both a very long rope and two facilitators (you know who) with very tired arms. A new idea was needed.

How about multiple ropes? Put them in a square formation and form a "box" around the participants. To escape from the box, one has to jump over a rope (any side will do). Time the activity to pump up people's energy and to provide an additional challenge. And to prevent anyone from getting tired arms, the twirlers are part of the group and have to be replaced so they can make a jump, too. Well, what a success!

Since that time, we've used *Hop Box* in many situations (with large groups). What's an active Initiative problem that will engage upwards of 150 people? *Hop Box* is your choice.

The Fastest Game of Tag Becomes the Game that Never Ends

I (Steve) used to work for the New Games Foundation and used to present the game *Everybody's It* as the world's fastest tag game. Tagging anyone within reach, the action is fast and furious and does tend to end quickly. It also means that some players don't have but a moment to move before being frozen by a well-placed tag. To allow for more action and increased playing time, the *Hospital Tag* version was created. Under the new rules, participants can "cure" a tag by covering it with a band-aid; i.e., one of their hands. When both hands are used up, they're frozen.

This initial change was made to create more fun. (More running, more tagging means more action, which translates into more fun.) Even with this change, the faster people still had an advantage. Not to say that life isn't full of

opportunities where one skill or ability gets you something faster or easier, and that's OK. But for the play experience, the challenge was to create a more even playing environment, and heighten the action, too.

So *Asteroids* (*Bottomless Bag Again*, pg. 77) was born. Give everyone a ball, toss them up in the air and then throw them at each other. If you're hit, you freeze. This adaptation produced joyous results. It was played at workshops and people enjoyed the frantic energy of running, throwing and dodging. But, as with *Everybody's It*, the game tends to end early for some players.

Soon a new wrinkle was added. *Anklebiters* (*Bottomless Bag Again*, pg. 78) allowed frozen players to be quick-thawed, or to reach out and ensnare one or more active players. The action increased, no one was left out of the game for any length of time. (Unless by personal choice — "I'm winded. I'm going to ignore that ball for a few minutes.") The smiles and laughter on people's faces got bigger and louder. I can't remember a time when *Anklebiters* didn't produce comments about it being a GREAT GAME!

Simply adding a ball to the game meant that more people were able to succeed at "tagging" someone, had a means for getting unfrozen, and the pace of the action increased. And since it almost never happens that all players are frozen at the same time, the game goes on indefinitely. Watching *Anklebiters*, it's difficult to remember that the original idea grew out of *Everybody's It*.

Creativity is a source of many wonderful Adventure activities. And you don't have to invent something totally new to be creative. In fact, if you just adapt some old game and call it something different, people will probably assume you're a genius. (Oops, there goes the mystique of our creativity.)

Make creativity a habit. Try to improve a game when it's not necessary, when it's just for the fun of it, when you just happen to have some new prop around, or when you need a little spark to get the old juices flowing again. This approach may seem like more work, and maybe it is. But it's also a lot more fun and it takes the pressure off of having to invent something new and different on the spot when you really *need* to. Besides, practicing creativity makes you better at it. Remember: Practice and experience develop mastery.

Game Change — Making Something Old Into Something New

If we don't change our direction, we're likely to end up where we're headed.

— *Chinese Proverb*

Every game that was ever invented by man consists in making the rules harder for the fun of it.

— *John Ciardi*

The preceding examples may not seem all that different from the following examples about game change. And for good reason: The two are closely linked. The difference between creativity and game change is that creativity implies a way of thinking, a mind-set, a lens through which to imagine all activities; game change is the method, the science of transforming activities to make them work better.

Why change a game? The rules are there for a reason — so you'll know what to do as you play. But sometimes the rules just don't seem to fit, or the game doesn't feel quite right, or maybe the game just isn't very exciting.

Here are a dozen reasons to change a game (though there certainly are more):

- There are more or fewer players than the set-up calls for;
- You don't have the right equipment;
- It's boring;
- It's too challenging;
- You have too little or too much time to play it;
- The players lack certain skills so the game isn't fun;

- The players are too skilled to enjoy the game;

- The space is too big or too small to play in;

- The outcome of the game — win/lose — causes people to feel bad at the end;

- The players need something the game doesn't provide (trust issues, no communication, no cooperation, etc.);

- It's too hot, cold, wet, snowy to play;

- It simply is NOT FUN!

Think of other reasons to change a game. Think back to the last time you were playing and it wasn't fun. What was wrong? What wasn't working for you? What could you have done differently to have made it more exciting, more challenging, more fun? Those are the questions you can ask to hone your game changing skills.

Changing a game allows for new possibilities. Altering the game components or rearranging the game's structure may make it more exciting and increase the interest of the people playing it. A good Adventure leader uses this skill to adapt activities to meet the needs of the group. (Refer to Points of Play #1 at the end of Section One.)

When to Change?

There are lots of practical reasons for changing games. Sometimes, many times in fact, activities need to be altered due to the unique circumstances of a program. Design considerations, program goals, participant's abilities, challenge level, number of people, playing area, etc., all can cause you to re-think the standard way of presenting an activity. This aspect of game change is more scientific, though intuition and a sense of what is fun are still helpful. The difference here is that you are premeditatingly altering the game due to the circumstances.

In many instances, the reason that prompts you to change a game is that the level of challenge exceeded or did not meet the ability level of the participants. In the first case, when the challenge level is too high, the group can become frustrated and anxious; they may not feel capable of completing the task. On the other hand, when the challenge level is too low, people feel bored; there is not enough action or activity to maintain their interest.

A man named Mihaly Csikszentmihalyi developed a theory about this match between challenge and ability. He calls it *flow*. He states in his book, *Beyond Boredom and Anxiety*, that when people are engaged in an activity that approximates a match between challenge versus ability, people enter this state of flow. He describes it as a feeling of timelessness, where all attention is focused on the task at hand, where concentration is directed solely at the activity. It's an interesting theory in that people often describe their feelings in a PA workshop in the same terms. People become so enveloped in the Adventure experience that they enter this state of flow.

How do you know if your group is in the flow or if it's time to change something? OBSERVE them. If you look around and see people standing listlessly, watching the sky or the floor, looking embarrassed or bewildered, trying to sneak away from the group, then you can be certain that something is not right. There may be many causes for the discomfort, but your leader's alert should be clamoring inside your brain telling you to think about what to do next. Noticing that something is lacking in the play experience is the critical first step in determining what to do about it.

Generally speaking, your level of interest and your sense of fun are both good reference points to measure the relative success of a game or activity. If you're feeling unsatisfied for whatever reason, chances are the participants will feel that way, too. As the leader, you are the one who needs to change the game before the fun quotient hits zero. Stay in touch with your own feelings as well as observing the situation.

When Not to Change?

There is, or should be in your mind, a distinction between a poor play experience and the group struggling to overcome a problem or issue. A group may find that a particular game or Initiative is causing them to work harder than you or they expected and making them feel uncomfortable. There's a difference between struggling to overcome the challenge versus feeling unhappy with the activity itself.

If a group is having to work hard and they are disagreeing, not communicating effectively, arguing, etc., that may not be *fun* for them. However, it *is* part of the Adventure experience. The fact that there is some conflict does not necessarily mean that the game is bad, that the activity needs to be changed, or that you need to intervene to alter the environment. Struggle and failure produce learning sometimes more than success. Be careful to notice the difference between a group attempting to work through its problems and a game that, because it is inappropriate for a group, creates problems that do not need to be there.

An example: You present *Warp Speed* to a group after 30 minutes of warm-ups and ice-breakers. They cannot come to an agreement on a solution and begin to argue over people's ideas. Some people in the group are standing in the circle not saying anything, others are talking but with an edge to their voices. What happened? Should the game be changed? Should you intervene?

Admittedly, it's hard to say for certain because you don't have all the information. Under the circumstances, though, after only 30 minutes together, a challenge like *Warp Speed* could produce some uncomfortable tension. If it's the first Initiative the group attempts and they are not working well together, that may indicate that they were not ready for such a challenge.

If the same situation occurs on the third day of a five-day workshop, and if the group had demonstrated some ability to work together and manage its process, you would probably allow the struggle to continue as a learning opportunity. The difference here being that the group should be better able to manage its own conflicts and disagreements after having spent two days together than they would be after only 30 minutes.

How to Change

Changes generally focus on game components, not on people. You want to alter the game, if necessary, to make it match the group's needs. Game components easily changed include:

- rules
- equipment
- locomotion (how people move)
- boundaries
- the fantasy
- roles of the players
- the goal.

Can you think of others? Altering one of these components doesn't cause any upset feelings — a beach ball doesn't mind being replaced by a balloon, a boundary doesn't care if it's big or small.

Some Hints about Making changes

If you want to determine the effect of a specific change, alter only one thing at a time. If you change two or three aspects of the game simultaneously, the game may or may not play better. Whatever happens, you won't know for certain what caused the play factor to change, good or bad.

Make changes at a time when it doesn't interfere with the outcome. If a group is about to score its one-hundredth point in *Moonball*, and you yell out they can only hit the ball with their feet, they may feel angry at you for changing the rules — especially if the change causes them to miss their goal.

Changes need to be fair for all players. If everyone is linked together to play *Tusker*, but several players decide it's OK for them to run as single participants, that change gives the single runners an unfair advantage. On the other hand, if I'm playing *Pairs Tag* with a partner on crutches, and we both have to hop on one foot, that equalizes the challenge for both of us. Instead of creating a mismatch of ability, we're trying to create an equal challenge for both players.

Practical Changes And Their Consequences

Boundaries

Changing the boundaries is a simple way of adjusting the activity level and perhaps the challenge of a game.

For *Pairs Tag*, a small space produces more bumping and jostling, the things people usually enjoy most. Larger boundaries may make it safer for younger players who are less likely to be aware of running over or through other people. It's safer, because with more space there is less chance of a collision. Making the boundaries really big, say a basketball court for 12 people, turns *Pairs Tag* into a walking marathon with little or no bumping into people; maybe good for aerobic training, but not very high on the fun index.

Another game where boundaries can be a critical factor is *Tusker* (*Silver Bullets,* pg. 42). If the boundaries are too big to begin with, it may be nearly impossible for the *Tusker* to catch anyone, especially when it's 4–8 people chasing linked pairs. At the end of the game, if

the boundaries are too small, the *Tusker* has an easy job catching the last remaining pairs. The solution that works best is to establish three, fixed boundaries while the fourth side moves (though the players may not realize it if you don't tell them). You become that fourth boundary. You can stay close to the action at the outset, assisting the *Tusker* by narrowing the playing area. As the *Tusker* grows and can cover more territory by fanning out, you can give the escaping pairs a reasonable chance of survival by preventing the *Tusker* from reaching both sides of the boundaries. With this game, boundaries a bit too small probably are better than too big. A group will be thankful to have the running cease a bit to soon than to experience the endless frustration of not catching new pairs.

In general boundaries should be *just right* — not too big, which can produce fatigue, frustration and a loss of camaraderie; not too small, which can cramp the action, increase risk of collisions and limit the challenge level; but somewhere in the middle, where there is both enough action yet not too much exertion of effort with little to show for it.

Fantasy

Changing or using a fantasy appeals to people's imaginations and is a powerful tool for inviting people to play.

Fantasy enhances the fun factor. Fantasies give permission for people to exhibit unusual behaviors. It allows people to participate when normally they might hesitate. (I may not want to play tag, but I'll certainly try my hardest to escape that voracious *Tusker*.)

Fantasies can heighten the sense of reality in a game, creating a scenario that simulates real world experiences and can increase the possible learnings from the activity. Or fantasies can allow people to leave behind the cares and concerns of the real world, thus potentially letting people gain a fresh perspective on their problems.

While fantasy can attract some people, it can repel others. The game *Killer* is a prime example. Many people enjoyed the thrill of playing that game, especially the extended multi-day version. Many people also complained about the fantasy and the imagery of death. The game gradually disappeared from workshops due to the hue and cry.

Before abandoning it, we altered the fantasy to being overcome by rapturous joy or being commandeered by an alien a la *Invasion of the Body Snatchers*. The game was still OK, but somehow the fun had disappeared. Not to argue the game's merits or faults, the choice became one of consideration. There are lots of other good games, so there was no need to continue playing this one.

Equipment

Changing the equipment used in a game can alter the activity level, the challenge level, and more than anything else potentially alter the whole game.

Frantic (*Silver Bullets*, pg. 65) is just as the name implies — frenetic. Pursuing the endlessly rolling Rabid Nuggets may not always seem like fun, but people do enjoy it.

The only drawbacks are that you need lots of tennis balls, which are heavy to cart around, and you need a large open floor, like a gym. *Balloon Frantic* was created to solve both of these problems. Balloons are a lot lighter and smaller than the same number of tennis balls, and you can play anywhere that balloons float in the air. The problem-solving aspect stayed the same, the rules stayed the same, but the flavor of the game changed dramatically. Anyone who has chased dirty tennis balls around the floor will glowingly describe the wonderful colors and the added intensity of diving for a falling balloon as a recommendation for this option.

Like a touch of seasoning to your favorite food, equipment sometimes adds just the right dose of playfulness to an otherwise good game. *Blob Tag* is fun, but spicing the game with two *tusks* adds a whole other flavor to the chase.

Escaping the *Tusker* is much more real than fleeing an unfanged *Blob*. The use of equipment (and fantasy) raises the fun factor a subtle but tantalizing notch.

Equipment, much like fantasy, can be an attractive invitation to play. Something novel and unusual arouses curiosity. If it's brightly colored, all the better. People like toys, even adults. Starting a program with some flashy (but inexpensive) equipment is a sound and well-respected practice. Equipment can sometimes divert attention away from people in the group. That may be helpful if people are shy and tentative starting a workshop and need to warm up; it may be an interference, though, if it prevents people from observing and dealing with tensions or anxieties of group members.

Goals

Changing the goal or purpose of the game can be a strong motivational technique or a method for reducing the stress of performance.

Including the time element in *Warp Speed* radically alters the feel of the game. With no time factor, people go through the motions but don't really apply themselves totally. Once they have a goal, achieving the fastest time, the process becomes much more intent on performance. The same can be said of *Moonball*, *Hop Box* and other timed events. A goal or stated challenge to the group often provides an added dose of motivation to participate at a high level. This approach can be overdone, though. A goal that is too difficult can be just as deflating to the group as a successful goal can raise spirits. Applying too much "motivation" can be a turn-off.

The game of *Monarch* alters the traditional aspect of dodgeball by including a strong measure of cooperation and teamwork. As the game progresses, more and more players become captured by the Monarchy, but rather than feeling badly about being hit or eliminated, the newest players to join the Monarch's side soon get caught up in the desire to capture their former confederates. The goal of the game is to work together to catch all the players, so being caught simply means shifting roles rather than elimination.

A different goal reframes the focus of the group. Play for fun, play for time, play to score points — each has its merits and rewards. Choosing which outcome best suits the group's needs is the balancing point on which to weigh your decision about how to frame an activity.

Roles

Changing the roles in a game can give new life to the players and the activity.

In *Ah-So-Ko,* players aren't really expelled from the game, just given a new role. Becoming a Heckler stimulates the noise and distraction quotient of the game, while also running counter to the traditional consequence of elimination. A person doesn't have to feel rejected or lose interest from inaction. An entirely new responsibility and persona await you.

Transformer Tag takes much the same tack — tag someone and he becomes your ally in the game. You're not only diminishing the numbers of the opposition, you're increasing the power of your team. WOW, what a concept.

Recycle old, tagged-out players into new, juiced-up teammates. Changing roles has a significant impact and positively alters the feel of this tag game.

Not every activity needs to prevent elimination, but it tends to keep people more interested in the game. The longer the players are attracted to the game, the longer they will continue playing. It's mostly a question of fun. If you're tired or bored with the game, choose to stop playing; but if your interest is high and you're having fun, why accept being eliminated from the action?

In *Foes & Questors*, we struggled mightily to balance having a consequence to being hit versus keeping people involved in the flow of the game. Yes, you can be frozen for periods of time and that can be frustrating (unless you need the rest), but there's always the potential for getting back in the action and seeking to turn the tables on those who temporarily stopped you. People always commented that the rejuvenation factor was one of the reasons why they enjoyed the game so much. You could take risks, even unreasonable ones, suffer the

consequences, and then do it all over again. Some people never learn. So much for experiential learning versus the fun curve.

Conclusion

Do these examples form any kind of pattern? The intent is to demonstrate the wide variety of changes that can be made to activities, some of the rationale for doing so, and some potential outcomes of altering games successfully. Can we get it into a simple little formula or credo? Try this:

Play is good.

Change is good.

Good play can be better with change.

There is something missing about this explanation of game change. Have you guessed it? You're right on the money if you said, "Hey wait a minute. All these changes produced success."

In all probability, we have made lots more changes that didn't work out to anything special than all the examples showcased here. We've thought about, created and played countless games that haven't given us much satisfaction. And we don't give up easily. If a game isn't right to begin with, you can bet that we'll tinker with it.

The point is that if you try to change a game or two, find the process isn't working, don't assume you don't have "the gift" or whatever else it takes to alter a game. Sometimes the insight for changing games is like a sixth sense. To develop that sense, you have to practice making changes. Practice and experience are required to do this well.

Perhaps more importantly, you need two other things: A willingness to try out different ideas and a desire to have fun. If you give yourself the opportunity to seek out fun in whatever you're doing, and we mean discover what is *really* fun for you, then your play sense will become a good guide for you to follow. Add to this awareness the permission to experiment and follow whimsical notions, and you may find more successful changes emerging from your efforts.

Since there are no guaranteed successes in life, or Adventure, or game change, you'll just have to accept whatever you create. There are no real failures if you try to make changes. You can always go back to the original activity.

Chapter Seven

Practical Tips – Two Leader's Bags of Tricks

Skipping from a model to reality, what produces success? The items below are a personal repertoire of skills, techniques and experience that help us with our work and play.

Things That Make A Workshop Work

"You can learn more about a person in an hour's worth of play than in a day of conversation."

— *Plato*

"How much work could a workshop shop if a workshop could shop work?"

— *Rohnke*

Starters

Have lots of fun throwables on hand right at the beginning of a workshop. Give me a mess of Twirlies and I'll have a stand-around group of people who don't know one another smiling, doing, sharing and talking within seconds. There's not much listening at this stage, just action. Other throwables of note:

- Soft Frisbees
- Whooshes
- Comet Balls
- Fleece Balls

Caveat: Remove all basketballs from the area if you are in a gym. Basketballs are like magnets to people who have limited imaginations; roundball is anathema to creativity.

Conversation

During the time when folks are just beginning to show up for your training session, talk *with* them, not *at* them. I've been emphasizing this technique for years, but I feel that most people disregard the advice because it seems so obvious; there's no "trick" to it. Talk about things that have nothing to do with the workshop: Movies, weather, bungee jumping, something funny or exciting that happened to you recently, gourmet coffee, etc.

Raconteurmanship

Tell stories (something you have experienced) to the group related to what you are teaching. Let them know that this is real-life stuff worth hearing about. DO NOT relate macabre war stories to elevate your status as an experienced person.

Casual Competence

While you are talking with the folks, don't say or bring up things to draw attention to yourself. This is not a YOU time, this is their time. You must gain respect via your actions, not self proclamations.

Self-Deprecating Humor

Use lots of laughter. A good way to initiate some non-intrusive humor is to casually tell a personally embarrassing story about something that you did. Make yourself the brunt of the laughter, and get people used to laughing *with* someone situationally, rather than *at* that person.

Gem Stock

Use only programmatic gems during the first couple hours. Unless you are very good and very practiced, experimenting with activities during the first few hours of a workshop can be disastrous.

Venue

Give me an empty gymnasium and I'll fill it with fun. People are usually comfortable in a gym setting because it's a known. If you take first-time-folks out on a field or into the woods they may be wondering, "What's going to happen to me out here? Everyone knows that ROPES COURSES are in the woods, and you know what happens there…" It's also easier to maintain a group's attention within a closed area. And look at all the boundary lines painted on the floor for your exclusive and unrestrained use.

Full-Time Fun

"Don't stop running or they may figure out that you don't know what you're doing." That's a bit facetious, but partly true, and it's why the first few hours of programs that I'm facilitating are so frenetic. Load 'em up with activity at first, there's lots of time later for questions and introspection. This is experiential education, so get into the experience.

Don't Teach; Facilitate

Present the learning scenario as simply, entertainingly and accurately as possible, then back off and become an observer. If the group gets into a bind, becomes frustrated, or wants to quit, remember it's not your role to save them or teach them how to… Your raison d'être is to extend the learning process by allowing them to experience the joys of discovery and the agonies of not reaching a desired goal. Let this happen, *it is the crux of Adventure programming.*

Process

Without debriefing, a dynamite experience is simply an outstanding recreational activity. In contrast, debriefing every experience will cause participants to dread the process. Think balance.

Simplicity

There is nothing complicated about the Adventure learning process.

Encourage communication, cooperation, challenge, enjoyment and trust. Ask for a commitment to make these concepts happen. Give each individual a choice about the timing and performance level of their attempts. Talk about the results. Surround the group in a milieu of fun. That's it... that's all... STOP!

Participate

Don't be afraid to join activities, especially early in a program. Your presence in a game identifies your interest. Your involvement allows you to model enthusiasm, silliness, cooperation, listening, coaching, supporting. Even if you don't join an activity, show that you're involved by encouraging, talking, interacting. If you ignore your ability to influence by actions rather than words, you will have to work harder as a leader. Who needs to work harder?

Be a FUNATIC

A fanatic is described as one who is "unreasonably enthusiastic, overly zealous." A *funatic* is a fun fanatic. You can never go wrong erring on the fun side of the tracks. Inject some fun and enjoyment into an experience, and people will learn in spite of themselves. They will be so enthralled by what they're doing that the learnings will creep up on them before they even know what hit them.

Colleague and friend Tim Churchard has a wonderful saying he sometimes uses at the beginning of a workshop: "Today, the worst thing that can happen to you is that you will have fun. The best thing that could happen is that you will have fun and learn something, too."

DDADA — A Simple Guide to Presenting Activities

The value of an idea lies in using it.

—Thomas Edison

If you're the type who needs an easy-to-remember process for presenting activities, this acronym is for you. DDADA was used by the New Games Foundation to teach people about leading activities. It's a step-by-step guideline for presenting any game.

Describe

Present the rules to the activity; making the rules as simple as possible is usually the best technique. Speak clearly so that everyone can hear you. Be creative in your presentation, but don't confuse people with too much detail. Use fantasy and humor when appropriate.

Demonstrate

Remember — *One picture is worth a thousand words.* No matter how effective your explanation, a brief demonstration will clarify the rules. Like the old Chinese proverb: "I hear, and I forget. I see, and I remember. I do, and I understand."

Ask Questions

Before starting the game, check to see if any of the participants need clarification. If you don't ask them, they may not ask you. If there are lots of questions, you may not need to answer all of them (particularly with younger children) before starting the game. Use your judgment. Generally, it's preferable to get people into the game quickly so that they can have some fun. Too many questions can disrupt the flow you're trying to achieve.

Do

Play it!! Even if people are uncertain about some of the rules, they will probably learn quickly once the action starts. If you still notice confused looks and little or no activity, stop and explain or demonstrate again. (Exception:

Foes & Questors. If you wait until everyone understands *all* the rules, you'll never play. Some confusion is part of the game. Live with it and have fun.)

Adapt

Check to see if people are having fun. If so, let the game unfold and continue to observe. If you suspect that people's energy or enthusiasm is flagging, either change the rules (see Chapter Six on Game Changes) or change to a different game.

This guide can help you by providing a structure to your presentation style. As you're learning and developing your own style, an aid like this is particularly useful. Just remember though, it's only a guide. Modify it to work best for the group you're with, the game you're presenting. A guide can lose its value if it dictates everything that you say and do.

A Leader's Dilemma — Enforcing the Rules

Part of an Adventure leader's role is presenting and enforcing rules. But knowing when and how to enforce the rules can present problems.

What do you do when rules are stretched or outright broken? What is your response when two or more people get involved in a disagreement or argument over the rules of a game?

The basic answer is that it depends on the circumstances. More specifically, what rule is being broken, what is the consequence to the individuals in the group, what impact might it have on your role, vis-a-vis the group, and what are the ramifications for future activities if you let the infraction go?

Creative Interpretations

In *Warp Speed* the basic rules are: 1) the object must start and stop with the same person, 2) touches must be sequential; i.e., not everyone can touch the object at the same time, and 3) everyone must have possession of the object at some time during the activity.

As the group begins to work towards a solution, people will usually question whether it is breaking the rules to rearrange their positions in the circle to achieve a faster time. In this instance there is no rule being broken despite the *perception* that moving people in the circle is changing the original pattern. This example is a clear case of creative, out-of-the-box thinking. PRAISE THE GROUP!

The group may also decide that it is OK for one person to hold the object, spin around and touch the object to every person's hand. Clearly this technique will produce a very fast time. Does this break a rule? Yes and no, depending on your perspective.

Yes, it changes the definition of "possession" from what it was at the start of the activity (each person catches and throws the object), and so it could be considered breaking the rules. This technique also involves at least two people touching the object at the same time. Is this illegal? Technically yes, but it is not everyone touching it simultaneously so it is still sequential.

No, if the group re-defines "possession" to mean just a touch (no matter how quickly), then this technique seems legitimate. And no again if the group interprets one person holding the object and then touching it to everyone else as sequential touching.

Ask yourself: What is the purpose of this activity? Are these "infractions" helping or hindering the group to learn?

Warp Speed is an activity intended to promote creativity. Reward groups that think creatively by allowing them the option to interpret the rules to their advantage. These two examples are legitimate creative solutions, especially if the group has decided that achieving the fastest possible time is their goal.

But don't ignore the other dynamics at play here. Ask in the debrief how people felt about the re-definition of possession. Oftentimes people do not like the fact that they have given up their individual roles, but they are willing to do it to achieve a faster time. The bottom line makes it worth sacrificing greater personal

involvement. Check to see what the group's goal was. If it's time, then maybe changing the rules is OK; if it's involvement and productivity, then maybe the trade-off is not so clear.

Either way, weigh the effect of the rules being altered against the cost of strictly adhering to the letter of the law. In this situation, lean more towards allowing interpretation.

In *Everybody's It* tag, people sometimes stand still when not frozen; when someone runs by, they reach out to tag them. Fair or foul? Creative strategy or cheating? People conserve their energy or utilize another skill besides speed and agility to gain an advantage. No rule explicitly states you cannot stand still unless you're frozen. When people are tagged by someone using this technique, they usually cry foul. It's one thing to be tagged, another to be outwitted and tagged. But the fact that anybody can adopt this strategy makes it fair, although it may sometimes detract from the game if people get upset. It's another example of people being creative.

In both these cases a stated rule has not been broken. The stated rules could be interpreted to prevent these techniques, and that is where your judgment as a facilitator comes into play. Ask yourself, "What are the pluses and minuses of allowing or disallowing the group to liberally interpret the rules?"

Breaking the Rules

Here's another example that may be very different. At the *Spider's Web*, the group has been working extremely hard at passing people through the openings. They know that any touch causes one or more people to have to go through again. You see a slight touch as they pass someone through for the third time. Maybe someone in the group saw the touch, maybe not. Would you allow them to continue?

You can ignore the touch if you feel that the group is working to their fullest potential and that they need to have some success. You may want to reward them for trying their best, and perhaps give them a break even though they might be able to do better. Recognize that in

this situation you may be lessening the sense of accomplishment that the group derives from the activity because you didn't push them to fulfill the strict interpretation of the rules.

If you feel the touch is due to carelessness or rushing due to pressure from a deadline, you will probably call them on the touch. The point is for the group to examine what it is doing. If they are being sloppy or reacting differently due to time pressures, then these mistakes are opportunities for the group to learn and grow. Even if sending them back causes them to fail, the benefits of understanding their behaviors will be more beneficial than achieving the goal and not comprehending the consequences of their actions.

Another aspect of the *Spider's Web* versus the *Warp Speed* situation is the effect on the development of the group. Allowing for creativity, and even fostering it, is beneficial. But if the group goes too far in interpreting the rules to its advantage, then it's a relatively simple matter to prohibit those interpretations. On the other hand, if you allow the group at the *Web* to think that you won't stick to a stated rule, then they may push you to be more lax in other situations as well. If you're loose with the rules at the beginning of an activity, they may expect that you will be loose at the end; if you change and become more strict, they may see you as the cause of their failure rather than their own actions.

It's OK to be strict with the rules. In fact, it's probably advantageous early in a program or on an Initiative. It's easier to loosen up after being strict then it is to clamp down after being lenient.

If you don't have a legitimate reason for backing off of a rule, it's probably not worth it. In most cases, backing away from a rule simply to insure a successful completion of the problem isn't a good rationale.

In general, there are five options regarding rule enforcement:

- Enforce the rule and its consequence.
- Observe the infraction and report it to the group (allowing the group to decide whether to abide by the consequence).
- Observe the infraction and not report it (potentially allowing the infraction to become part of the debrief by exploring issues of integrity and/or quality control).
- Modify the rule (perhaps adapting the rule and its consequence is the best alternative because it was misunderstood or misinterpreted).
- Ignore the rule.

A good leader understands the differences between these choices and recognizes the pluses and minuses of each method of enforcement. Each alternative has its place in a leader's role as enforcer of the rules. The key is knowing when to use the different choices.

Expanding Your Activity Repertoire

For every group there is an appropriate activity.

So, is a good leader someone who knows lots of games and activities? Not necessarily.

Someone may know hundreds of activities but if he doesn't make good choices to match the activity selection to the group's needs, then that leader isn't doing a good job.

Is a good leader someone who only knows a few activities but leads them well? Again, not necessarily. While someone may be successful with the activities she knows, this leader may not have the flexibility and knowledge to deal with the different needs of some groups.

A good leader doesn't have to know every activity in the world (or all the activities in Karl's books), but it helps. Why? Because you may find just the right activity for a specific setting from amongst the myriad of games that you learn. In some cases, many activities may fit the same situation; in certain cases, only one or two may be appropriate.

Good leaders need to be comfortable and confident presenting the activities they do know. Why? To be able to appear relaxed and knowledgeable in front of the group.

A large repertoire of activities to choose from gives you a safety net. If one activity you present bombs, you can immediately select another that will work. In planning an agenda, consider multiple options in sequencing games. Options offer a higher probability of success.

This need or desire for a large repertoire may seem like a Catch-22. How do you learn a lot of activities without having a lot of experience leading them? How can you become an experienced leader without knowing many activities in advance?

It's a question of balance. At first you probably need to limit the type of programs you lead. With a limited scope of activities, you can lead a smaller range of programs successfully. Start where you feel comfortable (unless you're into high levels of stress and anxiety). As you develop experience and begin to expand your repertoire, you can expand the range of programs you deliver because you will have more tools to use in addressing group issues.

Each individual will move along this developmental track at a different pace. While some people feel uncomfortable leading, others may

relish the risk of trying something new. Allow for a few butterflies to flutter in your stomach as you begin your session, but be wary of what you've undertaken if you end up lying awake for several nights out of anxiety.

If a large repertoire is desirable, how does one get it? You can't exactly go to a store and buy large, extra large and gargantuan repertoires of Adventure activities. So where does one find a trusty and flexible activity collection?

Workshops and Books

Workshops and training programs are the best resource. Learning by doing is always the best alternative since you can experience the game and discover any quirks or special rules needed to play it safely. You'll often hear people say, "That game sounded stupid or strange when I read it in the book, but now that

I've played it this game will be one of my favorites."

Books are the best secondary source. They are relatively cheap, readily available and full of good ideas. And while books don't give you the direct experience of an activity, the more experience you gain, the more valuable books become. You'll get better at reading between the lines and evaluating how a game will play out after just reading the description.

Books are a wonderful resource for ideas. You may not like everything about a particular game, but the general idea may spark you to create something better. Older game books focused on traditional, competitive activities. More often than not, such games need to be adapted to fit the Adventure philosophy. This technique of finding ideas and adapting them also works better once you have more experience. The more you know and understand about what makes a quality play experience, the more likely you can devise new ideas on your own.

Conferences and Other Ideas

Conferences, like workshops, offer opportunities to learn new ideas. AAHPERD (American Association of Health, Physical Education, Recreation and Dance) and AEE (the Association for Experiential Education) are two national organizations that host regional and national conferences where you are likely to discover sessions on Adventure activities. They also offer a wide variety of books and other resources.

Toy stores, recycling centers, sports equipment catalogs and children's museums are other places that we have found ideas for activities. Basically, anything that will juice up your creativity is a potential source of a new game or Initiative problem.

Another good reason for developing a large repertoire of activities is that it will help keep you fresh. The more options you can draw from, the less you have to play the same games over and over. Of course, you'll develop a list of favorites and play them more frequently. Nothing wrong with that. But beware of burnout from always presenting the same activities.

Large Groups

You want to know the secret to working with large groups? Don't do them.

You want more? You're sure? It's like the carpenter said: "Be careful how much you learn about working around the house. The more you know, and the more you demonstrate that you can do something, the more you're going to be asked to do."

We joke about leading large groups. Generally, it's not easy. For most people, the usual anxiety of leading increases exponentially as the numbers of faces before them increases.

10 — no problem…
20 — it's doable…
30 — maybe I need some help…
40 — is this really going to work…?

50+ — call a professional…
100+ — call Karl and Steve… they'll do anything.

Maybe.

I admit to enjoying presenting to large groups, sometimes. Large groups have incredible energy to expend; but they demand a lot in return. If you structure a large group program properly, it can be fun.

What to Consider

First, what is considered a large group? Anything over 25–30 requires a different style of presentation. For an average Initiative problem, 10–15 is the ideal to maximum size (though more than 20 people work on some Initiatives). For a *Trust Fall,* 12–16 is stretching the limits of people's capabilities to concentrate and to physically catch one another.

Remember, these numbers are just that — numbers. You take the group you get. But it's important to recognize that diminishing returns do set in as the size of the group increases. The more people, the more difficult it is for everyone to be actively involved in the experience and to share their personal opinion; in other words, the larger the group size the less able you are to have a meaningful discussion about the activities. Debriefing large groups can be done, but it may not produce the kind of sharing that you want from a group.

Second, how do you structure a large group experience? As the leader, you will be the focus of attention more so than with a smaller group. With a host of participants, your role is to hold their attention and keep them involved. In large groups it is easy for people to feel left out and bored, so try to keep the activity level high; i.e., lots of movement and action, and move from activity to activity quickly. A large group's attention span is definitely shorter than a smaller group's. Transitions between activities take longer, so you need to plan for fewer activities.

Third, large groups tend to limit the options of what activities work well, especially if you are indoors in a small space. An hour to ninety

minutes may be as long as one person can manage presenting to fifty plus people. More than that, and you better have a pretty extensive Bag of Tricks to draw on or plenty of experience with large group activities.

Know what the outcome of any session will be with a large group. What people learn is reduced (less potential for asking questions, less chance of everyone having time to talk and share) and the opportunity to pass along any skills is reduced. Basically, large group activities tend to focus on fun since there isn't much else that you can realistically achieve.

Can you effectively run Adventure experiences with larger groups? The answer is yes. To be successful, you need more creativity, more props and a lot of confidence.

Practical Stuff

Taking a large audience and presenting some games for fun is a very effective method of exposing new groups to Adventure.

Some favorites for larger groups include: *Pairs Tag* and *Pairs Squared*, *Boop*, *Categories*, *3-way Hog Call*, *Transformer Tag*, *Hustle Handle*, *Quick* and *Coop Line Up*, *Birthday*

Line Up, FFEACH/MOOCH, Hop Box, Mergers, Scrabble Babble, Egg Drop and the classic *Lap Sit*. Many of these activities can work favorably even with over a hundred people. If you don't believe it, don't try it.

Presenting Initiatives to larger groups poses an entirely different set of issues. When someone asks you to lead Initiatives for 30–40 people, normally you would want to try to convince them to consider another type of experience. Initiatives and most ropes course activities function more effectively with groups of 10–15. But when you can't work with such a small group, there are alternatives.

Present several Initiatives simultaneously. The key here is to be certain that the groups can monitor themselves adequately with split supervision. You need to select problems that can be done safely without immediate, direct supervision. You could include a *Spider's Web*, but you wouldn't want to be far away due to the safety concerns. Include *Traffic Jam* and you have no need to worry about physical safety, and you can monitor the group's efforts from a distance.

The down side to this plan is that you will not have close observation of each group. Debriefs may not be as effective or as thorough since you will not have detailed observations about the group process during the activities.

Set up *Stepping Stones*, *Trolleys* and *Tin Shoe* as three problems. Divide your large group into three units and give each smaller team only the props for their Initiative. Each group can function independently, or they can decide to collaborate to make their tasks easier. The wonderful aspect to this scenario is that all the groups have to cross the area, but each has a different set of props to employ. Creative collaboration can turn this dilemma into a successful lesson plan.

Another technique is to present the same activity to the entire group, but subdivide them into smaller teams to tackle the problem separately. Using *Stepping Stones* again, create a circular boundary with a safe zone in the center. Arrange enough props for three or more groups (depending on the size of the work teams that you want) around the perimeter of the boundary so that each team has an equal share of the materials. Again, groups can proceed independently or can choose to work together. Debriefs can focus on why the groups opted to go their own way, or on how and why they decided to help each other.

Create a Site Central variation to the problem. In this type of scenario, the group is divided into smaller units and each group is given a different function. If you divide your group into two smaller teams, one team (3–5 people) becomes the decision-makers and one team (the remainder of the group, 10–15 people) is the task force. The task force actually does the problem; the decision-makers must approve of any actions before the task force can act. One or more people from the decision-makers is designated as liason to the task force to discuss the plans. That person(s) cannot physically help with the task.

If you divide the group into three teams, you still have decision-makers and a task force, but the third group becomes consultants. Only the consultants can move back and forth between the decision-makers and the task force, and the consultants can only communicate — they are not allowed to physically involve themselves in the task.

Site Central scenarios emphasize the importance of communication and simulate many real life situations. The number of issues emerging from the activities increases and sometimes the complexity of the group dynamics makes it difficult to focus on all the relevant issues. Still, if you need techniques for keeping large groups actively involved in Initiatives, these strategies work well.

The key to large group situations is to remember that it's easier for people to lose focus and to feel lost in the crowd. Do whatever you can to maintain a high level of activity for all participants, provide more structure to help move things along smoothly, and keep discussions focused and brief to maintain interest.

What Can Cause a Bad Experience — Four Issues

Not every Adventure program is going to run smoothly or be completely successful. Problems can arise just as easily as the glowing faces of enthusiastic participants at the end of a good session. Leading activities can and is a challenge. When you plan and consider how to prepare for your Adventure sessions, be aware that trouble is out there waiting for you!

Where does a good idea, Adventure programming, go wrong? There are four distinct areas from which trouble springs:

- Leadership Style
- Sequencing
- Participant Behaviors
- Logistics

Some trouble spots are easily identified (though not easily solved), some problems are "givens" (you can't alter the space or the people as much as you may want to), and some difficulties remain unknown until after they surface (no matter how well you plan, sometimes things don't go as you hope or anticipate they will).

Adventure facilitators have many options available. Your knowledge, confidence level, repertoire and comfort in front of groups — both intangible factors and hard skills — can influence and manage the unknowns of participant's behaviors and the unchangeable nature of logistics. What you choose to do, or not do, has a great impact upon what happens with the group.

The following lists highlight some of the pitfalls faced by Adventure leaders. Some factors in one category (poor choice of game under Leadership can also be placed in another category, in this case Sequencing). In any event, these lists can identify some trouble spots. Being alert to the following factors will help you... identify potential problems before they happen.

Leadership Style	Sequencing	Participant Behavior	Logistics
poor presentation	poor timing — too much/too little challenge (poor choice for population)	poor timing	poor geography/ environment, nature (wind, noise, safety, etc.)
poor choice of game/bad		sensitivity issues (politically incorrect)	
sensitivity issues game	feeling unsafe	reality vs. fantasy (*Killer*)	bad game (not fun, not appropriate)
lack of imagination	lack of imagination (small repertoire)	feeling unsafe (*Striker*)	wrong equipment (unsafe)
reality versus fantasy (inappropriate scenario)	poor balance of competition/cooperation	lack of imagination	too many/too few people
pushing too hard or not enough	diminishing of trust	strict adherence to the rules	too much/not enough time
too serious or too silly	pushing too hard or not enough	cheating	onlookers
volume & enthusiasm	too serious or too silly, too active or too passive, etc.	success vs failure — calling your own touches	
		bend to peer pressure	
		unknown of people's psyches (hidden agendas)	
		diminishing of trust	

The Games List

I hear, and I forget.

I see, and I remember.

I do, and I understand.

— *Chinese Proverb*

The Professional's Memory Enhancer or The Novice's Crutch?

For years now I (Steve) have been carrying a worn page in my pocket as I head out to lead a program. On that page are the names of the hundreds of activities I know and use in my work. No, it's not the same piece of paper that has survived these fifteen years. Many have been lost, some given away, some worn to tatters by overuse. It is both my security blanket and my stress reducer.

Why have such a list? Here are a few good reasons:

1) It helps you remember all the games you know.

2) When you're mentally stuck for a game or activity, the list is a convenient memory enhancer/restorer.

3) A list allows you to categorize activities for easy reference in program planning and sequencing.

4) Consulting an impressive looking games list sure makes you look professional.

So are you sold on a games list? Have you already started scribbling? Wait just a minute and consider a couple of cautions about using lists.

Be careful that the list doesn't become a crutch. If the list and the categories start dictating how you lead and what activities you select all the time, then you're relying on it too heavily. The list should be a band-aid, not a miracle cure. Don't use the list to the point where you lose touch with spontaneity and creativity. Personalize your list. Choose activities that have meaning for you.

Don't get caught up in just adding more and more games to your list. Remember that learning more activities doesn't necessarily improve your leadership style and presence. Don't be distracted from developing your facilitation skills by the need to learn more and more games. Balance is the key. You should know enough activities and games that you can comfortably accommodate the needs of a group, but you also need to be a strong enough facilitator to manage the group process effectively.

Lastly, scan your entire list for activity choices during the planning phase. You can start with the games in the most relevant category, but you may be surprised that you find good ideas elsewhere on your list. For example, I often find good "starters" in my "large games" section. A list can restrict your thinking just as easily as it can enhance it. Know what the list is good for and use it liberally as you develop your skills; but also realize that it's only a tool and not a magic formula that can improve your ability to deal with a group.

Fine Tuning

Adventure leaders sometimes set themselves up, making their task harder than necessary. The following list of techniques may help you avoid some of the pitfalls we've encountered and observed.

Positioning

When the sun is shining down early or late in the day, it may prevent people from making direct eye contact with you during a presentation or debrief. If you position yourself so that *you* are facing into the sun, no one in the group will have difficulty seeing you. Yes, it does make it tough for you. But especially at the beginning of a program, you are trying to make it easy for people to relax and get comfortable, why allow the distraction of sun in their eyes.

Eye Contact

On a bright day, to alleviate your own eye strain, you may be tempted to wear sunglasses. Wearing sunglasses can put a barrier between you and me. There can be no eye contact. Is it worth possibly creating a barrier between yourself and people in the group?

Often it's these little things that make a big difference. Being a great facilitator means being open to the group, being accessible.

Anything that limits that feeling of connectedness seems worthy of evaluation.

Centering

Standing in the center of the group when explaining an activity seems logical, but it doesn't work in all situations. In circle games, which tend to be used a lot at the beginning of a program (probably as symbols of everyone being involved on an equal basis — did you think of that? Good Job!) standing in the center of the circle means some people are always behind you. They may not be able to hear you or see what you are demonstrating. Consider where you can have the best impact on the group; don't just assume one spot works best for everything.

But being in the center may be necessary for a game like *Swat Tag* (*More New Games,* pg. 45) because a demonstration is crucial for people to fully understand the action of the game. This being so, how do you manage the communication issues stated above?

Stand on the perimeter of the circle as you verbally explain the rules so that everyone can see and hear you. Then move into the center of the circle to give a visual demonstration. If questions are asked, rotate as you speak (so you address all the players), and speak LOUDLY so that everyone hears the answers.

Another activity where you should be in the center is a game like *Speed Rabbit* (*Cowstails II,* pg. 63). The same techniques above can work — explain from the perimeter and move to the center for demonstrations. But demonstrations can be more effective if you roam about the circle, using people to help create the animals. You're asking people to help you, and you're showing that it's OK to be silly. Both techniques may help this game reach its extraordinary laugh potential.

Another important reason to be the center is so that you can be the first one in the middle. There's often a lot of anxiety about being in the middle of a circle for a game, probably rooted in our memories of elementary school where we were IT and couldn't pass along this heavy

burden to someone else. Because *Speed Rabbit* involves looking silly, acting silly, being silly (and there really isn't much point to this game if you're not going to exude silliness), you being the first person to own the center sets a precedent. If you manage to get out of the middle, then people know it can be done. If you show them how, participants might develop a strategy to help themselves get out of the center once they're in. With you in the center, the players can feel more comfortable to start because they are relatively safe (momentarily of course) as part of the circle.

Centering Rule #1: Always assume the center position first if there is a risk (physical, emotional) for the participants.

A couple last tips about centering:

It is much less effective, usually ineffective, when done with a large group. The more people you have, the more difficult it is for them to hear because they are spread out. Bring them together, as close as possible, for the explanation. Speak VERY LOUDLY if necessary. Repeat the rules/directions several times to all parts of the circle or group to maximize the chances that people hear you and understand.

A rule of thumb that has served well over the years applies to any type of "tag" game where a person is in the center of a circle and must do something to get out. *Speed Rabbit,*

Swat Tag, Bumpity-Bump-Bump and *Wompum* are good examples. Whenever this situation arises, state that if you are the person in the middle, you can decide if the person you tagged is now it, whether or not you *really* did so. In other words, the center person has the ability to get out of the center simply by saying, "I got you." People respond favorably to this approach since no one likes the helpless feeling of being trapped in the middle and unable to escape.

Staying Close

Another situation where a leader can get into trouble is in explaining an activity like *Hog Call* (*Silver Bullets,* pg. 98) or *Hop Box* (a.k.a. *Jumpin' Jack Flash*). In each case, the formation for playing the game requires people to be spread out. You might think to separate them first to show them their positions before explaining to make it simpler to understand. This strategy dictates that you have a very loud voice, or a co-leader who can give the rules to the more distant group. Either way, there is potential for some confusion. You might try lining people up in the proper formation, but still have them stay close enough to you to hear the rules before going to the actual starting position.

POINTS OF PLAY

A few "keys" have emerged in discussing Adventure leadership. We offer them to you as these Points of Play. They are principles we believe in, ideas that may seem like common sense. They are a few last points to consider and dwell on as you finish reading, some thoughts to mull over as you peruse the remainder of the text looking for new activity ideas, and some nuggets of our collected experience that may cause you to think again about how you use the information in this book.

1) ***Do whatever needs to be done to create a fun moment.*** Know what you can do to allow people to have fun and do it; try to avoid doing too much and be sensitive to doing too little.

2) ***No matter how good (or bad) an activity is, your leadership can always make it better (or worse).*** Activities are pretty much interchangeable; it's what you do with them that is important. A good leader can probably make a bad game work, but a poor leader can stifle even the best of games.

3) ***The better you get at leading through Adventure, the better you have to be.*** In other words, the more skill you develop, the more complex the needs of the group become. You're using Adventure to meet more complex goals: The more awareness you have, the more focused you need to be on what the group needs and wants. The bigger your reputation becomes, the more will be expected from you.

4) ***No matter what else you do, remember that the point is to have fun.*** It's easy to get caught up in rules, equipment, debriefing issues and questions, rainy day plans, attitude problems, ...the list goes on and on. But so long as people are having fun, they will be interested and open to the learnings available to them. If the fun is missing, the learning opportunities are diminished.

5) ***Plan more activities than you need, especially when you are a novice leader (but always be ready to change the plan).*** Having more ideas than you could ever use may make you feel more secure and confident, but you need to remember that you can't always predict how groups and individuals will react to Adventure. You still need to give them whatever will make it fun.

6) ***The first 15–30 minutes of a program can make or ruin the experience.*** The first few minutes can have a large impact on the remainder of the program. Use your best activities, the sure-fire successes, to set the tone. In a longer program of several days, this entry period may not be so important since you have more time to recover. But in general, start every program with a bang.

7) ***Facilitate, don't recreate.*** Good debriefs can transform disappointing experiences into powerful and valuable learning opportunities. Fun for the sake of fun is OK; just remember that fun is simply the tool to access the learnings.

8) ***If what you are presenting to your audience isn't enjoyable, people will not return for more of what you have to offer.*** Point #7 not withstanding, fun is at the heart of all Adventure programs.

HAVE FUN!

Section Two

Activities

Using The Icons

We have used the following icons to help you see, at a quick glance, if an activity can be done indoors or out and whether it needs props, pre-built materials or ropes course elements. But do not discount any activities just by the icons. Many that display the indoor icon can also be done out of doors; the icon simply tells you that the activity is *traditionally* done indoors. The same is true of the outdoor designated activities, only a few of which (*Waiter Wars,* for example) really should be done outdoors. The same is true of the number of props needed. The Lots of Props designation may mean lots of different types of stuff (*Minefield*) or lots of the same item, like fleece balls. We suggest that you read all the activities (eventually, anyway) and adapt them, if necessary, to suit your individual circumstances.

 Indoors

 Outdoors

 One or a Few Props

 Lots of Props

 Pre-Built or Set Up Props or Ropes Course Elements

Ice Breakers

Commonalties

Looking for a quick mixer?

• •

A chance to experiment with diversity? Just an excuse for people to talk to each other for a few minutes? Give this a try.

Set-Up

Ask the group to arrange themselves into clusters of 2s, 3s, 6s, 8s or whatever suits the mood. Give each group a piece of paper and pen.

Play

The task is to generate a list of things that are common to all the people in the cluster but which you could not identify by looking at them. Ask people to come up with a specific number of commonalties or as many as they can in a couple of minutes.

Some examples:

• speak a foreign language;
• have the same number of brothers and/or sisters;
• traveled to a certain country;
• have the same letter starting their last names;
• are vegetarians;
• ride motorcycles;
• wear contact lenses, etc.

Some examples that you can see, and hence don't count: Wear glasses, have brown hair, have blue eyes, etc.

Given a few minutes, it's sometimes amazing how many commonalties people can find with each other. It's a simple way to begin learning about other people in a fun way.

Variation

As a means of dividing up teams or to pick partners, I'll ask a person to find a partner, someone they don't know but with whom they have something in common that is not visible. After all the people have a partner, I'll ask each pair to disclose what their common trait is. This technique can be used over and over and over. Did you know that the authors have both played *Foes & Questors*... rappelled off a bridge on a major interstate highway... dragged chains through the sand at Crane's Beach...

How We Differ

A *Get-To-Know-You* Game...

· ·

I've run into other games like this one (used to break the ice at the beginning of a workshop), but the variety and diversity of the questions available in this survey seem more interesting and revealing. Give it a try and I think you'll be impressed by the group's reaction. Make copies of these questions so that each smaller group gets only one: Less paper = more talk.

Categories (All 1 point)
Bonus Points

For each different birthday month recorded.
5 pts. — born on a holiday

Points for each birth state represented.
5 pts. — born overseas.

For each shoe size over 12 or under 4.
2 pts. — wearing sandals

For visiting each of the following:
Grand Canyon, Sears Tower, Epcot Center, Waikiki.
5 pts. — for three,
7 pts. — for four

Points for each different make car driven to this site today.
5 pts. — if you car pooled,
10 pts. — if you walked

For appearing on TV, radio, or newspaper. (You must be mentioned by name.)
7 pts. — all three

Points for each sibling, living or deceased. Includes adopted, step, and half-sibling.
10 pts. — for twins

For each continent visited. Requires 24-hour on-ground stay.
10 pts. — for 6, and
15 pts. — for all seven or Antarctica

Points for each last name starting with the letters Z, Q, K, or U.
7 pts. — for X letters;

Points for each language (other than native) that you speak *fluently*.
12 pts. — three or more

For each year married (1 person).
3 pts. — for 10 yrs.;
12 pts. — for 20

For each state that you have lived in. (Min. 6 months)
5 pts. — for 6 months overseas

Points for each living biological parent.
3 pts. — for each living grand-parent;
7 pts. — for each living great-grandparent

Subtract the youngest age in the group from the oldest, and allow one point for each calendar year between the two.
3 pts. — for anyone over 65

For each person NOT wearing a watch.
3 pts. — NO jewelry (wedding bands excluded)

For each person who can roll their tongue.
7 pts. — if you can turn your tongue upside down (in your mouth!)

Points for all those with colored underwear (patterns and floral count).
10 pts. — *No* underwear

Divide your original group into grouplets of 3–5 depending upon the total number of participants. When completed, ask the teams to add up their scores and compare final totals if they want to. At some point, ask them which was more fun; participating, talking, sharing, laughing — or winning. If they say, "Winning," take their trophies away and recycle them to make toothbrush handles.

Human Treasure Hunt

A nice low-key energizer for a group just meeting each other...

• •

Another mixer activity for groups large or small, where people may or may not know each other, where you want a little or a lot of interaction, and where people can have some fun.

This activity requires some preparation. Or you can simply photocopy the sample list in the text.

Create your own list, personalizing the facts to suit your audience. What you write for a group of adults, high schools students or elementary students would be different for each group.

What you want to create is a list of facts about people that will be representative of the group playing the game. Include facts that apply to some or most of the people in the group, with a few factoids mixed in that my have only a few responses or possibly none at all.

Play

Each person gets a treasure hunt list and a writing implement. The task is to circulate within the group and identify a different person for each fact on the list. If John fits "born in the same month as you," then you can't use John's name for another fact. Players attempt to complete their entire list utilizing different people. Specify that you must meet people individually if you write their name next to a fact.

To play competitively, tell people to finish their list ASAP. Then start your timer, or pretend to. Most players won't care, but the "Casio Whip" always acts as a prod to performance.

This game can last for 5 minutes to an hour, is great around meal times, fits most indoor

spaces and is a nice low-key energizer for a group just meeting each other. Sound like a winner? You're right again.

Variation

If you know a few things about your group before their arrival, you can create the list with specific facts about the participants. When I led trips overseas, I would take one fact from each student's application and generate a list of all the facts, one per student. That way, each student had to meet each person to complete the list and everyone learned something unique about everyone else during the process. It takes more work, but you get more results.

Use the attached list as a sample to guide your own development of a *Treasure Hunt* list.

Human Treasure Hunt

_____ is born in the same month as you

_____ can speak a foreign language

_____ has been on TV, radio or in the news (why:)

_____ has performed on stage anywhere

_____ has been elected to a political position

_____ volunteers for an organization or cause

_____ has been in a parade (why:)

_____ has a unique skill or talent (what:)

_____ has the same number of siblings as you

_____ wrote a letter to the editor (why:)

_____ has traveled outside the U.S. (where:)

_____ established a record

_____ can play a musical instrument

_____ climbed a mountain over 10,000 feet

_____ has lived outside the U.S. for more than a year

_____ knows someone famous (who:)

It Ain't Me Babe

With apologies to Bob Dylan...

• •

We're always looking for new and inventive ways for people to get to know each other. If you are too, check this out.

People are usually either open or tight about relating personal information to strangers. This activity may raise some anxieties, but it also can be very funny.

Instead of your typical get-to-know-each-other verbal introduction, try this non-verbal interaction.

Ask people to randomly pick a partner. Give them 5–10 minutes together to introduce themselves. They may not speak to one another during this time. Writing is also not allowed. As a compassionate gesture, allow paper and pen for drawing only (but it probably isn't needed).

Players needs to communicate whatever they feel is important about themselves to their partners. At the end, players report out to the group what they learned about their partners. What adds a little fun to the descriptions is to have each partner verbalize what they learned, and then allow a brief time for rebuttal and/or corrections from the person just described to insure accuracy of the introduction.

There are no points to score. It's all for fun. If you learn something about each other, so much the better. Enjoy the experience. You'll probably never have a chance to not speak to one another again.

Truth Is Stranger Than Fiction

This activity brings out a lot of unusual stories.

• •

That's why it's fun. That's also why it can take a long time for the game to play out if you pursue the stories in greater detail.

Play

Here's how to play (or at least one variation). Players share three stories about themselves. Two stories are true; one is a lie. The group then tries to determine which story is which.

Short Version

If you want the game to move quickly, allow a short period (30 seconds) for questions and then everyone votes for which story they think is true. After the vote, the storyteller reveals the truth. As soon as the truth is told (amidst comments of, "You gotta be kidding?" and, "You did that?"), a new person can share two stories.

Long Version

Once the stories are related, time is allowed for questioning of the storyteller. The intent is to verify the story by asking pertinent questions as to whether or not the tellers have enough information to back up their stories. People normally enjoy the questioning, and beleaguered tellers sometimes feel as though they are involved in the Inquisition. After a specified time (2–5 minutes) or when no more questions remain, the group votes on the stories and the teller tells all.

Once the truth is revealed, there may be a desire to delve into the story in more detail. Allow time for this; it's where the action's at.

The only drawback you may encounter is that novice raconteurs feel they have to come up with outlandish stories in order to be part of the game. Occasionally, people have felt awkward because their stories didn't display as much pizzazz as those of other players. As leader, be ready to start the story sequence with some tales of your own, or announce the game and then give people 5–10 minutes to think of some stories before play begins.

You will find that, inadvertently, most people almost always tell their true stories first, then finish up with some wild prevarication. Just human nature I suppose; i.e., feeling the need to be initially honest.

Karl and I have led all the games in this book at least once. Steve and I did not lead a workshop together in 1993. What do you think?

Who Are You?

What brought the biggest laugh or smile to your face recently?

• •

Imagine that you could ask people you just met anything you wanted to know in order to learn something about them. What would you ask?

Don't lose that question!! That's what this little activity is all about.

Ask the group to brainstorm a list of ten or so questions that people would like to ask each other. The questions should be appropriate for the setting, so monitor your group's choices.

Narrow the list down to two or three questions that people like best, then allow whatever length of time you want for mingling and conversing. Encourage people to try to meet everyone (if the size of the group allows).

Provide pens and paper in order to record the most interesting questions. If people want to ask more than two or three questions, have as many rounds as you have time for.

Consider trying for a balance of factual, personal (but not intrusive), humorous and unusual questions to provide an air of Adventure to the conversation. After all, lest you forget, this is an *Adventure* based experiential text.

So...

• What is the funniest situation you have encountered during the last two months?

• What famous person, living or dead, would you most want to have dinner with?

• Who do you consider to be a personal hero/heroine?

• What is your favorite film of all time?

• Who is one of your favorite fictional characters?

• What's your most recent embarrassing moment?

Warm-Ups

Bumpity Bump Bump

Ask your group to "line up in a circle..."

• •

Saying, "*Bumpity Bump Bump*" takes between .6 and .65 seconds (the average is close to .623). You need to know this.

Ask your group to "line up in a circle," then put yourself at circle center. The arced players should be about four to five steps away from you. Point decisively at one of the circled folks and say that person's first name with conviction, following their stated name immediately with the exclamation, "*Bumpity Bump Bump.*" The person that you pointed to and named must respond by saying the first name of the person to the left, before you finish exclaiming, "*Bumpity Bump Bump.*" If they flub the name

or completely forget who's who, that person takes your place in the center, and subsequently attempts to trap someone else.

It obviously pays to know who is on your left, unless the person in the center exclaims, "RIGHT!" before pointing and saying, "BBB," then you must name the person to your right. *However*, if the center person is male and exclaims, "Right!" you must reverse that command and name the person to the left, unless the center person is female and yells, "Left!" which is obviously right, right?

Sorry, I couldn't help it. You were doing such a good job of reading and concentrating, I should be ashamed. Everything before the Italicized word *however* above is for real, and constitutes a useful name game. Everything after *however* is me fooling around — just playing. Are you smiling? Hope so...

Billboard

Use this self-disclosure activity as a means of, "...getting to know you."

• •

Ask a just-met assemblage to brainstorm eight or ten characteristics that they would like to discover about other players in the group. Record these psyche factors on "blue tac" or flip-chart paper; print large with a felt-tipped pen so all can see. Asking for a show of majority (elevated hands, voice volume, basic intimidation), pick the top five or six listed items. These topics might include: Favorite fast food, favorite health food, best vacation spot, best book read in the last year, your top three movies of the year, favorite thing to hate, sexual

proclivities, pet pedagogical peeve, top recreational pursuit...

Provide each player with a sheet of chart paper and a marker, and ask individuals to respond to each topic as it pertains to themselves; i.e., make a personal list of what they like, using the headline items brainstormed above. Provide about five minutes for this soul-searching.

As you see players apparently finishing with their choices, help them tape their choices sheet to their shoulders (front or back; their choice). Indicate that they can now walk around the room and help others tape on their identity "billboards," or just observe and compare responses. Encourage individual vis-á-vis verbal exploration of the various choices. Think of this mingling as the quintessential liquorless cocktail party.

Categories

After you have been in the Adventure education business for a while, someone will eventually ask, "I hear that you do a good job facilitating groups, could you plan something significant for my weekend group?" Being a basically nice person, and responding to their flattery, you say, "Sure, this weekend would be fine. How many people are in your group?" "Well, quite a few will be skiing this weekend, so we shouldn't have more than 80 or 90."

AArgh! Gulp! HELP!!!

Here're two suggestions: 1) Don't work with groups larger than 25; 2) If you *have to*, start your large group session with *Categories*.

Set-Up

Ask the large group (if there are more than 100 people, you will have to use a loudspeaker — don't look at me... you got yourself into this)

to separate quickly into smaller groups that you are about to announce. Alternate 50/50 splits (only two groups) with multi-groups (many choices). Be upbeat and directive in your presentation; keep the groups moving. As soon as the milling around has slowed and distinctly smaller groups have established themselves, give the participants only time enough to look at one another, say hi, then hit 'em with another categorical split.

The following list is extensive and much larger than you would want to use during one presentation. When I'm doing *Categories*, I seldom present more than 10–12 groupings. Look through the list and pick those categories that appeal most to you. Be careful not to use an inappropriate choice considering the age or maturity level of the players. Deciding who scrunches or folds toilet paper might not be the best idea for a middle school group.

Categories List

Clasp your hands and fold your thumbs. Is your right or left thumb on top?

Fold your arms. Is your right or left arm on top?

Have someone look at your eyes and tell you what color they are.

Which leg do you put in your pants (shorts) first?

Are you wearing jewelry? Wristwatches and wedding rings don't count.

When you clap, is your right or left hand on top? Parallel hands?

When you tap your foot to music, do you use the right or left foot?

Do you print or use cursive when you write a letter?

Using your index finger as a pencil, draw an imaginary circle in the air. Does your finger travel clockwise or counterclockwise?

Again, using your index finger as a pencil, draw a profile of a dog. Is the dog facing right or left?

Which is your dominant eye? (Do dominant eye test procedure.)

With which eye do you give a spontaneous wink?

Thinking of clearing a ditch or low fence, off which leg do you jump?

Standing, facing the foot of the bed, on which side do you get in ? Which side do you sleep on, if you sleep with someone else?

What is your shoe size?

What month were you born in?

Can you roll your tongue? Can you turn your tongue upside down?

What is your astrological sign?

What is your blood type?

After a store purchase, do you count your change or not?

How many blood-related siblings are there in your family counting yourself?

After taking bread out of the bread bag, how do you reseal the bag? Spin? Fold? Which direction do you spin the bag? Or do you spin just the top?

When you apply a "twistie" to the top of a plastic bag, do you turn the twistie clockwise or counterclockwise?

When you lick an ice cream cone, which way do you rotate the cone?

When standing casually with your hands in your pockets, are they in your front or back pockets?

Do you pull toilet paper off the top or bottom of a roll? (Remember to establish a don't care category.)

Are you a scruncher or a folder — toilet paper?

What color underwear do you have on right now? (Make sure to signify a no underwear category.)

Do you pronounce tomato with a long or short a? Same question with aunt?

When you insert your mail into a mailbox, do you check to see if the mail has dropped, or do you just pop the envelopes into the slot and leave?

Do you pick up pennies from the ground or ignore them?

Do you shower primarily in the morning or at night?

When you perform the isometric exercise of trying to pull your joined hands apart, is your right or left hand on top?

Do you shave primarily with a blade or an electric razor (depilatories don't count)?

Do you generally wear auto seat belts or not? Do you put the seat belt on before or after you begin driving?

When you ride a bike, do you wear a helmet?

If someone asks you to turn around, which way do you turn?

When you sit down on the ground, which hand touches the ground first? When you get up do you use the same hand?

Which way do you swirl liquid in a glass (brandy in a snifter)?

When you open an envelope, do you use a letter opener (knife), or tear it open?

Hustle Bustle

Do you know what the word bustle means?

● ●

I didn't either. It's like the word *verge*. You know, being on the verge of doing something. Or similarly, the use of *fro*, as in, *to and fro*. Interesting words that we use all the time, but can't define. Well, *bustle* means, "Energetic and obtrusive activity," and in this case complements the word hustle. *Verge* and *fro* are up to you; I hope I've piqued your curiosity.

Hustle Bustle is an introductory activity I use often during the beginning phase of a workshop. Remember: Game names are only significant to the people using them; i.e., calling this game *Hustle Bustle* works better for me than thinking of it as activity #14. Call it whatever you want (empowerment), and change the rules if it makes sense for you and your players.

By presenting this game during the first couple of hours of a workshop, when people are still trying to figure out one another, I'm programmatically attempting to achieve a number of things: Cooperation, communication, trust, etc. To emphasize these various pedagogic points, let me talk you through how and why I

frame and use this engaging group challenge.

Try to pick a venue for your presentation that is relatively quiet and located in a somewhat removed area so that the group will feel comfortable trying a new activity. Snarling chainsaws, lawnmower exhaust, gawking students, or environmental discomfort (sunlight, wind, cold, rain, etc.), don't help to establish that optimum teaching moment. The only reason I'm mentioning this is because it's so obvious, but sometimes classroom teachers have a tendency to forget and so do I. If the sun is shining brightly and I'm presenting a group game in an open field situation, I have to consciously place myself so that the sun shines in *my* eyes, not into the forty or so eyes watching me.

Be animated. Everyone is initially keyed on you, and you are setting the tone for participation. If you can't get UP for these activities, don't bother reading any further, because everything you present will be just OK, kind of gray, and typical of what has made many students dread *fizz ed*.

Play

Announce that you think learning names within a working group is an excellent way to encourage communication and establish a friendlier tone amongst just-met people. For example, if you want to refer to someone in the group, it's much more congenial and acceptable to say, "Hey, Sally, can you give me a hand?" rather than, "Hey, *you* in the red dress..."

So, we're going to play a speed game that involves remembering *your* first name. Sounds easy enough, eh?

Set them up to feel initially uneasy about the potential of playing some embarrassing name recital ritual, then pull the fear right out from underfoot. Anticipate — relief, amusement, and a developing off-balance interest in what you have to say next.

I'm going to say my first name (Karl) so everyone can hear it. I would like the person to my left to state her first name immediately after I say mine, then the next person in line to the left continues with his name *toot sweet* and so-on all the way around the circle. Be efficient, be distinct, and let's give this a try. Ready? KARL!... Betsy... Todd... Janet... Josephine... Matt... and eventually back to me. A group of thirty people will take about 12–14 seconds to complete the circle. Did you remember most of the names? Good, neither did I.

I'd like you to repeat that identical sequence, but this time try to say the names as quickly and efficiently as possible, because I'm going to time you from start to finish. I need someone to do the timing. Does anyone in the group have a Casio stopwatch? Good, Drew you have one. (Make sure to have someone else do the timing so you can concentrate on building the competitive excitement, and so no controversy develops about whether the instructor pressed the button too soon or too late. Besides, it's more fun to blame someone else.)

Ready? **KARL!** Betsy, Todd, etc. Final time — 13.58 seconds; Excellent! A new world's record. (Announce why it's important that a digital stopwatch be used. Why? Simply because you need a chronometer that measures to the nearest hundredth of a second; world records require that kind of accuracy.) Also tell them at this juncture, that although 13.58 is a

considerable reduction of their initial time, their obvious potential for speed has in no way yet been challenged. Ask them to discuss among themselves what techniques could be utilized to bring their time down, and allow a minute or two for this sharing of ideas to take place. If recommendations are made to you, redirect all comments to the group. If no discussion is forthcoming, facilitate a bit, but don't take over.

When all seems ready, and just before the attempt, ask the group, from a realistic goal-setting standpoint, what they think could be eventually recorded as their ultimate lowest time. It's important they hear from one another; i.e., what individuals in the group think their level of achievement could be. Someone without much confidence may say 12 seconds, while a person who has no investment might guess five seconds to impress their friends. Try to remember who says what for future reference.

Try the circular speed route again and cheer their predictably lower time, but also stick to your enthusiastic, if not entirely realistic belief that the group can do better, perhaps even reach *warp speed*; that rarely achieved paradigm when the group enters a flow state that equates performance to recorded time; i.e., when a feel for performance precludes stopwatch validation.

Remember, part of the fun associated with these imaginative activities involves a dollop of added fantasy, and that you are largely responsible for "releasing the child..." within the group. The activities themselves have a magic to them, but they need some help getting started. Simply memorizing the rules and proctoring the activity just doesn't do it.

I'll usually encourage four to five attempts to reach "warp speed," announcing on the fourth try that if the group doesn't lower their time, it's only appropriate, from a competitive standpoint, to allow **group B** to have a chance at the established record. Now, rather than saying the names clockwise (to the left), look to your right and say, "KARL!" to start the

sequence. (If your name happens to be Fred, well...) Allow the counterclockwise **group B** a few turns to try and best the time set by clockwise **group A.**

As you sit there reading this, comfortably aloof from the emotional involvement of the challenge, pitting **team A** against **team B** (themselves) may seem facetious, perhaps even childish, but the developing intensity and paradoxical levity of the situation (don't take yourself or what you're doing too seriously) allows this type of reality tweaking. Afterwards, in a debrief session, talking and laughing about the ludicrous **A/B** competition attempts can lead to more introspective comments and concerns about the use and abuse of head-to-head competition and how it relates to sports, schools, families, etc.

This laughable pitting of nonexistent teams against one another also allows you to rhetorically ask a few questions about competition and its role within the confines of cooperative games. Does encouraging competition detract from the enjoyment of a game? Can you compete and still avoid the negative aspects of a win/lose scenario? Is competition bad?

Competition provides a spice and incentive for play that is hard to duplicate. The type of positive competition that I'm referring to, however, is not the win/lose finale that allows an individual or group to feel good about themselves while a second group experiences the "agony of defeat."

A group or individual can compete vigorously and with honest intensity against themselves to either try and better their own previously-set standard, or try and best a time, score, or record set by some nebulous group in a far-flung (but exotic) geographical location. This is why the initials PB are so well known by master athletes. Most master age-level athletes will never set genuine world records or win national titles, but they can compete against their own best times to try and establish a rewarding PB (personal best).

Groups should not be pitted against themselves to excess (even positive competition can be overdone), but the benefits of having a goal adds considerably to the incentive of whatever is being attempted. Go for the gold, even if it is your own.

Pairs Squared (Pairs²)

sh

Watch the pandemonium erupt as people attempt to tag, escape and hide from their partners.

• •

Do you love *Pairs Tag*? If you don't, you probably haven't played it. It's a great game for large numbers in small spaces.

Briefly (since it is written up in a previous volume of PA game literature), *Pairs Tag* consists of the following rules:

- everyone has a partner to start the game;
- the game is tag; if you're it, you must tag your partner — no one else;
- when you are tagged, you must spin 360 degrees, or count to three before tagging your partner back;
- there is NO RUNNING allowed during the game, walking only;
- you may not go outside of the boundaries during the game.

It sounds too simple and too dull to be exciting, right? Try it. Put about 30 people inside a 20'x20' space and watch the pandemonium erupt as people attempt to tag, escape and hide from their partners.

So what does all this have to do with Pairs²? As we've said many times, if it's worth doing, it's worth overdoing. We couldn't resist. If it

plays so well with partners, what's the next logical step?

Play

Ask each pair of people to choose another pair as new partners, hence two pairs of two will be a quad or *Pairs Squared*. One pair is designated as *IT*, the others must escape. If a tag occurs, the newly tagged pair must perform the requisite spin before tagging back. Walking is the only form of movement. One very important additional rule to consider: You may want to prohibit people from trying to move between two people who are linked together. Squeezing between two people holding hands can produce a choking movement and/or can wrench people's shoulders and wrists. Use your discretion.

This variation creates an added element of chaos to the movement of the game that seems to enhance the fun factor. It also may be a method for slightly slowing down the speed of the players if you find that they're not adhering to the no running rule.

You can bet that if this game takes off, the next book will contain *Pairs ³*. But you'll have to wait till then for the official rules. You can make up your own in the meantime.

Transformer Tag (or Heads/Tails Tag)

It's a quick burst of running.

Demonstrate to the participants two body positions (suitable for running, of course). The historical choices have been: One hand on top of the head, one hand attached to the gluteus (right or left behind). Each person will have to decide which accepted body position is "right" at the start of the activity.

After a moment for players to determine their game identity, indicate the start of the game by shouting, "Declare!" or by flipping a coin in the air (any other suitably designed starting mechanism is acceptable). Players then immediately declare their identity by adopting one of the body positions.

The action involves one *team* — the heads, for instance — trying to tag and transform all the tails. If a head tags a tail, the tail becomes a head, and vice versa. Once transformed, the person continues to tag anyone of the opposing team. The game continues until one team successfully dominates the world! Then, rematch after rematch until the action loses its appeal. Usually 3–4 rounds is sufficient.

It's a quick burst of running, unless there are no boundaries, in which case you may notice a head chasing a tail across state lines. Such interstate pursuit should only be conducted by highly-trained personnel.

Variation

Equipment for this variation, *Heads/Tails Tag*, requires a coin, preferably a large one (quarters work nicely). Identify the two body positions outlined above for the *Heads and Tails*. Once the group knows the two positions, the action starts as soon as the coin has been flipped in the air.

As the coin hovers above the group, everyone must declare as either a Head or a Tail. When the coin lands on the ground, people need to know what side is up. If it's Heads, Heads are *it* and try to tag all the Tails. Any Tail that is tagged is frozen. The action stops once all the Tails are immobilized. If Tails shows on the coin, the action is reversed.

This variation tends to be shorter, but the fun is in how people learn what side of the coin comes up. This moment of uncertainty adds a bit of a thrill to the game, especially if the coin rolls along the floor.

Both versions together make for a pleasing interlude of body-conscious exertion.

Games

Aerial Four Square

Ever play Four Square on the playground when you were a kid? Probably, it was hard to avoid.

• •

Four Square is one of those ubiquitous nostalgia games, like *Kick the Can,* that many played or observed during recess or around the neighborhood. If you weren't part of the ubiquitous kid scene back then, Four Square is played by four people standing in a chalk outlined play area. Reproducing the chalk-on-asphalt (hot-top, tarmac, bitumen) grid did not require a degree in mechanical drawing.

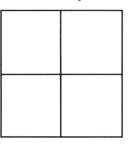

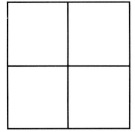

... or upside down it looks like this.

Players stood in one of the squares (the squares varied in size as to the imagination, implied challenge, or amount of chalk available) and tried to hit a red playground ball into one of the other squares so that their opponent could not return it. Players who missed left their quadrant, and someone waiting in line to play took their place.

Set-Up

Aerial Four Square is set up practically the same way... no, that's not true, it's quite different, actually.

You will be setting the four square grid overhead at a height of about 12'. To arrange this aerial grid, dig 4 two-foot deep holes in a north, east, south, west arrangement, so that the holes outlining the square are about twenty feet apart. Drop four 4"x 4"x16' pressure-treated boards into these holes, then fill and tamp firmly. Using lengths of 1/4" bungee cord, connect the tops of the N. and S. boards, and do the same with the E. and W. boards. This connecting and right angle crossing of bungee cord outlines your *Aerial Four Square* playing grid. (You don't really need an illustration of this, do you?) Be sure to stretch the bungee somewhat before you tie the securing knots, so that the cords don't sag.

Play

Split your group into four smaller equal groups, and suggest they arrange themselves approximately under *their* quad section of the "pie." Using a beach ball as the object of play, each team tries to not have a point scored against them. This negative point is disawarded as the result of not being able to return a ball that arrives via that team's quarter section.

Rules

- Each team is allowed to hit the ball three times after it arrives. A fourth hit receives a negative score.

- No individual can hit the ball twice in a row. If this happens, the offending player is jeered and cheered.

- If the ball hits the bungee cord and is rebounded back to the hitting team, that team gets an additional three hits to get it out of their section.

- A shot into another quadrant does not count unless the ball is hit up and over a section of bungee cord.

- When a team has 10 points scored against them they continue playing, but cannot accrue any more negative points. As a reward for having followed the rules faithfully for ten points, that feckless team is encouraged to hit the ball with a bandon (a bandon looks like an ethafoam bat), not having to worry about direction or ground contact. This team has entered the pure play, funn phase of competition, and because of their irreverent and ineffective game response, usually cause the other teams to give up any semblance of seriousness, making future scoring impossible. Good-O!

Ultra Non-Competitive Variation

This time everyone is on the same team, and the game objective is to see how many 1 to 4 circuits can be made from quadrant to quadrant before the ball hits the ground.

- There is no limit to the number of hits under or over the bungee height, but no points are scored unless the ball eventually drops into the quadrants in a 1 to 4 predetermined sequence. This might be a smidgen confusing, so just remember: The ball can go anywhere and into any quadrant, but no points are scored until the ball has made it through all four quadrants in sequence.

- If the ball hits the ground, all accumulated points are lost.

- All other rules are up to you.

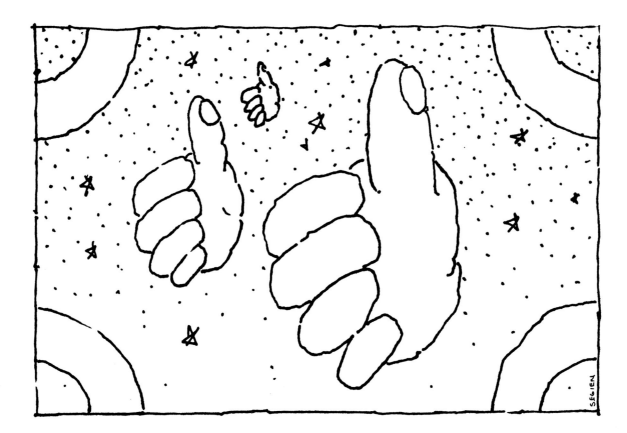

Alienation

The action and anticipation still approach neurotic proportions.

• •

The game *Killer* is explained on page 77 of *The Bottomless Bag*. It's not a bad game, and with the right group can be loads of fun. But, with the evening news invariably reporting another murder, the name and context of the game had fallen into disfavor, particularly with the parents of young student players who have mostly forgotten what it's like to be a young student player.

So, here's a variation that involves a different name and subtly different rules, but for you aficionados and true *Killer* fans, fear not, the action and anticipation still approach neurotic proportions.

Game Objective

At the end of an established time period (24 hours), for you to be on a team that has either the most humans or aliens; the greater population obviously takes over the earth, and, even more significantly, WINS.

Set-Up

One player is designated as the *Ultimate Alien* (UA) at the beginning of the game.

If you want to be included in the play action, here's how to pick an *Ultimate Alien* so even you don't know who that nefarious person is. **All players stand in a tight circle with their eyes closed and extend one hand forward with their thumb sticking up — like a hitchhiker.** You reach into that mass of thumbs and squeeze one (1) thumb definitively. Then with dispatch, the person with squozen thumb (eyes still closed), finds another available thumb amongst the many and squeezes it *twice* (2). The person with the twice pressured thumb is IT. Get it? Good!

If people want to play, but don't necessarily want to be the UA, all they have to do is not extend their thumb; no thumb, no squeeze. Perfect.

The UA is given eight 1/2" slug washers (these are about the size of a quarter, 1-3/8" in diameter). One person, not playing the game, is responsible for delivery of the washers to the UA. This person's identity is revealed to all at the beginning of the squeezing sequence so that the UA can make appropriate and unobtrusive contact. If the number of players exceeds 20, add more alienation washers to maintain the action.

Rules

- In order to alienate someone (turn that player into an alien), the UA must try to deliver a washer to that person without being seen. The criteria for a successful transfer is that the washer must be found by the player after the transfer is made; i.e., without knowing where it came from. A proper alienation scenario involves physical contact with the washer by the person finding it, although this rule is often ignored by slipshod players.

- If players recognize that an alien is trying to alienate them, to protect themselves, all they have to do is point at the alien and quietly say, *"You're human."* At that juncture the alien returns to human form and operates as a human until either the time is up or they once again get alienated.

- If a human catches the UA passing a washer, and says, *"You're human,"* the UA will acquiesce and calmly pretend to resume a human demeanor, BUT that condemned alien can never become human and will lie or do whatever is necessary to make the other players believe that he or she has joined their human condition. The UA then, when appropriate, continues to pass on alienating washers.

Consideration

This is basically an anti-trust game and should be announced as such. If everyone is aware of the game's objective (having agreed-upon fun), then the potentially pejorative aspect of the game simply becomes part of the excitement. If every game you play resembles *Save The Whales*, a certain level of off-the-wall, counter-culture play will be excluded from your Bag of Games. I'm emphasizing variety of fun here, not confrontational scenarios of philosophical concern. Remember F.U.N.N.?

Auto Tag

Coupling left and right hand throwers establishes a truly formidable combo.

• •

Sandy Morley, currently in the Guilderland, NY area sent in a variation of a variation of a variation, which she calls *Auto Tag*. It's simple (finest kind) and active — looks like a variation of a winner.

Play

Running pairs have to hold on to one another. Holding hands is without doubt the most efficient and comfortable way to go, but if you can't get the players to overcome the polarizing tendencies of their particular age, offer a short length of *Buddy Rope* to preclude sweaty palms and inevitable expressions of *Eeeuuw!*

Each member of the IT pair will have one free hand. Fill IT's free hands with soft, throwable balls, like a fleece balls — something *you* wouldn't mind getting hit with. (Coupling left and right hand throwers establishes a truly formidable combo.) A "tag" is made if the IT auto-pair hits someone with one of their balls. When this occurs, the other IT player drops his ball (headlight), which must be retrieved by the hit pair, who are now IT, and the game continues.

More than one car can be IT, obviously, or obviously IT. Sandy says, "Each pair chooses a make, model, and color of car to be, then makes appropriate noises associated with their auto."

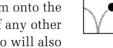

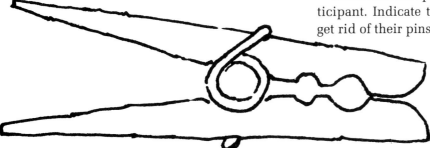

Back Stabbers

This is an easy game to dislike, but the majority of folks will play with giggling abandon.

• •

I think some people may be turned off by the potential combative level that can occur during the game, but let me explain the object of play and a few rules before I turn you off altogether.

Set-Up

You will need about 50 spring-loaded laundry pins; wooden or plastic. They cost maybe two to four cents apiece. The old, no-spring wooden type (the kind used to make little play people or put on your nose in case of a skunk attack), don't work for this game. If you buy some by accident, make some little wooden people for your own children — or nephews and nieces...

If the pins come in different colors, that's a bonus for eventual team designation. You can spray paint the wood pins to achieve the team colors needed.

Me Against The World

Hand out three pins of any color to each participant. Indicate that players are to try and get rid of their pins by clipping them onto the clothing of any other player, who will also be trying to do the same. As soon as a player legally gets rid of all three clips, he jumps up and down, simultaneously shouting that he has accomplished this, and if anyone is listening, that person is eventually recognized as the winner. Emphasis is obviously on the action rather than the outcome.

To avoid the predictable embarrassment of inappropriate ventral pin attachment (translates to purposefully aiming for erroneous zones), allow only dorsal clip contact above the waist; i.e., on the back. As such, all the clippers begin to look like matadors attempting to place bandarillos in the bull — if that didn't make sense, forget it.

Rules

• Only dorsal attachments of clips are allowed.

• Clipping or entangling hair is a no-no.

• If a clip stays on for 5 seconds, it is considered a legal clip.

• If a clip spontaneously falls off before 4.99 seconds have elapsed, it must be picked up by the clipper for another try. Clips on the floor cannot be stepped on to cancel their spring-loaded capacity; i.e., conveniently smooshed.

• Clipees may not rub their clipped body against another person, or the wall, or whatever in order to dislodge a legal clip.

• Clothing cannot be grabbed to slow down a running player, or to facilitate a clip.

• Boundaries must be compassionately set to prevent long-distance running by the fast few.

- Do not be overly strict about rule enforcement, except the rule about inappropriate corporal placement of the clips (no crotch-shots).
- Everyone must wear a loose fitting shirt or sweater. Lycra tank tops are out.

Team Clip

Essentially the same rules as before, except:

- Players operate in teams of three.
- A team must collectively get rid of all their clips. If one player on a team gets rid of all her clips, that empty-handed person must help her teammates rid themselves of the remainder, until all nine pins have been legally set.

Variation

A team is not finished until they have used up all their assigned pins and the ones that have been attached to their own team shirts. A pin can only be removed by a teammate.

This variation obviously adds considerable playing time to the game. If the action slows down, announce a one to two minute time limit extension from that juncture, and at the end of that extension, designate the team with the least pins attached as, clothes pin *todo el mundo* champ emeritus; for which achievement they receive the coveted "nice going" award.

If, after playing *Back Stabber,* it becomes obvious that the group (or a vocal portion thereof) hates the action, don't play it anymore. Or, as the TV puppet character Alf so succinctly noted, "Find out what you don't do well, then don't do it."

Beach Ball Bingo

ker

Divide into two teams without choosing up sides. Choosing up sides is a sociopathic travesty (I'm not sure what that means, but it translates that I don't like the results of choosing up sides). Having the two best friends or the best athletes choosing sides seldom produces even (equally skilled) teams, but does cause the slowest, heaviest, most inept, least popular to be chosen last — again! Try using one of the *Category* techniques listed in the *Warm-Ups* section. The two teams then number off and line up facing one another about 25 feet apart

Place two sets of three inflated, 20" beach balls (total six) on the ground midway between the two flanking lines. Call out two numbers. Two members from each team of those numbers

(total four) rapidly move out toward a set of beach balls and, through wild gyrations and morphologic manipulations that defy explanation, attempt to hold all three balls simultaneously off the ground for five seconds. If a group drops a ball in the attempt, the other group wins and gains a point for their team.

Without hesitation call out another set of numbers. This should be a rapid-fire game, so if there seems to be too much standing around or too many chomping-at-the-bit observers, place another set of three balls or as many sets as necessary to maintain interest.

If teams are having trouble keeping the beach balls off the ground (nobody is winning), let some air out of the balls; softer balls are more controllable.

Bean Bag Tag

This is really simple. Put a bean bag on your head and play *Everybody's It*. If your bag falls off, you're out. If you're tagged, you're out. It doesn't take long to recognize that longevity in this game depends upon keen peripheral vision and the ability to move fast in slow motion.

Bounce Dodgeball

What if I could combine Dodgeball and Musical Chairs without the music and without the chairs?

• •

Waaay back, I wrote about a humane version of that old Everybody-For-Themselves game called Dodge Ball (AKA Murder Ball, Bombardment). Since then I have noticed through observation and questioning that Dodge Ball is probably THE favorite playground game for children of all ages, which, of course, makes perfect sense since the game is so reviled by adults.

Murder Ball encourages all the traits that teachers abhor (me-against-the-world attitude, gang mentality, compassion is a weakness, the most adept always wins, hurting someone is a plus), but occasionally encourages the more humanistic elements that educators encourage: *COOPERATION* (Fred's down, everybody throw at the same time!); *COMMUNICATION* (When I say *throw*, everybody whip their ball at Fred.); *TRUST* (Let's stick together so Fred can't get us.); *FUN* (Did you see me knock that guy right off his feet? Was that great?)

Following what Harry Truman once said concerning how to teach children, (a paraphrase) "Find out what the kids want to do, then tell them to do it." Here's an acceptable variation of what they obviously want to do. I suspect Harry would have liked this game.

This innovative variation comes from Dwayne Aycock of the Covington, Georgia, Project Adventure office. He writes, "I was watching a group of children play Dodgeball when suddenly an idea struck me. What if I could combine Dodgeball and Musical Chairs without the music and without the chairs?" Dwayne, I *like* that kind of thinking! Here's the fast-paced results of that original thought line.

Dwayne's nifty variation maintains the fast pace of throwing and ducking, also includes some decision making, but nicely avoids the direct-hit ball and more significantly precludes the let's-GET-somebody mentality of Bombardment.

The following is essentially what Dwayne passed along to me.

Play

The object of the game is not to get hit by a bounced ball (the bigger the ball, the less potent the throw), while you are moving between safe zones. Being safe requires that a player stand on a gym spot (the type that PA sells in their equipment catalog on page 28). If you think about it, this could be a very boring game, with 20 people standing on 20 gym spots listening to their Walkmans. The catch is that there is one spot less than the number of people playing. Simple rules are the best rules.

Mark out the boundaries before the game starts, remembering that a smaller playing area invariably results in more action, less elitism, and a faster paced game. Anyone who runs outside the boundaries automatically becomes a bouncer. To begin, designate two people as bouncers.

Rules

- All Bouncers must remain outside the boundaries of the playing area. If a ball stops inside the boundaries, a Bouncer may retrieve it, but the ball must be thrown to a Bouncer on the outside or carried to the outside before it can be thrown again.

- A ball must bounce at least once, as the result of a throw, before it effectively makes contact with a player below the waist.

- Ball strikes above the waist do not count.

- A ball cannot be blocked with the hands; this counts as a hit.

- If hit players are moving between gym spots, they are eliminated from the game and become bouncers.

- If eliminated, a player must remove an empty spot from the playing field before becoming a bouncer.

- Every time a throw is made, the players must move off their spot to another spot.

Don't try to read any fancy rule embellishments, hidden agendas, or psychological twists into this game — there aren't any, it plays like it reads.

Dwayne adds, "Though it seems somewhat chaotic at first, the game actually fosters cooperation and teamwork among the participants."

Variation

Pat Kemp wrote recently, saying that she allows the kids to play a variation of Bombardment called *Cross Over Dodgeball*. She writes, "When hit, a player moves to the other team, thus eliminating the need to eliminate. Also, those who need the most practice at throwing and dodging aren't instantly knocked out of the game. The team with the most players after a specified time, or the team with eventually everyone on it — WINS! Pat emphasized that she uses only Nerf balls for these whackum-smackum games.

BING-BANG-BUZZ

This is an OK game for a rainy day, but don't expect most kids to want to play for the entire period; they might suddenly realize that they are learning something.

• •

I learned how to play *Buzz* as a freshman in college. A buzz is what you got, because *Buzz* was (is) a drinking game. Since that time I have seen the game played in a number of ways, and have read about the game used as a mathematics curriculum tool. Buzzed or not, the game offers some fast-paced thinking fun.

Play

One game option goes like this: Everyone sits in a circle and someone starts counting. Each person sequentially says a number in a clockwise or counterclockwise direction until the number 7 is reached, and instead of saying 7, that person says BUZZ. The counting direction then reverses until the next number that has a 7 in it or is a multiple of 7 is reached; that person also says BUZZ. The direction again reverses, and the sequence continues until someone makes a mistake (not saying BUZZ or saying BUZZ at the wrong time). As a college frosh, a mistake meant sloshing down a beer resulting in a sloshed frosh, a traditional example of that time-honored pastime, froshsloshing. As a pedagogic tool, it just means that the group must begin again from one.

For example:

    1, 2, 3, 4, 5, 6 - BUZZ (reverse)

    8, 9, 10, 11, 12, 13 - BUZZ (reverse)

    15, 16 - BUZZ (reverse)

    18, 19, 20 - BUZZ (reverse), etc.

After some practice, a group may surprise themselves as to how high a counting sequence can be reached before a mistake is made. Remember, when you reach 77, the response is BUZZ-BUZZ; now which direction are you headed?

To make the game more difficult, add the word BANG for 5's and multiples of 5.

    For example:

    1, 2, 3, 4 - BANG

    6 - BUZZ

    8, 9 - BANG

    11, 12, 13 - BUZZ

    BANG

    16 - BUZZ

    18, 19 - BANG

    BUZZ - 22, etc.

Variation

The ultimate advanced game, for mental masochistics only, includes the word BING for 3's and multiples of 3. If any number can be a combination of 3, 5, or 7, each BING, BANG, or BUZZ must be said. Anticipate that this sequence will move slowly.

For example:

    1, 2 - BING

    4 - BANG

    BING

    BUZZ

    8 - BING

    BANG

    11 - BING

    BING

    BUZZ

    BING/BANG

    16 - BUZZ

    BING

    19 - BANG

    BING/BUZZ

    22 - BING

    BING

    BANG, etc.

Saaloshing… froshling… wozzlebozzle.

Because there are so many potential changes of direction, allow BING-BANG-BUZZ game variations to continue in the same direction. If frequent returns to the start occur, and they will, allow the start to begin anywhere in the circle in order to include those people, who up to this point have just been watching. This uni-direction rule makes the BANG and BUZZ variations easier also.

Cave In

Bill Thompson, of Project Adventure Australia, thought up and wrote up this Initiative problem.

Set-Up

Props required:

- 4 to 6 hula hoops;
- 1 or 2 rope rings;
- two 8-meter lengths of rope.

To set up the problem, lay both eight-meter lengths of rope on the ground so they are parallel to one another and about two meters apart. This represents the *tunnel* of the cave. Space the hoops and rope ring(s) inside the tunnel to represent the collapsed tunnel or *Cave-In.*

Play

Have the group sit comfortably at one end of the tunnel and close their eyes. Ask them to imagine that they are on a caving expedition and have just crawled through a narrow tunnel to a large underground cavern. Ask them to think about or describe the type of environment that would surround them. Now inform them that there has been a cave-in and the only way out is to crawl through the collapsed tunnel simulated by the hoops and rope rings.

Rules

- Group members must pass through all the rings (hoops or spliced rope quoits) in sequence.

- The only thing allowed to come in contact with the rings are feet, bare or shod.
- If anything other than feet contact the ring, the offending participant must return to the beginning.
- If the hoops come into contact with one another, the supports are obviously too close together and another cave-in will occur, sending all group members back to the beginning.

Variations

A limited supply of air could add to the task (say up to 45 minutes worth for 30 participants).

Blindfold the participants to simulate working in the dark. Adapt the rules above to make the passage of sightless participants possible.

Restrict use of various anatomical parts to simulate injuries.

SEGIEN

Claydoughnary or Claytionary

ker

If you have played the popular party game Pictionary, this histrionic variation should appeal.

· ·

Play

Provide each small group of three to six people with a small container of Play Dough. There's a bundle of nostalgia (some good memories, some not so great) in just smelling the stuff.

[Author's Aside: Do you know why Play Dough smells so bad? I didn't either. It's because the manufacturer doesn't want kids to *eat* it. If you like the smell of Play Dough, you are an anomaly, and if you eat Play Dough... well, PD breath will likely cause you to lose some friends.]

Each group selects a modeler. The leader gives a topic (sotto voce) to these collected members of each group. You can establish as many groups as you can afford containers of Play Dough. For what it costs, seems to me they could have made it smell better.

The modelers scurry back to their respective group, grab the pre-warmed chunk of dough and attempt to sculpt or model the word or phrase that all the other modelers are also attempting to squeeze into a recognizable shape. This is a very frenetic time, much given to spontaneous comments and unbridled humor.

The first team to shout the correct answer is the winner for that round. Another moldable word is then offered to a new group of eager listeners, and off we go for round two. Score is kept, so that when all members of a group have each had two turns, a final score is announced amidst miscellaneous recriminations, gnashing of teeth and huzzahs from the quick-witted high scorers.

Some studiously silly categories might include: *Famous Places* (Grand Canyon, Great Wall, Golden Gate Bridge, Eiffel Tower, Taj Mahal, Great Sphinx, Mount Rushmore, etc.); *Things Around The House* (compact disc player, lawn mower, bicycle, vacuum cleaner, etc.); *Animal Kingdom* (python, kangaroo, dolphin, flamingo, giraffe, etc.). Make up your own categories for even more fun.

This game is a hands-on winner, courtesy of Ann Driscoll.

SEGIEN

Commons

Do you believe,
I mean really believe in ESP
(Extra Sensory Perception)?

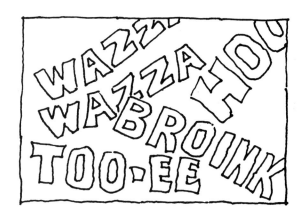

• •

Do you think intuition is a bunch of hooie? *Commons* is an example of the synergy of multiple minds melding and the power of positive thinking. At least it is most of the time.

Set-Up

Divide your group into three sections. Arrange each section to form the three sides of a triangle. You can give bonus points to the group for forming either a perfect equilateral, a ninety-degree isosceles, or for knowing how to compute the area of the triangle they formed. Refer to your high school geometry text or the nearest math teacher for assistance with this aspect of the activity, if necessary.

Play

With the group in three lines facing each other, ask them to take a couple of minutes to create a **SOUND** and a **MOTION** that they think will make the other two teams laugh. The Sound/Motion they invent should not last more than two to three seconds, should be something everyone can do without risking injury, and should meet all relevant standards for common decency as proposed by the International Adventure Morals and Righteous Behavior Commission.

Allow a few minutes for the three teams to separate and create their humorous presentations.

Once the groups are ready, reform the triangle and ask each team — one by one — to demonstrate its Sound/Motion. After each demo, ask the two observing teams to reproduce what they saw to the original team so that the creators can have a chance to see what they looked like.

After viewing and practicing all three Sound/Motions, here's the challenge. The three teams must meet separately (no communication between teams other than telepathy and mind melding), and try to determine what they feel the other two teams will do. The goal is for all three teams to stand in the triangle and on the count of three, have *all* the teams do the same Sound/Motion together. Each team must select from only the three sounds and motions demonstrated to determine which one they will reproduce.

The group can have as many rounds (each team selecting a sound/motion individually and then doing it all together) as they need. Three to five rounds is normally sufficient to either reach consensus or to drive people mad. Most groups will intuitively decide that one of the three presentations is funnier and choose to reproduce that one and everyone will be amazed at the power of group think.

Sometimes a particular team may get locked into their own sound/motion and refuse to change despite what the other two groups do. This hard-headed, stubborn refusal to compromise can cause some confusion and conflict to emerge. Remind people what the objective is — to have fun and to do the same thing — and try a few more rounds. If the desired result doesn't emerge, end the game, tear this page out of the book, and send the entire group to see the principal for being disruptive.

Copy Cat

Copy Cat

sb

What's fun is to watch the movement.

• •

Here's a game for born-leaders. Or is it a game to create followers? Perhaps it's a method of brainwashing that leads to mass conformity. All I know is that it makes people laugh.

Set-Up

Ask your group to form a circle. During your explanation of the rules, ask each person to choose someone in the circle to be their leader but not to tell anyone who their leader is. Explain that once the activity starts, if the person you chose as a leader moves or changes position in any way, you must do exactly as she does. Whenever she moves, you mirror her. Ask that people try to watch their leaders without staring directly at them so that leaders won't know who (if anyone) is following them.

After explaining and asking for questions, check to be certain that everyone has a leader chosen. Before beginning, have people close their eyes and get in a comfortable pose. As soon as everyone opens their eyes on your command, they should change their pose to duplicate that of their leader.

Play

Once people open their eyes, patterns of movement begin to ripple around the circle. Sometimes this activity will last for several minutes, sometimes it will seem frenzied — at other times quiet. The end result is usually everyone in the same pose, though sometimes you get two or three groups of people doing different poses.

What's fun is to watch the movement — seeing someone start in a pose and then others changing to it, only to suddenly change to something new they have just seen.

If the fun of it isn't enough, you can debrief the significance of conformity versus independence, the challenge of selecting a qualified leader and the consequence of one or more people deciding to act on their own and what impact that has on the rest of the group. You can, but I wouldn't.

Eye Got You Circled

ker

This is one of those diabolical games that deserve forewarning.

• •

I am quoting the following paragraphs somewhat verbatim from the individual who was kind enough to share his time and *joie du vivre* to have faxed this game. The author is Dovid Grossman from Yeshiva College, an all boys' school in Sydney, Australia; I suspect an excellent teacher with a keen sense of humor.

This lifetime, ongoing activity resembles a couple other needless activities that you may be familiar with from other Adventure workshops or publications — The game, *Killer* and *Count Coup* come to mind — but there's enough difference here to warrant the space, besides Dovid's writing style is fun to read.

"This is one of those diabolical games that deserve forewarning. Should you read further, you are committed for life (to whatever degree you choose, of course, by the immutable precepts of 'chickening out' outlined in the oft-quoted shibboleth *Challenge By Choice*).

I warned my students, but they are young and foolish and did not heed my blandishments. They resemble their teacher. What more need be said? Oh, yes... The Game!

Objective: To attempt to form a circle below your waist, and get someone to make eye contact with the circle. Should you look directly at the circle that I am responsible for forming; I score a point. However, should you see the circle, put your finger inside the circumference and get your finger safely out; you score a point. If I am quick enough to grasp your intrusive finger; the point remains mine. The circle can be made of anything that is obviously circular.

Location: As you are now playing a lifetime game, time and venue cease to exist as you and your adversary are vulnerable NO MATTER WHERE YOU ARE AND AT ALL TIMES.

Rules and Clarifications

The eye-balled circle must be homemade. You may take a hamburger bun, draw a circle with the ketchup on the burger, close the bun and present it to a friend asking him/her to, "Wow, check out the size of the patty on this 3/4 pounder!"

The circle must be presented below your victim's waist. This has worked very well for me in the mornings as my students are walking up the stairs ahead of me. I call out a student's name, simultaneously placing a finger circle around my eye, so that as he looks back to answer, I score. Yet, I have almost been had by the student who put a large circle on his homework paper and calmly waited for me to walk around the classroom checking the papers. He would have definitely scored a point if I hadn't been alert and poked a hole through his homework; my point!

There are a few other rules about not spitting through the circle, and punching people, that I chose not to include due to the zealous nature of my charges.

I did add the rule that all points must be scored as unobtrusively as possible, recognizing that a subtle circle score is much more satisfying than a loud, splashy neon circumference. Should a score cause a class disturbance, someone will be warned or punished as with any other unwarranted disruption of school time. I have been scored against while lecturing by a student who quietly held his hand out in the aisle with the OK finger gesture. I continued pontificating, recognizing his score with a brief nod of my head, all the while fuming inside that I had been so easily HAD. The student stopped doing this soon thereafter, as the student behind him kept getting his finger in and out of the finger circle and scoring against HIM.

I have also suggested the ruling that you cannot tell your victim that he looked. If he does not admit to it, then and there, what's the point? We are learning about honesty here, and if a yes-I-did, no-you-didn't scenario ensures, what's the use? We also discussed how peripheral vision works and that someone might know the circle is there without actually looking at it. This is true.

Those who would cheat are quickly discouraged by the value put on scoring. No ongoing score is kept, so nobody bothers keeping track.

The game is really ludicrous, and therefore we are having a lot of fun with it. Just the other day I was fulfilling an adult senior staff responsibility of reprimanding a student for one of those terrible things that we all did when we were kids. When the repentant sinner had fully bowed his head in remorse... I shot him a circle right at the waist. Score another one for me *and* for the big broad smile of a repentant sinner who knows that even GOD enjoys a good game.

Fantasy Tag

Ask players to write down a fantasy on the paper.

• •

This game can produce some hilarious results depending on the mood of the group and the timing of when it's played. It tends to work better with small groups (10-12) but I have done it with up to 26 people successfully.

Set-Up

Start by giving each person a piece of scrap paper, preferably paper that is similar so no one can identify someone else's piece by size, shape or color. Ask players to write down a fantasy on the paper; the fantasy should be something that they have always wanted to do and that *they won't mind being read publicly*. It can be anything, real or fanciful, so long as it is something each person has a desire to do.

Collect all the pieces of paper and then read the fantasies one by one. After reading them all, re-read them to be certain that everyone playing has heard them all.

Play

Divide the group up into teams of three or four players. One group starts by trying to identify who belongs to a specific fantasy. If their guess is correct, that person becomes a member of the guessing team and the guessers get another chance. The same team keeps guessing until they make a guess that is wrong.

The Cardinal Rule: People must be honest in "owning" their fantasy when it is guessed.

There has been much laughter, amazement and incredible demonstrations of EFG (Extraordinary Fantasy Guesswork) during this activity. Be sure to submit your best fantasies to the Intergalactic Fantasy Collection Center.

FFEACH & MOOCH

An unlikely pair of histrionic games...

• • • • • • • • • • • • • • • • • • • •

Steve invented and regularly plays a pantomime game called *FFEACH* (Fast Foods - Electrical Appliances - Comic Book Heroes). For unbridled intensity, coupled with fast thinking and action, this activity is hard to beat.

Play

To play, divide your group into smaller groups of five to seven and separate them by a few yards. Situate yourself somewhat apart and between the groups. See Diagram.

Announce to all the players that you will secretly and separately reveal a topic (fast foods [quarter pounder, fries, etc.], electrical appliances [blender, vacuum, etc.], comic book heroes [Superman, The Hulk, etc.]) to one player from each group. That player must swiftly return to her group and charade (non-verbal, but supportive sounds can be made) the topic to their waiting and attentive team members. As soon as the topic is guessed, another

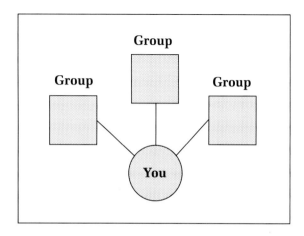

member of the group dashes up to verbally receive his topic from you. The first team to guess the topic of each team member wins. (Whatever that means.)

If *winning* seems inappropriate, ask the first team finished to hurry over to whatever group is still charading, and offer their obvious world class expertise. In this way, the groups are not competing against one another, but eventually cooperating until all are finished, with everyone cheering on each other.

It is important for facilitators to either have a developed and recorded list of topics or to have played the game often enough so that the topics are on the tip of their thalamus. As the game intensity increases, players will probably come up to you in twos and threes, eagerly — no frantically — anticipating their miming topic. There are not many games where you can observe such animated intensity on the faces of the players: good photographic stuff.

Gloree Rohnke recently developed an interesting and entertaining variation of *FFEACH* called *MOOCH* (Movies, Occupations, and Humms). The games are played identically, with different topic headings. The *tweak* results from having the option to hum or charade the tune topics that are offered as a parachallenge. Humming while you are laughing or trying to be serious causes giggles all around.

Variation

As a variation, allow the two or three competing teams to make up their own list of:

1. short quotations
2. book titles
3. advertising slogans
4. proverbs, etc.

The captains of each team bring their lists to you. (Don't take more than two to three seconds to choose a "captain.")

On *GO,* the teams send one representative to you for the first topic and those people rush back to charade the topic to their team. When the quotation, etc., is discovered, another person in the group rushes back to get the next topic until everyone has had a chance to be theatrically frustrated and/or exhilarated. The first team done is heralded as "Le Petit Champion" — so that no one becomes too impressed with themselves.

Fork-Wad (Four-Quad)

You can use either cord, rope, or bungee for this game, but I like 1/4" bungee best.

• •

Set-Up

To set up the playing venue, ask two people to hold a 20' section of 1/4" diameter bungee between them, then suggest they step back until there's some tension placed on the cord. Ask an additional two bungee holders to do the same, so that the two sections of bungee run perpendicular to one another, essentially forming a four-square grid, with no outside boundaries.

Distribute enough colored plastic *sensory balls** to the remainder of the group so that each player gets two balls. Make sure the balls are four distinctly different colors, but don't mention anything about color to the group. If someone specifically asks what color balls they should take, just tell them to grab whatever two come to hand.

Choose your favorite way to divide a large group into four smaller equal groups. Then ask each group (balls in hand) to occupy one of the four bungee-outlined grids. A less imaginative quartering, but usually quicker, is to divide the players by just asking everyone to pick one of the four grid areas and go there, mingling and merging until there are four equal groups.

Play

Finally — the problem. The task is to see how long it takes to divide the colored balls into four separate grids, then for the grids opposing one another to exchange balls. This is obviously a timed event.

Rules

- *All* ball exchanges must result from receiving a tossed ball rather than a hand-to-hand passed ball.
- Dropped balls result in a five-second penalty per drop. A dropped ball must remain on the ground until a final time has been determined.
- A ten-second penalty is incurred for touching any of the bungee cords.
- No one is allowed to break the plane of the grid with any part of their body in order to facilitate tossing a ball.
- A ball cannot be passed beneath the cord.

- The balls must be kept in-hand, they cannot be tucked into clothing or held, for example, between the arm and body.
- Increase the action and problem-solving by asking each player to initially pick up three or four balls rather than just two. (More balls, more action.)

* ***Sensory balls*** are those multi-hued plastic balls that are used by recreational facilities, psychological centers, and fast food restaurants to fill a small pool-like container and serve as an ersatz "flotation" medium — like at MacDonalds. Sensory balls can be purchased through Project Adventure's equipment catalog.

These inexpensive balls also lend themselves to the games/Initiatives — *Frantic, Up Chuck, Paul's Balls, Pick & Choose,* and *Phones & Faxes.* Not to be used for games that require throwing the balls at another person, like... *Asteroids, Ankle Biters, Monarch.* Sensory Balls are lightweight, but a hard thrown ball twixt the eyes (and lots of other places) will hurt.

Happy Landings

Ask the players to make their own paper airplanes.

In a gymnasium, large room, cafeteria, football field, rugby pitch, parking lot, Logan Airport, etc., pass out some recycled sheets of paper. Wrinkled sheets won't work, so leave those in the circular file.

Ask the players to make their own paper airplane. If they don't know how, refer them to those people in the group who do. If *no one* knows, show them. I shouldn't have to write sentences like the last one, but with kids watching so much TV, many of them have never done

some of the things that were commonplace when I was their age. My own children find it hard to believe that there was essentially no TV when I was in elementary school. Paper airplanes at that time were no big deal, but everyone knew how to make at least one kind (usually the pointy-tipped, swept-wing rocket type that was a cinch to glide from the back of the room to the teacher's desk).

Using one of the convenient lines on the gym floor as a base line, ask the paper pilots to try and propel their planes beyond a line (rope on the floor/ground) that you have set 30' beyond the base line. The low-tech idea is to see which team can fly the majority of their creations beyond the 30' boundary.

This competition is obviously set up for many flights, so if your team didn't do well the first time, "get back to the drawing board" and engineer something Bernoulli might have come up with — he's the guy down at the corner deli that makes such a great turkey-breast sub (hold the onions).

As always, performance takes a back seat to process. Working together on the planes (cooperation, communication, decision making) has more pedagogic punch than measuring where the origamic gliders end up.

Par Avion

Since you are already fooling around with paper airplanes, try the following as a communications ploy. Write something on a paper airplane (all airplanes should be made identically; same shape, same paper) that you have always wanted to *hear*. Ask the group, eyes closed for five seconds, to throw their airplanes into the air at the same time. Everyone picks up an airplane and reads the message out loud — if a quick scan by the facilitator deems it appropriate. The group should be large enough so that flight plans cannot be logged or followed.

Obviously, this whimsical idea can quickly deteriorate because of inappropriate messages (confidences revealed, smut, etc.), or if friends seek only other friends' airplanes. This is a high-flying game for a group that trusts one another and wants to have a good time, not be devastated by inappropriate ditties or embarrassed by Top Gun innuendoes.

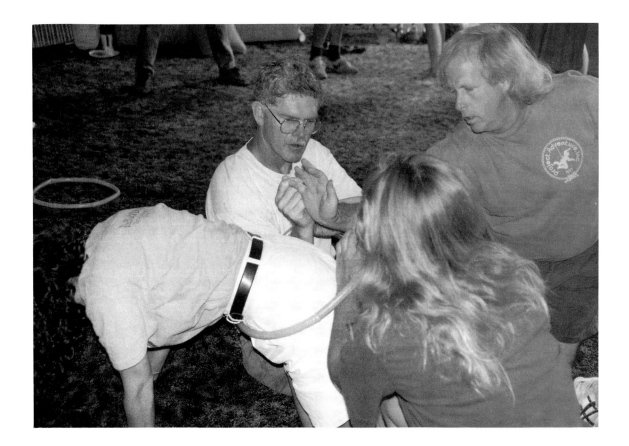

Hoop Loops

It's a tried and true winner as a warm-up/challenge.

. . . .

You'll need some hoola hoops that come in sections (found on page 32 of the PA equipment catalog), or some rope loops that can be adjusted in size to attempt this activity. One size fits all diminishes the attractiveness and the challenge level of this problem dramatically.

If you're familiar with *Circle the Circle*, then you know how people enjoy passing hula hoops around the circle in a hand-holding formation. It's a tried and true winner as a warm-up/challenge. So why not take it to the next level?

Play

Present the group with several hoops of various sizes. To begin with, it's appropriate and compassionate to have hoops large enough to accommodate anyone in the group.

Ask the group what size hoop they want to start with. Then ask them to send the hoop all the way around the circle, thus completing a *Hoop Loop*. If the group is successful, then pick successively smaller hoops until the hoop sections break apart as the group makes its attempt.

The only rule is that if the hoop breaks, the game ends.

Games **117**

The challenge of working with progressively smaller hoops lends itself to lots of talking, laughing, coaching and innovative stratagizing amongst the group members. Working towards the smallest possible hoop often leads the group to succeed at a hoop size that is tinier than they would have imagined possible.

Variation

Ask two (or more) people to work together for this version. Maintaining at least one body part from each person in the hoop at all times, the pairs must try to pass themselves through the smallest hoop possible. People do not need to be holding hands in this variation; in fact it tends to work best when pairs are given hoop sections and given the opportunity to work/play at their own speed.

Considerations

When presenting this activity, you may need to give some thought to people's comfort with their own bodies. Despite having played this game with some very large individuals, I've never seen anyone uncomfortable attempting this challenge. However, if body image is an issue for any member of the group, the fact that this game always ends with someone breaking the hoop may make it inappropriate.

If approached with a fun-loving attitude and no emphasis on "completion and success" other than giving it a try, I think this idea works. And the expressions and laughter of the groups I've observed lead me to believe there's value in them hoop sections.

Instant Impulse

sb

The competitive juices are usually flowing freely in this game.

. . . .

Adventure is non-competitive? Don't present this activity if you believe that statement.

Set-Up

You will need:

- a large coin (quarters and nickels work well)
- a fleece ball
- blindfolds (or the group can just keep their eyes closed)

Divide your group into two teams, equal numbers on each side. Ask each team to sit down facing each other with approximately 12" between the teams. Each team must link together by holding hands so that all the players on a team are connected. (NOTE: Buddy Ropes will not work for this activity, so if your group won't hold hands, forget it.)

The fleece ball is placed exactly between the last two people at the ends of the lines. The ball should be equidistant from both players, and the last players need to rest their free hands on their knees at the start of the game.

At the head of the line, the first players on each team keep their eyes open. All other players are either blindfolded or close their eyes. Position yourself as leader close to the two sighted people at the start of the lines.

Play

Flip a coin. When it lands, *heads* is the signal to send an impulse down the line; *tails* means nothing and the coin is flipped again.

When heads turns up, the two sighted players immediately squeeze the hand of the next player in line. This impulse is passed down the line as quickly as possible to the last person. As soon as the last person receives it, she tries to grab the fleece ball. Whichever person gets the ball, that team wins the round.

Winning a round means the player at the head of the line (the sighted person) rotates to the end of the line (the grabber), and all players move up one spot in the sequence. A team wins the game when the person who started as the sighted player returns to the head of the line and wins a second round.

When *tails* turns up on the coin flip, should a nervous player send an impulse down the line and grab the ball, that team is assessed a penalty. They must reverse rotate one spot. Assess this penalty any time an infraction occurs.

Considerations

An ideal number for this game seems to be 5–10 players per team. With larger groups, perhaps create four teams — two competing against each other and then have a final match between the two winners.

Kangaroo Catch

Guess where this game came from?

• •

Wrong! It was first played in Vancouver, WA, just over the OR border, but the continent-connector indicates that Kangaroo Catch was introduced to the U.S. by Simon Hanson, an Adventure training specialist from Merribrook (a development training center in Cowaramup, WA: that's Western Australia, not Washington this time) which, to end all this, is about a 23-hour flight and three-hour drive from where I'm sitting right now.

This running, hopping game is played somewhat similarly to *Italian Golf*, (*Cowstails and Cobras II*, pg. 67) — enough so that you should look it up and compare.

Play

Played in pairs, the objective is to reach a distant goal (perhaps 100 meters away) with your partner in the fastest possible way, with the least penalties accrued, while adhering to the following rules.

Rules

• At the start, only one person may move toward the goal, and that person may only hop (double footed, as per the marsupial after which this game is named).

- The second person cannot move until they have thrown a hula hoop over the body of the hopping person. Actually the hopping person isn't hopping, because the chance for success in hooping a hopping person is about zip — but that's up to you, of course. (The de rigueur catching pose is to stand in an available manner with both arms held rigidly above the head; pointing your fingers helps.) The extended catcher may maneuver his or her body to and fro in an attempt to coax the hoop over their hips — essentially the crux of an acceptable catch.

- After a successful throw and catch, the initial thrower becomes the hopper, bouncing with alacrity toward that point where they

think the next throw and catch can be consummated, recognizing that a 50-meter throw and/or catch is unrealistic, and that the penalty for missing is to repeat the throw until it's made. Ten repeated 40-meter throws and misses can substantially reduce the fun aspect of this game for even the most persistent funophiles.

- If you are competing or want to establish PB's or WR's (Personal Bests/World Records), record the time from start to finish and add a ten-second penalty for each miss. If you want to down-play competition, jump up and down a lot and announce at a high decibel that everyone did GREAT, and would they like to try again?

Klingon Tag

This game might remind you of Back Stabbers.

• •

To play this extended tag game you need a bunch of colored stick-on dots. A bunch, in this case, is about 100 each of four colors; get more if you plan to play this game more than once. You can purchase these dots at a stationery store (Paperama in the Boston area).

Set-Up

The beginning groupings necessitate 4 teams of five or six people each. Each team gets 100 Klingon Dots of the same color. You can differentiate teams by marking their foreheads (big round circle of appropriate color) with a non-permanent felt marker. Or, for a team with less commitment, use colored arm or head bands.

Rules and Such

- Have each team distribute their Klingon Dots (KDs) among the team members.

- The object of the game is for players to stick their KDs on members of the other teams. No hard slapping or poking applications, and only on acceptable parts of the anatomy. (Acceptable to you, not your libidinous players.)

- KDs must be applied singly — no machine gun applications.

- While you are merrily applying KDs, remember that players on the other teams are trying to do the same to you.

- When a player has applied all of his KDs, allow that person to retreat to a neutral corner of Federation space and be immune from further KD attacks.

- When the action slows (time limit) or ceases (oxygen debt and glycogen depletion), have the teams remove their acquired KDs, place them on the wall for all to see, and count them.

- Game proctors (not necessarily you) publicly count and compare the number of KDs accumulated, then describe (as below) the groups in ascending or descending order.

Most KDs — Your group members are obviously very attractive, and people naturally gravitate toward you.

Least KDs — Your aloofness and attention to the task at hand allows you to avoid negative business associations.

Median # of KDs — Generally your group is well balanced and able to work with other groups at a comfortable median/mode standard.

This game might remind you of *Back Stabbers*, where, rather than using KDs the players attempt to attach spring-loaded clothespins to a competitor's shirt or jumper.

The Last Detail

It's rumored that Sherlock Holmes played this game.

· ·

If someone broke into your house while you were there, grabbed something right in front of you and then ran out the door, would you be able to describe the thief to the authorities? Let's find out.

Set-Up

You can play this activity in partners, but it also works very well with teams. In a team format, have two groups of three to seven players line up facing each other with about three feet in between the lines. Select one line as the observers, one as the changers.

Play

First, the observers get two minutes to carefully study the opposing team (or just one player if that makes the game more manageable for younger students). After they have finished their observations, the observers turn their backs to the other line.

The changers now have sixty seconds to alter up to ten things about their appearance. The team has a total of ten changes to make. One person could make all ten changes, everyone could make two... this rule is adaptable to encourage people to be involved. Once all the

changes have been made, the changers stand still again.

The observers turn back to face their opponents and they try to discover as many of the changes as possible within a time limit (two to four minutes is usually plenty). The observers can work together or individually to examine the other team.

Once the guessing is over and any undiscovered changes are revealed, the two groups switch roles and repeat the process.

One caution: Remind people when they are making changes that they must be visible (no fair changing your state of mind or putting your loose change in another pocket) and that the changing team needs to return as closely as possible to the position they were in to start the game or else the observers may guess that a change in posture or location in the line is intended to fool them.

It's rumored that Sherlock Holmes, Miss Marple, Perry Mason and Sam Spade all played this game in their formative years and look where it got them, aside from the fact that they are all deceased.

 # Minnesota Mosquito

Select one or two players to act as mosquitoes.

· ·

Ron Ball writes that the Minnesota state bird is the mosquito and having, many years ago, experienced that state *bird* in some abundance at the Minnesota Outward Bound School (now the Voyageur OB School), I'd have to agree. Ron offers the following tag game based on this famous "bird."

Select one or two players to act as mosquitoes, and equip each mosquito with an ethafoam sword (stingers). When a player is stung (no head hits) she is frozen, and remains so cryogenetically suspended until two unfrozen players encircle the afflicted player with their arms and shout DEEP WOODS OFF, or DI-ETHYL META TOLUMIDE before being stung themselves.

If a viable player can touch a mosquito above the waist without getting hit saying, "take that, you DEET-ridden hemo freak!" — that brave player can unfreeze one immobilized probosisized player.

The players trying to keep from getting stung can band together hand-in-hand in groups of eight (minimum). When this is accomplished and players simultaneously *whack* their partners on the back (before the mosquito can sting anyone in the octo-group) that's the end of the skeeter (scratch/scratch), and the game (scratch/scratch) until you start again.

Monarch

Allow a goodly amount of running room...

· ·

This game is written up in one of the *New Games* books, but I don't have one right here to copy from, so you are going to have to put up with my version of the activity. Actually, it's Steve's version, because I (Karl) learned the rules from him and have watched him present the game any number of times. Not a bad game all-in-all, if you don't make the mistake of using a red playground ball in place of a Nerf-type ball. Boundaries are variable as to the size of your group, but allow a goodly amount of running room.

Play

The Monarch (the person IT) starts off with a Nerf ball (symbol of the Monarchy) in hand. Choose the Monarch however you please, but don't pick the slowest, dead-armed thrower to start. The assigned Monarch tries to hit an Anarchist (any other player) with the ball, at which juncture the just-hit Anarchist becomes a joint-Monarch. The two Monarchs then try to work together to hit another Anarchist, etc., etc.

Include two balls (two Monarchs) at the start of the game if the group numbers more than 20 players.

Rules

- If Anarchists run out of bounds, they automatically become Monarchs.

- Monarchs cannot run if they have the ball in their possession, except when they are alone at the beginning of the game. The ball can be passed to another Monarch, however.

The game continues until all the Anarchists have been convinced to change their political affiliation.

Consideration

Monarch is kind of a no-boundary, bombardment-type game and can be a disaster if you use a ball that no one wants to be hit by.

Name By Name

Tired of the same old name games?
Give this challenge a try.

• •

Have a group that doesn't know each other?

Play

Inform the group in your typical Adventure style that you have a challenge for them that will help them get to know each other. In order to proceed with the problem, everyone needs to say their name once. First name only please! It should be said loudly (be proud about your name and all that good stuff); but if *anyone* can't hear the name clearly, that person calls out *REPEAT*! in a loud voice. Hearing this embarrassing call forces the quiet person to say the name again loudly enough so that the Repeat command does not follow the name.

After all the names have been said, announce the challenge. All players must now rearrange themselves so that the circle is alphabetical by first name. No talking, no signing or gesturing (visually indicating letters), no showing ID cards, etc. Helpful pointing or repositioning is allowed, but the challenge is for individuals to place themselves in the circle in the appropriate place.

Once the group has moved and the circle is re-formed, that ends *Round One*. Take a test. Listen as all the names are said again. If people are out of sequence and corrections need to be made, allow people to move a second time (again with no speaking, etc.). Take another test. So ends *Round Two*. The challenge is to form an alphabetical circle in the fewest number of rounds; i.e., having spoken the names the fewest number of times.

Generally, groups respond well to this challenge and people do tend to remember the people close to them in the alphabet. Having done this activity with up to 40 people, it usually takes fewer rounds than you might imagine. (The most I've ever seen was 4 Rounds. I've seen many groups do it on the first round — AMAZING!)

Helpful Hints

• Don't play this game after doing name games or if the group knows each other unless you substitute middle names for first names. This

variation is fun, but it will confuse and confound you trying to remember first names later on. Be forewarned.

- If you want the challenge to be a bit easier, tell the group what the goal is before they hear all the names once. They will pay more attention and remember more names. If you want the challenge to be more difficult, tell them the goal after they hear the names.

To set the record for this activity, allow people to communicate their names only by mental telepathy, then ask them to move. If your group is 100% accurate, forget what you're doing and pool your money on a few lottery tickets.

Name Five

Here's a way to have some fun and learn something, too.

• •

This game appeared at a workshop a while back, and it seems to be more useful now than ever. This format allows for a lot of flexibility in terms of subject matter, and with more emphasis being placed on cross-disciplinary teaching, here's a way to have some fun and learn something, too. Now I know that some of you will say, "Hold on, that's giving us too much to think about." Come on, give us a break. We have to have something to write about other than just the rules to a few games. Besides, this is useful training for TV shows like *Jeopardy* where you can win some real prizes.

Set-Up

Have everyone sit in a circle, with one person in the center. You'll need one object that will be passed around the circle.

Play

The person in the middle starts the action by closing his or her eyes; the players in the circle begin passing the ball at this time. When the person in the middle has a challenge question ready, she says, "Stop." and opens her eyes. The person holding the ball is the one to whom the challenge is directed.

The center person now asks a question. The challenge is to name a specified number of things from a specific category. For example:

name five foreign cars, name seven rivers outside of the United States, name all the planets in the Solar System, name four knots used on a ropes course, name ten people in the class, say fifteen words in a foreign language… The person with the ball must immediately pass the ball to the person beside her and the ball continues around the circle until it returns to whoever started it. The player answering the challenge must provide the complete answer before the ball returns. If they cannot, that person goes into the middle and the middle person moves into the circle.

The circle can adjust the speed of the ball depending on the difficulty of the challenge. But it's best to maintain a moderate speed all the time to prevent people from feeling they're being picked on.

To prevent someone in the center from asking a question that is impossible to answer (name 30 dinosaurs — not including Barney or Bam-Bam, name every professional sports team), you can allow *The Challenge*. When the ball returns to the person answering the question, they say, "I challenge." Now the center person must answer the question before the object has moved all the way around the circle. If they cannot answer their own question, they must stay in the circle for another round.

OK, Karl, here's one for you, name six characters from *F&Q* before I shout Count Coup! "COUNT COUP!" Gotcha back!!

"Not fair, Steve! That's a travesty — you really didn't shout *Count Coup*! And since you just read this, I got you back."

Needle'n'Thread Tag

Strategy and planning are the keys to success.

• •

If you're looking for a tag game that's more than just running and chasing, this is much more than it seems at first play. As you read these rules, it may not sound like anything special. The proof is in the playing.

Set-Up

Create a circle with all but two of your players. The people in the circle need to stand close enough so that if they hold out their arms to each other they can hold hands comfortably. Asking people to hold hands to form the circle is usually the best way to start (unless your group is of an age where holding hands conjures up gruesome images of Cooties, in which case *Buddy Ropes* may be necessary). The two players not in the circle will provide the action for the first round.

Play

One player is chosen to be IT; the other to escape from the IT. Whenever the "not-it" (hereafter called the NI) runs between two people in the circle, those two people immediately link hands to create a barrier which the IT cannot break. People in the circle must close their hands as quickly as possible and try to prevent the IT from crossing between them. The NI is given the option of choosing where to start, either inside or outside the circle, and the IT must start wherever the NI is not; the IT starts the game by yelling a suitably appropriate phrase or word.

The objective for the NI is to sew up the circle without being caught by the IT. If the IT tags the NI, that ends the round. The options at that point are:

a) The players switch roles.

b) The IT becomes the NI and the NI joins the circle and someone from the circle becomes the new IT.

c) Two new players from the circle become NI and IT.

d) The game ends. You can probably determine some other options as well — try whatever sounds fun.

If the NI succeeds in closing all the gaps without being tagged, one of two things typically occurs. The NI and the IT will both be on the same side of the barrier (meaning an endless pursuit if they're on the outside and a certain capture if they're inside the circle); or, the NI will be safe forever since the IT is permanently on the other side of the barrier. HOORAY! Either way, it's exciting.

A Hint

The success or failure of this game seems to depend on the NI's ability to understand the strategy of effectively hiding behind closed gaps in the circle. If the NI relies entirely on speed, the IT almost inevitably catches the NI (sooner rather than later in most cases). Strategy and planning are the keys to success.

Usually the most advantageous position for the NI to start is inside the circle with the IT somewhere on the outside. This starting position assures the NI of being able to close at least one pair of hands before being forced to run away.

Without some reliance on strategy, the game has a tendency to become boring, since no one ever comes close to sewing up the circle. Not to worry. The game provides some good action and people tend to learn from other peoples' ideas and plans. Allow the game to play out for several rounds before deciding if it's working or not, especially with younger children.

A Couple Other Ideas

One other way to add in some excitement would be to invent a fanciful story to go with the game. The circle represents a village that is trying to protect itself. The IT is a rogue Kumquat trying to capture all the inhabitants of the village. The NI is a brave and stalwart villager who tries to divert the rabid Kumquat while the village assembles a security fence to protect itself. Players of all ages seem to enjoy the added thrill of the chase when they understand the significance of the pursuit.

Another way to add challenge and motivation to the game might be to total the number of "stitches" an individual or group can make in a class. They can earn points for each successful stitch and this record is something they can strive to break each time they play. Check out the description of *Score Board* for some other considerations of this idea.

Nesting Balls

A fast-paced, thinking game…

● ●

Mark Murray mentioned this active game to me as one that he has been using with corporate groups for some time; which is not to say that it wouldn't be well received by any group that enjoys a fast-paced, thinking game.

You will need *beau coup* balls. (I took French 101 in college and got a D, but it doesn't dissuade me from using and misusing an occasional French word or phrase. You have to admit, "*beau coup balls*" exhibits more panache than "lots of balls"? Would you ever actually say beau coup balls? I doubt it, but written words are to play with, and there's definitely more *joie* to writing, than just key-boarding expository how-tos. John Updike said, "Writing was meant to be an act of joyful play." — or something like that.)

Set-Up

Unloading your bounteous bag of balls (alliteration appeals, also) on the ground, take a magic marker and begin printing a large capital letter on each ball (tennis ball). Use the game SCRABBLE as a guide to how many letters you will need for the game. You will need more E's than C's, and more A's than K's, only one Z and X, etc.

When your fuzzy balls have all been scribed in your best bold Helvetica font style, place them all within the hula hoop that's on the ground directly in front of you. (Oh yeah, you also need five hula hoops.) Thinking of that hoop as the center dot on a five di, place four more hoops on the ground as to represent the other four dots on the five di — right …two dis make a pair of dice. There's no dice here, this is just to orient the hoops.

The four outside corner hoops should be distanced about 10 yards from one another, recognizing that the further the hoops are placed

apart, the more running will be involved.

Considering that it's important to actively include yourself in these games from time to time, what kind of shape do we find ourselves in? Sorry if I'm treading on excess adipose, but seriously, this group/sharing/empathetic approach depends upon your personal involvement; no you, no student enthusiasm.

Divide your group into four smaller groups, utilizing some imaginative quad-splitting routine that has nothing to do with best friends choosing up sides or splitting males and females.

Play

Indicate that each of the four equal groups should stand by one of the four outside hoops. On GO, one person from each group can run to the center hoop. These players pick up one ball and return to their home hoop. The picked-up ball must be immediately deposited in the home hoop and cannot be protected from opposing players. As soon as the ball is deposited in the home hoop, any other player on the home team (only one) can take off to grab another ball from the center hoop, OR from any of the other hoops.

This frenetic level of ball scoping and scooping continues until one of the teams achieves its goal (five hooped balls that spell a word) and yells, "SEQUENTIAL BALLS!" There might be 6, 7, or 8 balls in the hoop, but five of them in combination must spell a word. That team wins the round. To begin again, all the balls are collected and placed back in the center hoop.

This game is like *Four-Letter Word* (*Cowstails & Cobras II*, pg. 66), except balls are substituted for 4"x6" cards, and there is considerably more running involved.

This game can also be played with unlettered balls. Then the criteria for winning is simply to collect a predetermined number of balls within a hoop. Same rules, same frantic pace — less thinking.

No Name Game

Non-stop action and total involvement...

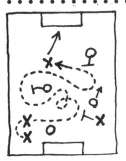

I know some good teachers. If one of them sends me a game to share, with the following kind of comment attached, you can bet it's a winner. "This unnamed, student-generated game was very popular with almost everyone, providing non-stop action and total involvement as passing to teammates and teamwork improved."

This no-name game (finest kind... let the kids name it) comes from David Joseph, an elementary teacher from Concord-Carlisle, MA, who also happens to be a Project Adventure trainer.

Play

You need a soccer field and goals. Got some? Good!

The object of the game is to throw a Nerf football into the other team's soccer net using the following kid-generated, group-facilitated rules.

Rules

- Put a goalie in front of the goal.
- Anyone, except the goalie, can run and score with the ball. The goalie is the only person allowed to pick up a ball off the ground.
- When a player is tagged (two hands above the waist), the other team gets possession and must complete a pass before running or scoring. A free throw is then allowed; i.e., no blocking or close coverage.
- If the ball lands on the ground, for whatever reason, it must be hand-batted in the air to another player, who can then run with the ball. Kicking the ball is not allowed for safety reasons. Hand-batting does not allow guiding the ball; i.e., the ball strike must not resemble a throw.
- If the ball goes out of bounds, it is inbounded by the other team by punting. Blocking this punt is not allowed.
- If the ball is thrown over or beyond the net, the goalie gets possession and inbounds the ball from anywhere beyond the end line.

David's students, "...also decided that keeping score was not necessary and that running and play action were more important." Yeah, kids! Yeah, David!

Ready, Aim,...

I read about this game once, then I mentally misplaced the idea (I can't share how many times that's happened). Earl Davis, PA trainer, reminded me of the rules, so now I'm going to write them down so they won't synaptically disappear again.

Set-Up

Divide people into pairs. Give each pair one blindfold and two soft throwables. Define an appropriate boundary for the number of players — you don't want it too big if you want a high level of action.

Each pair has a sighted person — who cannot touch any throwables — and a blindfolded partner — who throws, retrieves and tries to avoid being hit by the throwables. The sighted person can give unlimited verbal instructions but may not physically assist the blindfolded partners.

Play

The goal for each pair is to throw an object and hit a blindfolded player from another twosome. Hitting a sighted person is meaningless, but can invoke a suitable exclamation like "Missed me!" If a hit occurs, the two partners swap roles and immediately resume action. Or if you're heavily into real-life consequences this week, you can make them be frozen for 30 seconds before they become re-active.

No players, sighted or otherwise, should leave the boundaries. If throwables manage to cross that sacred line, you should promptly scoop them back into the field of play. Adding some extra balls as the game progresses can only enliven the experience.

Trust me here, there is a lot of energy in this contest. People are moving, laughing and generally having a high ole time. Tuck it away in your memory banks for a time when you need to lighten up the mood, reduce the tension, practice communication skills, or just want to flat-out have some silly fun.

DO NOT use tennis balls or lacrosse balls as throwables, or it's *game over man!*

Red-Handed

This game involves passing some objects swiftly around a circle.

. . . .

This small group, sit-down activity works best with soft objects because of the hectic nature of the passing. Adding more objects creates more bedlam and action, so start with a few until people get the hang of it and then add more until your arms get too tired to continue.

Sound intriguing? No? Simply handled, turn the page. Yes? Here's what to do. This game involves swiftly passing some objects around a circle. The goal is to get two objects *at the same time* in the lap of a player sitting beside you. *What you don't want* is for two objects to arrive simultaneously in your own lap.

Play

- Objects are distributed around the circle and evenly spaced so that someone won't get caught at the outset.
- Objects can be passed to the right or left at the discretion of the person holding it.
- Objects may only be passed to the player next to you; you may not skip a player nor may you throw it across the circle.
- At any time players may reverse the direction of an object that has been given to them.

If a player finds two objects in his lap, that player must emit a loud noise to indicate he is caught *red-handed* — the noise should sound like sparks flying when a wire short-circuits. There is no consequence other than making the noise (after all, why eliminate someone when sooner or later it will happen to you). Once players make the appropriate noise, they pass the balls in opposite directions to begin the action again.

Once a group plays this laughter-inducing give-away, they may feel the need for a slightly greater challenge. Ask everyone to close their eyes and continue passing the objects. An alarm sound for being caught red-handed is

still *de rigeur*, but now the game proceeds punctuated at irregular intervals by the sound of two objects arriving unannounced in someone's lap.

If you want to get tough, add the competitive element; caught red-handed, you're eliminated from the circle. But if you choose this consequence, find something engaging to do for those lap-challenged individuals who were distrusted and made aware of the real purpose behind this game — to GET someone!

And remember the motto of the game: "To give one worthy gift is far better than to receive two yourself!" Or, "An object in hand is worth two in the lap."

R_ic^oc_het

The bouncing action is about as unpredictable as you can imagine.

• •

This action game was invented by Chris Cavert who owns a company called *Passport For Adventure*. He introduced *Ricochet* to me at a workshop in Boulder, CO. This write up of the vocabulary and rules is largely taken from a letter Chris sent to me, that also included a Ricochet ball. Thanks — great game, good sharing. Take a deep breath and wear a cup, you're going to need both for this game.

Before we get into the rules and vocabulary for *Ricochet*, you need to know about the *Ricochet* ball. Chris suspects, and I think he's right, that the ball (…and it's not really a ball, rather six smaller balls melded into one larger ball) is sold in pet stores as a dog (macho cat) toy. The action potential of these balls-within-a-ball is such that when the "ball" is dropped or caused to strike an unyielding surface (gym floor, concrete surface, etc.) it does not rebound in a predictable way, in fact, the bouncing action is about as unpredictable as you can imagine.

Call PA's catalog department to get a hold of your own *Ricochet* balls.

In order to communicate with *Ricochet* players around the world, and in your gym, you need some common vocabulary to bandy about. To wit:

• **Rocket** — Throwing the warted ball as high as space is available; obviously not an indoor ploy.

• **A Short** — The lowest throw allowed; about 10 feet.

• **Sky-Scraper** — A throw that's in-between a Rocket and a Short.

• **Ricochet** — When the ball angles drastically away from the potential catcher after a bounce.

• **Cup Carom** (Back-Lash) — When the ball angles drastically back towards the catcher after the first bounce; therein my suggestion of wearing a cup, guys!

• **Rabbit** — When the ball takes off at a low, fast trajectory, exhibiting numerous uncatchable bounces.

• **Roller** — This is considered a "dead" ball; i.e., obviously uncatchable. The Rabbit is actually a Roller, but players *think* they can catch a Rabbit.

- **Dud** — A ball that comes to a "dead" stop because it hits a yielding surface — like grass, clothing, bodies, etc.

Play

Get together with a maximum of eight people. Creatively choose the first thrower and then sequentially number off the remainder of the players. This throw/catch sequence must be maintained throughout the game.

Choose a winning score; 10 points represents an average short game. First player to 10 points finishes as numero uno; everyone else automatically ties for second place. Start again with a new thrower — not the winner.

To begin play, the assigned catcher must call the throw, as per the vocabulary designations above. The thrower honors the catcher's request with as accurate a toss as possible, and aimed toward striking the ground close to the center of the group. The catcher has the right to call a re-throw *before* the ball hits the ground if they feel that the throw is unacceptable.

Each time the ball strikes the playing surface one point is scored, IF the catcher eventually catches the ball before it becomes a *Roller*. The total number of bounces makes up the score for that throw. If the ball becomes a *Roller* or if the ball is missed, no points are scored. During this zig-zag pursuit, the other players do their best to stay out of the way. If a ball does hit a player by mistake (*Dud*), that play is over with no score recorded, but one point is subtracted from the hit player's score.

If a player needs two points to reach 10, but scores three points, then everyone else gets another throw to try and get their total to 10. The winner must win by two, so that first thrower now needs one point to win. If that doesn't make sense, or if you want a simplistic victory, first player to ten wins.

Chris indicates that his favorite playing venue is a wide sidewalk with grass on either side, allowing spectacular diving catches. Play

in a racquetball court allows many more striking surfaces, considerably more action, and a higher score.

If you want to spot the risk takers in your group, observe who's waiting the longest to snare the bouncing ball. Chris writes that the record for one turn is 9 bounces — awesome! (The new record [no bonus points] as of 5/94, is held by an Australian, Jerry Barnes: 11 certified bounces — double awesome!!)

A post script, resulting from many PA lunch time (anytime) games.

A Casual

This requires that the receiver stands casually waiting for the ball, resulting from whatever type of throw that they requested, and that they remain casually affixed (both feet must remain planted) until the ball has rebounded two times. If casual players move their feet before the second bounce, a point is subtracted from their total score.

Successfully completing a *Casual* adds two points to whatever regular score is accumulated.

A Rebound

The receiver requests that the throw be rebounded off a wall. An extra point is added to the receiver's regular score in this case. When playing near walls (in a gym, for example) any inadvertent ball contact with a wall adds a point to the total.

Blind Throw

The receiver must stand with his eyes closed until the ball has made it's first contact with a horizontal surface. Successfully completing a bouncing blind sequence adds one point to the player's total.

(One of our staff is hearing impaired. For this person to play the blind throw, another player taps him on the shoulder after the first ball/floor contact.)

These various "throws" can be combined in an attempt to garner more points. Combined receptions are usually attempted toward the end of a game when it becomes obvious that you either score big or go out in a blaze of glory.

For example, if a player asks for a blind, casual, rebounding skyscraper, the thrower delivers a rebounding high throw off a wall (asking for this throw guarantees four points before the ball even hits the floor). Receivers must keep their eyes closed until the ball has made first floor contact, and then must stay in place until the ball has hit the horizontal playing surface once more.

This is a very difficult shot to play, and if successfully completed the catcher certainly deserves the extra points and wild applause. The derisive laughter resulting from a spectacular miss is also well received by players and spectators alike.

Striker

Score one for the let's-play-catch fans.

Remember when you were first learning to play soccer? "Hey… No hands there kid… use your feet!" **PHWEET!** "Penalty — hand ball. Come on… this is soccer, not football — use your FEET!" **PHWEEEEEET!!!**

Remember? Are you kidding? I remember spending every scheduled physical education moment in gym class, (except for ogling Lucy Strifalino) learning how to throw, catch and smack balls of various types — and now my hands are appendages-non-grata?

Here's a game I made up specifically to confound the foot fetish aficionados — STRIKER — you are *not allowed* to kick the ball. Score one for the let's-play-catch fans.

Play

Obtain a 20" diameter beach ball ($1.27 at Woolworths) and inflate it roundly. Halve your group, without choosing sides, on a playing field or gymnasium and ask the two teams to separate by about ten yards.

The team with the oldest or youngest player can elect to either receive or smack the ball. The team that initially delivers the ball (called a Smack-Off) initiates the action by having one player toss the ball aloft, allowing another player to hand-strike the descending soft sphere so that it sails toward the other team. (An alternate START has the two shortest players pair off for a jump ball.) Play has begun, so here's a few rules to maintain some semblance of competition.

A score is achieved by hitting the ball over an end line (if playing outdoors) or making ball/

wall contact at the end of the gym. After a goal is made, a member of the defending team is allowed to pick up the ball and, without interference, strike the ball toward the far wall. There is no time out after a score — play is continuous.

Rules

- The ball cannot be hit with any part of the body except hands and arms. (Don't argue, this is MY game and Rohnke rules — I'm getting even for all those years of hearing "...keep your hands down!")

- No purposeful body contact is allowed. Hip checks and the like cannot be allowed or this game quickly becomes antithetical to what you are trying to accomplish and almost dictates an unacceptable number of injuries; i.e., somebody's going to get creamed. Explaining the rules and play expectations

for *Striker* allows the opportunity to emphasize the concept of *compassionate competition*; being able to compete with gusto, but not taking advantage of size or competitive zeal to impede or diminish an opposing player's sense of fun and safety. This concept is most important, but once understood and accepted by the participants, will permit a level of strenuous play that would otherwise have been impossible to allow.

- There are no time outs, penalties (self-enforced rules), or whistles. The action does not stop just because half the players are sucking wind.

- Contact with the ball is made only with an open hand — no fists. Inadvertent body contact with the ball is OK, but purposeful and continued use of feet, knees, head, etc. results in disparaging comments (including hoots and whistles) by the opposing players.

If more than 18 people are on the court (field) add another beach ball. Two balls in play = two separate offensive and defensive teams, and a

useful dispersal of bodies. After a team makes a goal, yell **SCORE!** (teams love to hear that kind of stuff), and continue play. After awhile most people will have no idea what the total score is, or care.

If someone wants to know what the score is, without hesitation and with confidence yell out some numbers that are fairly close. Say, "It's 12 to 14, you're ahead." Close, non-committal ...perfect.

Noticing that there's more than a few tongues on the floor, end the game by announcing, "Next score wins." Not bad, eh? Winning by one point feels good and makes you respect the other team for playing so hard. Losing by one point is heroic and makes you respect the other team for playing so hard...

Consideration

This is a highly active and attractive game for young people. If someone decides to not play by the rules, removing that person for a few minutes to watch (no play = no fun) usually solves the problem.

Twizzle and/or Competition Elimination Twizzle

This is a Simon Says type of game with a literal twist.

• •

This was offered to me by Tom Fuchs of Cortland SUNY, which scholastic venue is also inhabited by those other persistent players and PA trainers, Tom Quinn and Tom Steele. So when I refer to *Tom* in this write up, I *really* mean Tom.

Play

Beginning Formation: Large circle, all students facing clockwise and NOT holding hands.

Terminology:

GO	– Walk in the direction that you are facing.
STOP	– Stop moving and *freeze*!
TURN	– Make a half turn (180°) and *freeze*!
JUMP	– Jump and make a half turn (180°) and *freeze*!
TWIZZLE	– Jump and make a full (360°) turn and *freeze*!

Instructor says: "The name of the game we are about to play is *Twizzle*. After we try some basic twizzling, we will attempt a couple rounds of *Competition Elimination Twizzle* — which is just plain old *Twizzle* with an

arbitrary rule that eliminates you from the universe if you mess up."

Explain the terminology, then have the students practice each command as you loudly bark out a few, GO, STOPs and TURNs. The important thing to emphasize is that players must totally FREEZE after each command — with the exception, of GO. Can't GO if you're frozen, if you know what I mean.

After some practice time, actually play a game where no one is eliminated, to emphasize the fun of the game. When you think everyone understands the rules and commands, announce that, "We are now going to play COMPETITION ELIMINATION TWIZZLE, but first we must all take the player's oath. So, raise your right foot and repeat after me." (Sample oath follows.)

"I (your name), do solemnly swear from time to time, (but I'm trying to watch my tongue) do solemnly swear to do my best, to give it that ole college try, to demonstrate the utmost integrity, honesty, sportsmanship, perseverance, and endurance while participating in this world renowned game of *COMPETITION ELIMINATION TWIZZLE!* I promise that if it is discovered by the referees that I do not totally freeze in my tracks, and am therefore honestly eliminated from this game that I truly love, I will not moan, cry, whine, freak out, carry on, chastise or criticize, even if someone near by accidentally lets one go.

I promise to smile, laugh and idiotically giggle upon being caught and to take my assigned and rightful new place in the center of the circle, thus positioning me to seek personal revenge and justification for having been so rudely snatched from my comfortable playing position."

So it has been spoken. So it shall be done.

Arrange your students so that they are lined up in a circle and let the game begin.

When students are caught, have them come to the middle of the circle and join you as co-referees. If you hear grumblings or complaints, remind the transgressors about the oath just administered and accepted.

Continue playing until there are about three or four people left. Designate these lucky people as members of an endangered species and remind them that it is their solemn responsibility to repopulate the earth with their kind.

Tom reports that, "This fun activity was borrowed from Donnie Osman, and that he got it from someone else. Oh well, that's how most things get passed along." Too true!

Waiter Wars

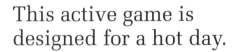 ker

This active game is designed for a hot day.

• •

I'm sure you can identify lots of valid reasons for playing *Waiter Wars*, but the level of laughter and flat out fun is enough for me.

Here's the props you will need for a group of about 20 people.

- eight –12 oz. unbreakable plastic tumblers (drinking glasses)

- four – unbreakable dinner dishes or plastic serving trays
- fleece balls to equal the number of people playing the game
- ropes or sections of ropes long enough to outline the playing areas
- a #10 tin can with wire bail attached
- about 15 feet of 1/4" bungee cord
- a water source near the beginning
- a candle

Objective — Le raison du play

To try and fill a bungee-cord suspended #10 tin can with water, until the can bungees down to a level that puts out a lighted candle situated directly under the can.

Scenario: A klatch (chic name for coffee drinking union members) of California-based waiters are angry and upset after having learned that their counterparts in Rhode Island are receiving higher pay and better benefits for identical Waiting work. They have decided to strike. As is often the situation, many out of work Waiters, sensing the potential for some under-the-table wages, have broken the picket line and established themselves as much denigrated scabs. The on-strike Waiters are determined not to let the scab Waiters complete their occupational responsibilities, setting the stage for the role-play warring game situation that ensues.

Set-Up

Divide your group in half; half striking Waiters, half scabs. The Waiters are led to the end of a rope outlined corridor that is approximately 10' wide and 75' long. There needs to be a water source at the starting end. The Waiters are given the tumblers and plates and are told that these containers are to be used to carry water to the far end of the corridor, so that the water can be transferred into the suspended #10 tin can.

The scabs are given the fleece balls and told to stand outside the corridor ropes.

Rules

• The Waiters must carry the provided tray (plate) on top of their five finger tips, with the glass on top of the plate. The other hand may not be used to balance the tray.

- The Waiters are free to put as much water into the glass as they like.
- The tumblers cannot be physically held on top of the plate, but must be balanced there.
- There is a two glass maximum per plate.
- Each Waiter is allowed one bodyguard to accompany him through the gauntlet corridor. Using the bodyguard is not required.
- Waiters are not allowed to *circle the wagons* with other waiters; they must run the gauntlet alone (or with their one bodyguard).
- Scabs can only throw the fleece balls from outside the corridor rope barriers. They may enter the corridor to retrieve a ball.
- If a scab blatantly steps within the corridor to gain an advantage, a ball is removed from the game by one of two referees.
- Scabs cannot throw at the waiter's glass until a start line has been crossed.
- If a glass is knocked off a plate, the Waiters must toss that glass (not the plate) from Waiter to Waiter back to the water source. Running with the empty glass is not allowed.

Tossing the glass must be accomplished outside the corridor. Tossing the glass back to the start may not be interfered with by the scabs.

- If a glass is emptied successfully into the #10 can, that glass can be carried directly back to the water source, but this must also be done outside the corridor boundaries (a safety consideration).
- All of this action is timed, so that the teams may switch roles in order to compare decisions and efficiency — and get revenge.
- Body contact (team against team) is not allowed.
- Soaking the fleece balls to increase their efficiency is *definitely not allowed*.

Consideration

If you can't find appropriate glasses to use for the game, try cutting off the bottom third of a one quart (liter) plastic soft drink bottle. The cutting is easily done with a sharp knife and the resultant container is not only inexpensive but safe to use.

Whizz-Bang ker

The orb continues to whizz from person to person...

• •

This fast action, no prop, no reason game came to me via Jim Grout, via Mark Murray, via college drinking games genre, and I'm happy to pass it along to you — Whizzzz!

Play

Line up in a circle! Tell the person to your right or left that you are going to pass them a movement and a sound. Cup your hands and indicate that you have captured an energy orb.

Show the group your cupped hands. What more could you do to prove your veracity? Open your hands? OK you asked for it.

When you take your hands apart to prove to the skeptics that an energy source is indeed within your grasp, the kinetic energized orb escapes and moves immediately in a whizzing fashion either to your right or left. The direction is indicated by which way you pass the existential orb. (You should know that kindled orbs cannot maintain flesh contact for more that .007 seconds or irreversible palm purulence ensues, which insidious condition manifests itself in acne of the palms. Don't let this happen to you, as a handful of Clearacil is no panacea; get rid of the infectious orb *fast*.)

The orb continues to whizz from person to person until someone, about to receive the flashing sphere, cocks her arm and raises her fist exclaiming concurrently, "BANG!" This definitive movement and sound stops the orb and reverses it's direction.

If the orb comes whizzing to you, and you sense the need for a change of pace, grab the orb and slowly initiate a two handed basketball-type set shot toward someone else in the circle (making eye contact), entoning at the same time, "VA-VOOOM." The person receiving the arcing orb pulls it in with an obvious sound of satisfaction, "AAAAHHHHH"; then the orb once again spirals with dispatch around the circle.

Redirection Variations

Perform a one-handed jump shot with the orb toward someone, (say his name). That person must make a basket with his arms, and as the orb comes arcing through, says, "SWISH!"

Considering that everyone seems to like hearing the word *score*, the person with the orb makes a hockey stick sweeping movement toward someone else simultaneously saying,

"SMACK!" That target person must bow her legs, throw both hands over her head, and shout, "SCORE!"

Here's your chance to embellish a game. Think up an action/reaction sequence that fits in with the fast-paced format established above. As you're thinking, remember that whatever you come up with doesn't necessarily have to make sense, but you need to establish a feeling of fun and appropriateness so that there's more fun flow than dumb flow.

Wizards and Gelflings

In the universe (as defined by the boundaries of this game actually), there are two forces at work. Each force is represented by a unique species of beings. As is often the case when two species co-exist, there is tension and competition.

The first species is the Wizards. Wizards tend to be pretty serious because they are always thinking — creating spells, calculating formulas, analyzing experiments, chanting ancient rituals... you know the type. They like their work a lot and don't like to be distracted.

On the other hand, Gelflings live to have FUN (with a capital F!). They frolic, fantasize,

sing, dance, merrily enjoying themselves without a care in the world. Well, almost not a care. They must watch out for Wizards.

Wizards have a fixated mindset about Gelflings. See a Gelfling, freeze it! NOW! Wizards constantly try to freeze Gelflings by touching them with their magic ball/wand/orb.

As soon as a Gelfling is frozen, it immediately reacts to the suspension of its ability to frolic by emitting the Universal Gelfling Distress Call: A very high pitched wail (think of Tiny Tim doing "Tiptoe through the tulips..."), "Help Me, Help Me, Help Me ..."

A physical motion emphasizes this distress

call. Use a fist with the thumb extended up, raising and lowering it into the palm of your other hand — the universally recognized Gelfling symbol for "help." This call repeats itself over and over until at least two unfrozen Gelflings surround their frozen partner, join hands and hug that person calling out, "Go free, little Gelfling, go free." At this joyful juncture, the frozen Gelfling is free to frolic once again.

Wizards hate to see all their cryogenic work undone, so they get particularly upset as Gelflings become unfrozen. Wizards exhibit extra amounts of serious freezing energy when Gelflings congregate around a frozen partner.

The challenge in this activity is to find the proper balance between seriousness and fun. Too many Wizards, the game ends quickly and the Gelflings feel overwhelmed. Too few Wizards, the Gelflings get bored and the Wizards need CPR. Experiment with your group, but 2–3 Wizards for about 15–20 Gelflings seems to be an appropriate ecological starting point. Just goes to show that environmental planning is an inexact science.

One last suggestion; allow the Wizards to change their identity. Any time they get tired of chasing Gelflings, they can tag a Gelfling and then give them the Wizard's magic ball. The Gelfling is immediately transformed into a Wizard, the Wizard into a Gelfling. This technique has been proven to prevent major stress breakdowns in Wizards.

May you and yours find excitement and joy in the eternal battle between WORK and PLAY! May the FUN be with you…

Zombie

Zombie status
is punctuated and finalized
with a Voodoo scream.

• •

Everyone knows that a zombie represents a creepy manifestation of the undead; i.e., a sloth-like, socially dreary individual who has ostensibly died but, being socially devoid of all couth, hasn't made the decision to permanently lie down. However, breathing as we know it has ceased, causing rampant tissue decay, raging halitosis and purulent drooling. The game of *Zombie* is based on this paradoxical flat-line creature.

Play

Ask everyone to collect in an open area (not many things to run into) and to close their eyes, assuming the hands up/palms forward *bumpers up* position. Indicate that you are going to assign *ZOMBIE* status to one of the players, and that it is this creature's responsibility to seek other "blindfolded" members in order to transform them into Jr. Zombies. (This is a nasty habit of Voodoo Vampires that I forgot to mention above, sorry.) After the initial/original Zombie makes physical contact with a normal player, the transformation to joint Zombie status is punctuated and finalized with a Voodoo scream. Then, in keeping with Zombie tradition, the newly anointed Jr. Zombie (still sightless) stalks off seeking another body to transform with their own laconic touch and demonic scream.

However, if a Zombie meets a Zombie, *coming through the rye,* and concurrent screams are forthcoming, both players are immediately humanized, continuing play as rejuvenated, ambulatory, back-from-the-dead humanoids. At the end of 5+ minutes of play, stop the action and see which sect (Zombies or pro-life) has the most active voting members, then draw whatever win/lose conclusions you wish from the results.

A final note: In evaluating a game like the one above, I find that if the players enjoy the game format, the rules, and the flow, you have a winner. If they balk at the rules, become verbally abusive to one another, and sneak out of class, I'll generally look for a way out myself. Bye...

Initiatives

3-D Mine Field

People seem to like the unique combination of trust, communication, empowerment and risk-taking.

• •

I've been presenting a communication-trust exercise called the *Mine Field* for a number of years. I thought it was an OK activity for the right group, but it wasn't by any means a workshop standby or a personal favorite. From time to time, I'll ask a workshop group, "During the last few days, which game or Initiative problem was the most fun or potentially most useful of all the activities (40–60) that you have tried?" Surprisingly, the answer has often been the *Mine Field.* People seem to like the unique combination of trust, communication, empowerment and risk-taking that characterizes the activity.

When I first started presenting the *Mine Field,* I used only tennis balls as props, set in a random pattern within an outlined area on the ground. On one occasion, as the result of not having tennis balls available during a workshop presentation, I asked the participants to help me spread the contents of my traveling Bag of Tricks onto the area outlined by a rope. (I don't use exact dimensions for the *Mine Field,* but the rectangular area is about 8' wide by 30' long.) The participants liked the idea of creating their own obstacle and particularly enjoyed spreading fleece balls, rubber chickens, rubber rings, beach balls, etc., onto a "blank canvas" patch of gym floor. Obviously, each time the obstacle path is set up, a new *Mine Field* pattern is established.

Rules

Here are a few rules and helpful hints to help you get started on your own *Mine Field:*

1. Use more or less obstacles to increase or decrease the difficulty of getting to the end of the *Mine Field.*

2. Operate in pairs. One participant is blindfolded (eyes closed) and is located within the *Mine Field* enclosure. The second member of the pair is sighted and must stay outside the obstacle enclosure. Only verbal clues are allowed; the sighted player cannot touch the blind player. Allow all the blindfolded players to enter the obstacle course simultaneously to increase the difficulty of careful movement and of being heard.

3. If the blindfolded player touches any obstacle, he must return to the beginning and try again, or simply count the touches for later comparison.

4. After a successful traverse or at the end of a time period, ask the players to switch roles.

5. As an added challenge, ask two blindfolded players to attempt a hand-in-hand traverse. Other challenges include: See how few steps can be taken; see how fast the traverse can be made.

Variation

Recently, I tried suspending various lightweight obstacles within the confines of the outlined *Mine Field* area in order to increase the difficulty of the traverse and also to reduce the predictability of the task. Examples of this "drop art" included a rubber chicken, a length of well-cows-tailed rope, a horizontally hung 24" length of pipe insulation, a crazy dunce hat, a tennis ball, a shrunken head, a plastic spider, etc.

Use four lengths of 4"x4" boards, placed vertically in post holes, to act as the corner supports for overhead lengths of #4 nylon cord. Connect the cord around the periphery near the top of the boards and also continue the cord from corner to corner, crossing in the middle. This overhead set-up will allow you to suspend your playful obstacles practically anywhere over the *Mine Field*. Be sure to vary the hanging distance of each item, using the Goldilocks Rule; i.e., some high, some low, and some in-between.

Balloon Trolleys

Trolleys have never been one of my most favorite activities, partly because of the weight and bulk of the *Trolleys* themselves. This lightweight activity is included here because it alleviates the major concern of doing *Trolleys* as a portable problem.

Set-Up

Blow up enough balloons so that you have one to fit between every person if they stand in a single file line. For example, if X is a person and O is a balloon, the line would look like this: XOXOXOXOXOX.

Play

The challenge is to move the entire group across an area, partially obstructed with "flotsam and jetsam," without allowing any of the balloons to hit the floor.

Sound simple? It sounded and looked that way the first time we experimented with this idea but it didn't work out that way. There was a lot more work involved than anticipated. You can even increase the difficulty by prohibiting people from hugging the players in front of them; in other words, you have to move simultaneously but without being linked together physically.

Rules

A balloon touching the floor or ground may result in:

• The entire group having to start again;

• The two people who dropped the balloon having to go to the front or end of the line and replace the balloon;

• The group having to figure out a method to pick up the balloon and re-insert it where it was without losing any other balloons;

• All of the above. Use whatever consequence coincides with your keen sense of challenge, tempered with a dollop of compassion.

Including obstacles in the space for the group to negotiate around definitely adds more flavor to this mix. They don't have to be elaborate, but you might consider: Going over a wrestling mat rolled up on the floor, going under a table or balance beam, stepping through a large hoola hoop, stepping over a small barrier of milk crates, etc.

The best part of this activity is the ease of carrying a bag of balloons (back pocket stuff) versus struggling with two, 6–8 foot 4"x4"s. Try it and you'll appreciate it, too.

Birthday Shuffle

For those of you familiar with the low ropes Initiative *TP (Telephone Pole) Shuffle,* here's a great twist to add a different challenge. If you don't remember, refer to *Cowstails and Cobras,* by you-know-who, on page 112.

Set-Up

Instead of the usual challenge of dividing the group in half and asking them to switch sides, tell the group to get up on the pole randomly. Once they're up, you can give them a chance to practice switching techniques if it's the first time for them on the pole. Be sure everyone understands the safety parameters and knows about spotting before presenting the challenge.

Play

Ask them to line up in order, after having situated themselves on the pole, according to the month and day of their birth.

This type of challenge presents another level of problem-solving to the activity. The group must determine the information and then make a decision as to which end of the calendar year belongs at what end of the pole, depending on where people start. The challenge of passing people hasn't changed much — sometimes it's more difficult, sometimes less so, than the original version. It's been my observation that a group has to work harder to succeed at a random order than just switching sides.

If you like the idea, think up some sequential categories of your own. Some other random line-ups might be: By height, by number of siblings, by shoe size, etc.

The Corporate Connection

Here's an example of how a simple Initiative problem can be made more *meaningful* for a corporate market. When you are deciding how you can justify charging a corporate client more $$$, remember it's not necessarily what you say, it's how you say it.

Thanks to Lee Peters at Weber State University in Ogden, Utah, for this variation of Deming's "Red Bead/White Bead Experience."

Goals

- To help participants become aware of the impact of statistical probability in the work world.

- To let participants experience group problem-solving with input representing all aspects of a process.

Group Size

- 10–20 participants

Time Required

- 45 to 60 minutes

Materials

- Three milk crates or solid wastebaskets
- 60–80 identical soft throwable objects
- Masking tape
- Newsprint and a felt-tipped marker

Physical Setting

- A cleared space at least 20 feet wide by 40 feet long. A wall at one end of this space is helpful but not necessary.

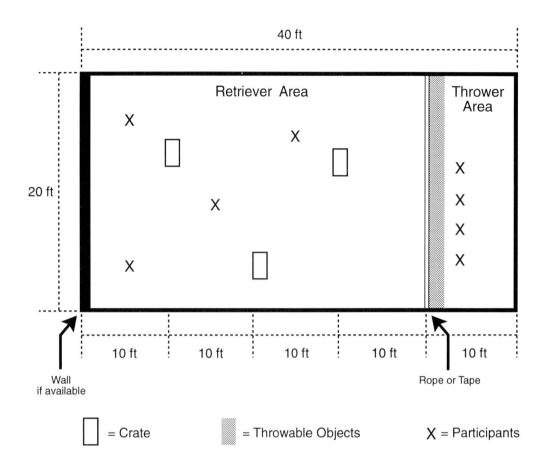

40 ft

Retriever Area

Thrower Area

X

X

X

X

X

X

X

X

X

20 ft

10 ft   10 ft   10 ft   10 ft   10 ft

Wall
if available

Rope or Tape

☐ = Crate   ▨ = Throwable Objects   X = Participants

Set-Up

Arrange the 20x40 space as shown in the diagram, and choose a group of 10–20 participants to put in the throwing area.

Explain that the group is now a company that produces a high-tech product — call it ALPHA. (Creativity tip: Let the group decide on a company name and product).

The goal of the group is to produce as many defect-free ALPHAs as possible per cycle. A cycle is defined as two minutes for the exercise (representing a monthly cycle). The group receives credit for one defect-free ALPHA for each object that they throw into the nearest milk crate, and credit for three defect-free ALPHAS for each object that they throw into the middle crate, and credit for five defect-free ALPHAS for each object that they throw into the farthest crate.

The only rules are that there are two distinct working groups in their company, "throwers" and "retrievers." *Throwers* must stand behind the taped line and are the only ones who can "score" by throwing an object into a crate. *Retrievers* must stand on the other side of the line and can retrieve misses, but they cannot score, nor can a thrown object bounce off any part of their bodies and into a crate for a score. The company can decide on any number of throwers or retrievers before the cycle begins, but once the cycle is in operation, they cannot change jobs. (Five minutes)

Give the employees time to decide on their roles and to ask any questions. (Five minutes)

Begin the cycle by stating *begin* and end after two minutes with *stop*. Participants count the completed ALPHAs and tell the facilitator,

ALPHA COMPANY							
Cycle	Crate 1	Sub-total	Crate 3	Sub-total	Crate 5	Sub-total	Total
1							
2							
3							
4							
5							
6							

who records on a newsprint chart prepared in the following way. (Five minutes)

Announce the total and ask the company if they would like to respond. Then give the company three minutes to decide how to change the process for the better. (Three minutes)

Repeat steps 4 and 5 as many times as necessary for the group to discover that they will do better as they focus on the crates with a higher probability of success (closer vs. farther). [Editor's note — Having used this game dozens of times, I have found that if a group commits to aiming for only the farthest crate, that they will score higher than if they concentrate their shots only on the closest crate. Big risk/big return.] (Eight minutes per time)

When the activity is ended, discuss the experience utilizing the following questions.

Debrief

• What were the barriers to success?

• What did you do that made you more successful?

• How did probability of statistics influence your decision making?

• How did leadership of the company impact the outcome?

• Who gave significant input; why was it significant?

Variation

The facilitator may appoint a *boss* and direct the boss to make all decisions on company operations during the first two cycles, then allow for the *workers* to give input.

So there you have it! Now you know the *real* difference between facilitating middle school students and a corporate group. Good luck with your new career.

Do-I-Go?

ker

I love ideas like this one, same-ole-stuff but approached in a different way, providing an alternative solution to a well-known Initiative. Credit Ross Merrett of PA New Zealand with the germ of this idea.

Set-Up

Arrange four *All Aboard* platforms (each measures about 2'x2') at the corners of an imaginary square, and in the center of that conceptual square, hang a swing rope. If you have trouble visualizing this, think of the dots on a die that indicate the number five; the four outside dots represent the platforms and the center dot is the swing rope.

Play

Divide and situate your group so that there are an equal number of people standing on each of the corner platforms. Indicate that the established problem is for each person to move to another platform; i.e., when finished, all participants must be on a platform other than the one from which they started.

I trust you have been involved in enough of these fabricated scenarios to recognize that the area between the platforms represents some ghastly noxious material that cannot be touched, and if so contacted, immediately results in return of the obnoxious person to their starting platform (…to clean off the gunk, of course).

Also contraindicated — no heroic, self-sacrificing travesty ploys (walking through the gunk to retrieve the rope), no props other than what the people have with them, and no cheating while the instructor compassionately attends to someone's "rope burn."

Variation

A variation requires two swing ropes hanging about five feet apart, with a fifth platform centered directly between the two ropes. The four corner platforms are a constant. If making or purchasing platforms seems excessive, try using four used bicycle or motorcycle tires at the corners. The bike tires are easily transportable, inexpensive (free), and will not skid easily on the floor, as hula hoops are apt to do.

The object of this moving Initiative problem is the same as above, but the center platform remains vacant at the beginning and must be vacated at the end. Be sure to splice a generous loop in the bottom of the swing ropes to aid those participants who don't have the arm strength to hold on for the duration of the swing arc.

This Initiative lends itself well, I think, to an indoor setting, where the ropes can be hung from just about any location because of the crisscrossing overhead beams and joists. It's a money-saver, too, because you are utilizing props that are already in place for other Initiatives.

The name makes more sense if you preface *Do I Go* with the word When, and put a question mark after Go.

Don't Touch Me!!!

Every now and then I come across a game that is so deceptively simple I almost dismiss it as being too blah, or too easy. After having used *Don't Touch Me* with a couple groups, I'm beginning to think that it has the feel of a potential classic. Perhaps I'm being too enthusiastic too soon, but judge for yourself and definitely give this one a try.

Set-Up

Ask the group to "line up in a circle" (this is always good for a bit of confused levity), and once circled up, indicate that each person is to "eyeball" someone on the far side of the circle and to call their name. If two people end up saying each others' names repeatedly, you have a pair. If there is an odd number, pop into the circle yourself and be a partner. Place a hula hoop or used bicycle tire (you can use a new one if you want — a 27"x1-1/4" works well) in the center of the people circle, so that it becomes the center of the center.

Play

Now that you are set up, here's the problem. Ask the pairs to change sides of the circle; i.e., to reverse positions, and while making this change to make physical contact (one foot's OK) with the interior of the hula hoop. Tell them that you will time this exchange so that a "world's record" can be established, and that every time someone inadvertently touches someone else during the inevitable initial melee, a one-second penalty will be charged. For example, if the exchange is made in eight seconds and six touches are admitted to, the total

time is 14 seconds. To emphasize each person's desire to make a clean crossing during the frenetic exchange, players should strongly state their desire to maintain personal space by exclaiming, "Don't Touch Me!" simultaneously and holding hands up, palms out — bumpers up!

Don't dismiss this opportunity for histrionics as just another opportunity for Karl to be weird. Barking out, "DON'T TOUCH ME!" has an individual therapeutic feel to it, and hearing twenty such exclamations used almost simultaneously is just plain funny.

There is more than one way to flay a kitty, so let the group talk about their attempts and strategize a more efficient, faster technique for the exchange.

Earthwinds

This is a very simple but effective warm-up sequence.

• •

Peter Steele, now retired from Fox Lane Middle School in New York, sent me this variation of *Circle The Circle* (*Silver Bullets,* pg. 60). If you don't recognize that old pass-the-hula-hoop-in-a-circle game, s'okay, you can't be expected to know them all, and it doesn't really matter since *Earthwinds* is a stand-alone activity.

Set-Up

You need eight bicycle inner tubes for this activity. The easy way to get them is budget for them and buy the least expensive 27" tube you can find. The best and most adventurous way is to visit your local bike dealer and ask him for his throw-away tubes and then do your best to patch them. There are other activities involving use of bicycle inner tubes, so don't discard any extras.

Color code four of the inflated tubes by wrapping colored tape around the tube and again 180° beyond, so that you have tape in two locations. Each of these four colored tubes represent a cardinal wind: NORTH (blue), EAST (orange), SOUTH (yellow), and WEST (red). Leave the other four tubes uncolored, which then represent the Northeast, Northwest, Southeast, and Southwest winds.

Play

Ask all the participants (12–50) to form a circle, holding hands. This circle represents the EARTH. Next, place all (8) of the inflated tubes inside outstretched held arms (make the necessary temporary breaks to do this) at NORTH, NORTHEAST, SOUTHEAST, SOUTH, SOUTHWEST, WEST, and NORTHWEST compass directions.

Instructions for the participants are as follows: Without breaking the circle, the NORTH wind inner tube blows (moves) clockwise [**cw**] toward the EAST wind tube, while the EAST wind tube blows counterclockwise [**ccw**] towards the NORTH wind tube. Simultaneously, the SOUTH wind tube blows **cw** towards the WEST tube, while the WEST tube blows **ccw** toward the SOUTH wind tube. Each of these cardinal winds must continue to move in the original blowing direction until they return to their starting points. The uncolored tubes stay put due to the **cw** and **ccw** motion of the cardinal compass wind points.

Object

The objective of this activity is to see which wind returns back home first, thereby determining which cardinal wind is blowing fastest. Another objective is to see if the instructor can explain the procedure and criteria for success without becoming misdirected by the obviously manifested Coriolis effect. (Southern hemisphere readers be of good cheer, as the Coriolis only affects flushed toilets, not hand-held inner or outer tube rotation. This is obviously because of a reversed polarity due to a skin/rubber athemia.)

If, during the process of being windblown, any inner tube wind becomes tied up or intertwined with another tube, you simply describe this as a temporary passing tornado.

Eggspeediency

You will need to time the group's efforts to track their improvement.

· ·

While leading a corporate training a few months ago, I was presenting the activity *Warp Speed.* The group did an exemplary job of working together to improve its time and when they were done I wanted to give them an additional challenge. I knew that I had six eggs left over from the *Great Egg Drop,* and in a flash of inspiration, I devised something new and unusual for them to try, albeit a bit risky.

If you don't know *Warp Speed,* here's a quick review. (Hey, this is a bargain — you're getting two games here for the rules to one.)

Play

Arrange your group in a circle and begin by explaining that each person is going to receive the ball (catch it) and then toss it to someone else (who hasn't previously caught it), with the last person who receives it returning it to you to complete the cycle. Be certain to tell the players that they must remember who throws it to them and to whom they throw it. If everyone remembers correctly, you've established a pattern where each person catches the ball from one person and tosses it to another.

Once the pattern is established (practice it once or twice to insure that people remember where the ball goes), you can present the *Warp Speed* Initiative. The challenge is to see how fast the group can move the ball through the pattern from start to finish with these rules in force.

Rules

- The object must start and stop with the same person (whoever starts it must get it back to complete the activity).

- The object must move sequentially from person to person (not everyone can touch it at the same time).

- Everyone must have "possession" of the object as it moves through the pattern. (I usually do not define possession nor do I tell the group that it is up to them to determine what possession means. That is part of the problem.)

You will need to time the group's efforts to track their improvement. If you choose to be a participant in the circle, you may want to ask someone else to start the object in motion, or you may find it very difficult to start and stop your timepiece.

If you like the sound of this activity, you have a good ear for fun and challenge. *Warp Speed* is one of the best all-around portable Initiative problems. If you want to consider something a bit more "off-the-wall" to spice up your program, read on.

Once the group has attempted *Warp Speed, Eggspeediency* offers you and them a higher level of challenge and risk. I usually find it appropriate to remind people of the Challenge By Choice concept and ask them if they want to consider a greater challenge before presenting this task.

The activity is simple. Substitute one (or more, if you and the group are daring) raw egg(s) as the object to be passed around the circle. The task is to pass the egg (and any other objects the group wants to work with) through the pattern without breaking the egg.

Often I will ask the group to work with five objects, and they can choose how many of the five are eggs. They need to "juggle" all the objects and insure the safety of the egg.

You may read this and say, "NOT! It can't possibly work." What if my (choose the one you're most concerned about): a) principal, b) co-worker, c) boss, d) school committee chairperson, should see me?

The rules are basically the same. The egg starts and stops with the same person, must move sequentially, and everyone must handle the egg. To keep the challenge level higher, I will not allow the group to readjust their position in the circle so that they are standing next to the person who passes the egg to them (a favorite, and extremely effective solution for the *Warp Speed* problem).

Let me say, to assuage your scrambled egg fears, that groups can do it quite easily if they work together and concentrate. Since there is a real consequence to failure (usually someone with egg on their chin), you should fully assess the impact this result may have on your group before asking them to try it.

I've seen groups succeed; I've had groups break the eggs. I've seen groups thrilled by their efforts, and I've had groups share good insights about how they worked together to achieve what appeared to be a risky goal. What appeals to me about this idea is that the group must collectively work out how much risk is OK, how they are going to manage it, and then act on their ideas. Some groups do it for fun and don't really care what happens to the egg or where it ends up.

The only word of caution I would give you is don't try this activity if you think people in the group will deliberately try to break the egg on someone else. The value of a fun challenge under those conditions probably doesn't measure up to the risk of undermining trust within the group.

The Ego Walk

Just Plain Fun!

• •

Earl Davis, a PA certified trainer, created this activity as a metaphor for understanding the impact one's ego can have on a group. It's a neat idea; but if the metaphor is too serious for you, change it and just have some fun. It's a great variation of *Pitfall*.

Set-Up

You will need to create a course before starting the activity. Tying a rope between two trees about 30 feet apart is a good start. Then suspend some ropes from this horizontal cross piece so that they hang down close to or touch the ground. Leave about 2–3 feet between these vertical ropes. (The proper spacing will be determined by what object you choose for the participants to carry — read on.) Last, create two lines on the ground, about 2–3 feet on either side of the horizontal rope to act as side boundaries. The walkers cannot go outside of these boundaries.

Divide your group so that everyone has a partner, or is in a group of three. Players entering the course must carry on their shoulders a pole at least 10 feet long. (2"x3"s work well.) The instructor (you!) places the pole on the person's shoulder at the start so that a portion of the pole is extending in front and a section of the pole is sticking out behind. Obviously, how much of the pole you leave extending behind the person determines the degree of difficulty of the exercise.

As players walk the course, they cannot turn around or glance backwards to see the section of pole behind, only forward.

Play

The objective is for people to walk the entire course, zigzagging between the vertical pieces of rope, without touching anything with either their body or the pole. On the first attempt, ask players to walk the course without any assistance or communication from their partner. The partner is responsible for counting how many touches occur. Touches should be counted, but no communication about how many or where and when they happened should take place until the walk is completed.

On the second round, the partners may give the walkers feedback (non-verbal is recommended) to try to help them negotiate the course without a touch. Devising hand signals and/or other forms of communication prior to starting is allowed and encouraged. In addition to giving feedback, the partner counts any touches that occur during the walk. The observers may not walk inside the boundaries with their partners.

This activity can be presented as an individual challenge as outlined here, or you might adapt it into a team challenge by asking how few touches a group can establish with everyone taking one turn walking the course. You can also create a different type of problem by asking the walkers to be blindfolded and allowing verbal feedback from their partners.

This activity may not sound like much, but it produces some good fun and is challenging. For younger groups not ready for or interested in the notion of feedback, presenting it as an opportunity for coaching or helping may get the message across more effectively.

Lest you forget after reading these rules the original idea that Earl had, the point of the exercise is to demonstrate to people how easy it is to touch someone unknowingly if you're not aware of your own actions. With some coaching and good feedback from your peers, you should be more successful at negotiating the course, exemplifying the notion that the more you know about yourself, the less likely you are to hit someone with an unseen/unknown part of your ego. It's a good metaphor, but it's also just plain fun.

Hammeroids

From the land almost down under, Project Adventure New Zealand (PA/NZ) trainer, Eric Schusser, offers this bit of Initiative legerdemain. The name is his fault also; you knew I wouldn't come up with anything quite so crass and plebeian.

Play

Using only the materials that have been provided, suspend all the objects in mid-air. Only the last inch of the ruler is allowed to touch the top of the desk, table, etc. That means the ruler must be on top of the desk, not jammed into a drawer or other sneaky Initiative stuff like that.

Materials allowed — A steel (wood's OK) 12" ruler; a rubber-handled carpenter's hammer (the rubber handle is optional); a 14" section of nylon (manila or jute is fine) cord.

See below for the solution illustration, which I did not draw, and the photo, which I did graph...

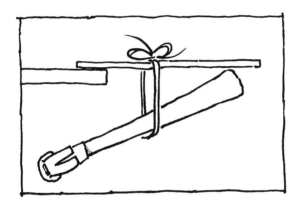

Hawser

This is a no-hands, Action Jackson game that requires a team to work hard and cooperate toward doing something that no one on the team has ever tried before.

Set-Up

You do need a 20'–25' length of hawser for the game. Hawser is defined as large diameter (circumference) rope, and that means, in the case of this activity, minimum 2" diameter — bigger if you can get it. Rope this size is generally very expensive if you buy a long length, but rope manufacturers often have remnants left over from a special order or from the end of a large spool that they are willing to sell for at least 50% off. Ask for remnant hawser.

Just to give you an idea of size and weight, I received a 26' long section of 9.5" circumference, braided nylon hawser recently. It weighs 57 pounds. A section of rope this size is perfect for the game *Hawser*.

Play

Here's how to play:

A team of six must move the *Hawser* 100 feet without using their hands and without maneuvering the rope onto their bodies. The rope must be moved by feet only.

Starting position is standing within a circle made by the *Hawser*. Finishing requires moving the *Hawser* the required 100 feet and then re-establishing the circular configuration with all team members inside. This is obviously a timed event.

Afterwards, give each end of your *Hawser* to a player and ask them to see who can tie the fastest bowline around the waist.

No reason — just fun.

Initiative Team Circuit

The players must individually jump or vault.

• •

This demanding Initiative circuit is a recent variation of an old variation. In 1969, I was doing some ropes course repair work while employed at the North Carolina Outward Bound School. When the work was completed, I still had some material and energy left, so I fabricated what I thought would be a challenging series of tasks, and strung them together in a sequence that I called *The Initiative Run*. The tasks were meant to cause the group to think and react efficiently. None of the individual stations were particularly difficult, but most of them required a team effort to get everyone through efficiently, and in some cases the team was necessary to help less adept members complete the circuit.

About twenty years later in Sydney, Australia, I was responsible for the facilitation of a group of Telecom employees; Australia's largest telecommunication company. I had been working with a particular group the day before, and wanted to challenge them the next day with a unique series of events that would require an unequivocal level of participation and cooperation. I put together an *Initiative Run* adapted to the indigenous eucalyptus environment that proved to be challenging and unique, and which very much resembled something I had done 240 months earlier, sequenced 'twixt rhododendron and mountain laurel.

Here's an amalgam of what I remember as the best activities from both environments and a list of props and material you'll need to have on hand before your group gathers:

```
 3 – cardboard paper rolls or
 1 – 3' diameter cable spool
 2 – auto tires
 4 – 10' sections of 1/2" multiline to
       suspend the tires
 1 – 2'x2' portable platform
 1 – 3'x3' portable platform
 1 – 4'x4' portable platform
 2 – 8' saplings (or stout aluminum poles)
10' – 3/8" multiline
 1 – 1/2" rapid link
 2 – 12' Trolley boards
 1 – class 5, 20' utility pole
20' – 1/4" bungee cord
```

This is a timed event, but if you think more will be gained by a methodical, less frenetic approach, present it that way, and save the stopwatch for a later time. A corporate group almost expects a time constraint, but a school assemblage might appreciate a run-through before you bring out the Casio "whip."

I'll verbally run you through the events, but follow the words via the illustration for the best synaptic in-context results.

Before we begin, let's talk about penalties. If someone makes contact with the turf, or whatever type of ground you are moving over, the

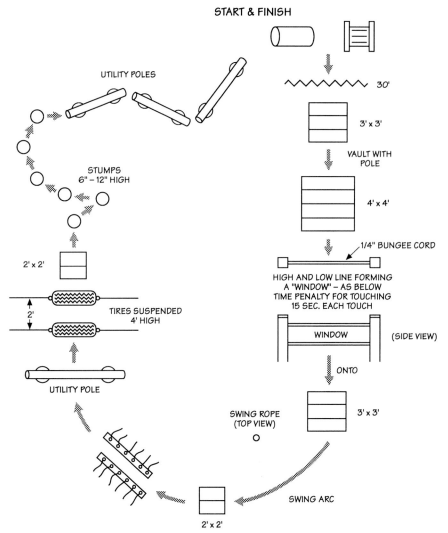

START & FINISH

UTILITY POLES

STUMPS
6" – 12" HIGH

2' x 2'

2'

TIRES SUSPENDED
4' HIGH

UTILITY POLE

30'

3' x 3'

VAULT WITH
POLE

4' x 4'

1/4" BUNGEE CORD

HIGH AND LOW LINE FORMING
A "WINDOW" – AS BELOW
TIME PENALTY FOR TOUCHING
15 SEC. EACH TOUCH

WINDOW   (SIDE VIEW)

ONTO

SWING ROPE
(TOP VIEW)

3' x 3'

SWING ARC

2' x 2'

TIME PENALTY FOR EACH TURF TOUCH –30 SEC.

offending player must return to the beginning of that particular segment of the challenge event and try again. If the bungee cord is touched while attempting the High/Low event, the person touching and all connected players (electricity), must return to the platform and try again. There are no time penalties other than the extra time involved in pursuing a second (third, fourth, etc.) attempt.

If the amount of time available to complete the circuit is a concern, you may want to assign a time penalty for each infraction, rather than having the individual or group begin again after each mistake.

Set-Up

Using 2 or 3 International Paper Co. cardboard rollers, or a large empty cable spool, roll from a starting line (short section of rope), across about 10 yards of grass (not concrete) until the people balancing on the rollers or spool can step/jump onto a 3'x3' wooden platform (like the one you use for *Prouty's Landing*).

Place a 4'x4' platform seven feet away in a continuing straight line from the first platform. This moderate distance between platforms was chosen because 7' is close enough to tempt an adept person to jump, but far enough away so that they probably won't make it. To assist the crossing, an 8' pole (stout sapling) is provided (on the ground next to the first platform), so that a vault can be attempted. Once 2–3 people are on the far platform, perhaps the pole can be utilized as an aid for those that choose not to vault...or just can't. The pole cannot be walked on.

Take a look at the top and side views of the following challenge, called the High/Low Line. The object is to get everyone through the bungee-outlined "window" onto the far platform without touching the cords or the wooden supports. Place the two platforms below and close enough to the "window" so that propelling people through the opening is not necessary.

Immediately next to the 3'x3' platform, place a 10' length of small diameter rope with a 1/2" rapid link affixed to the end. Participants can use this rope length to whip/snare the swing rope that provides access to the next 2'x2' platform.

After a successful swing, a player walks out onto the *Trolley Boards* and waits for enough help to transport the boards and themselves to the perpendicularly-placed utility pole. How many people are used to move the trolleys and how they eventually plan to return the boards for the next shuttle trip, is obviously part of the decision-making dynamic of the problem.

People can collect on the utility pole and plan how to move the group most effectively through the two suspended auto tires. The tires are suspended at two different heights and two feet apart in order to stimulate discussion and decision-making.

From the 2'x2' platform, just beyond the tires, the players must individually jump or vault (a vault pole, similar to the platform-to-platform vault pole, is made available) from stump to stump and then walk (run) and jump from pole to pole to the finish line (which is also the start line). The vault pole can also be used to support people during the utility pole crossings, if the group wishes to choose that option.

People helping people, verbally and physically, is an important part of this experience. As always, the process of getting from A to B is more important than completion or how fast they got there. Timing the group can act as a performance incentive, but if it's obvious that the group is turned off by this type of digital LED prod, be perceptive, don't time them.

Islands Moonball

ker

Another great variation of the original idea.

Eventually, *Moonball* may become the entire core curriculum of an Adventure experience.

You will need a moonball and enough hula hoops (or rope loops) so that all players can have one foot inside a hoop to start. A good ratio seems to be 2–4 people per hoop at the start.

Set-Up

For the first round, set the hoops out in a circular pattern with about 5–10 feet between the hoops. Or if you want to increase the challenge level, create a more difficult pattern for the first round.

Rules

- Once a player has put a foot inside a hoop, she cannot change hoops until the next round.

- Any player within a hoop may hit the ball, but two players from the same hoop may not hit the ball consecutively. If players from the same hoop make consecutive hits, the score returns to zero.

- Working together as a whole group; i.e., all the hoops together form the team, the team tries to record the largest number of hits before the moonball hits the ground. Whenever the ball hits the ground, the score returns to zero.

- During the play, if a player steps out of a hoop the score returns to zero.

The team will have three rounds of two minutes each to achieve their highest score. Once a round starts, the time is running and does not stop even when the ball is on the ground. The team, and the facilitator can choose to help, is responsible for retrieving the ball when it hits the ground and re-starting it.

The first two-minute round is played using whatever pattern you laid out. Between each two-minute playing round, the group has one minute for strategizing and discussion. During these strategy breaks, players can move the hoops, rearrange the number of people in a hoop, re-distribute the players to different hoops, and devise whatever plans they think will help achieve a higher point total.

Considerations

The shortness of the time periods provides a real focus to the problem and requires the group to make decisions quickly. Adjusting the length of the time periods or providing more rounds of play are certainly possibilities based on the goals and outcomes you want for the group.

Islands Moonball adds a new dimension to this Adventure favorite. It works well as an Initiative that can be accomplished in a short time frame.

Jumping Jack Flash or Hop Box

Here's another variation of an action socialization experience called *The Turnstile,* a very popular (with me) Initiative that's outlined on pg. 128 in *The Bottomless Bag* book.

The performance objective of *The Turnstile* is easy for an individual, but often frustrating for a group of them, individuals I mean. As part of the criteria for success, everyone must jump one at a time through a spinning rope so that the rope never turns without someone being in there to take a jump; i.e., a player cannot just run through, a jump must be taken. If the rope makes a turn without someone completing a jump, everyone must begin again, even those who have successfully made it through.

The problem is essentially one of effective leadership, planning, and efficient implementation. (Thanks guys, that helps a lot.) It's also a valuable teaching aid, because when the group finally decides to work together, the efficiency and sense of flow that's observed and experienced provides more hands-on learning about teamwork than you can verbalize, or swing a rope at. Anyway, the reason you're there is to remind them about what's happening, not preach about what's supposed to happen.

So what would happen if you took four 20' jump ropes and fashioned a jumping square, with the whole group inside the square trying to jump out? Good things.

Here are a few rules to help frame the problem (*Hop Box*) and prevent the more creative students from using too much initiative.

Rules

- All eight rope turners must also jump through one of the four ropes.

- Everyone has the choice of jumping through whichever of the four ropes they choose.

- Multiple jumps can be attempted; i.e., more than one person can jump through during one turn of the rope.

- This is a timed event. The clock starts at GO, and ends when the final person has made a successful jump.

- Misses are not counted or recorded as time penalties.

- The ropes must be turning when the timing starts. Ropes can be turned in either direction, clockwise or counterclockwise; it's the group's choice.

Allow at least two timed attempts at this intriguing group Initiative task.

This variation came about because Steve and I agreed there had to be a tweaked version that would function as well, if not better, than the original. "If it's worth doing, it's worth over doing." Too true.

Junk Yard Traverse

ker

There's always enough stuff around to act as props.

• •

This is an Initiative problem that I have used successfully, when it fit the occasion, but I have never thought of it as a "regular," because I had the mindset that mucho junk was necessary to make the magic happen. But what you really need is the chutzpah to make it happen no matter where you are.

Play

The group must move themselves and their anti-acid resistant junk (props) from one safe area to another while not directly touching the ground; boiling acid pit. (I'm sure just plain concentrated acid rain is sufficient, as boiling acid gives off highly noxious fumes and would

make the crossing uncomfortable for people with a predisposition for upper respiratory distress.)

Props: Unmounted tires, milk crates, boards, and other acid-resistant junk. (Try to include types of junk that can be torn or cut apart so that the participants have the choice of making those kind of truncated decisions.)

The distance negotiated should be significantly longer than the distance of all the acid-resistant junk laid out in a line. This will, of course, necessitate passing junk from the end of the line to the new beginning, and we're talkin' decent distance here — at least 50 yards. If you don't think the players can stretch the materials at hand that far, make more junk available. Everyone should be able to choose, from the plethora of available stuff, a personal bit of acid-resistant, step-on junk.

This is a good team-builder event and one that can be used to effectively determine where a group stands in terms of cohesiveness. And, perhaps even more significantly, the action provides a hands-on opportunity to assist in the confusing decision-making process of determining occupational direction: one could do worse than be a sanitation engineer or swinger of birches.

Key Punch
(a.k.a. The Calculator)

Read it, try it — you'll like it.

• •

Don't be put off by the length of this description! *Key Punch* is easy to present and is more difficult to do than it seems (always a programmatic plus in my book). Trust us, *Key Punch* is a winner.

Put on your new Nike quick-starts — you're going to need them in order to participate effectively in this fast-paced group Initiative.

Set-Up

Using a permanent, felt-tipped marker, consecutively number thirty gym-spot markers, one to thirty.

With a 90' length of retired rope (or whatever non-climbing rope is available), establish a 15'x30' rectangle on the gym floor or field.

Inside the rectangle, place the numbered spot markers (starting with #1) and orient them as illustrated. The plan is to have all even numbers on one side of the rectangle and all odd numbers on the other side. Also zig-zag the numbers up and down the rectangle. As you place the numbers, try to arrange them so that your odd/even and zig-zag planning is not obvious. (Note that numbers 1 and 30 are located at the end of the rectangle, farthest away from the starting line.)

When placing the spots, put them more than one step inside the boundary. This added distance forces the people touching the keypads to step inside the boundary, not just reach over the edge.

Thirty feet from the end of the gym-spotted rectangle, put down a length of tape or rope to designate a starting line and to mark the planning area.

Objective

The object of this Initiative is for a group of 10–15 people to solve the requirements of a "computer debugging procedure." Establish a futuristic scenario that involves a militant group of nihilistic hackers who have injected a very-virulent-virus into the government's Socially Serious program. The group represents the government's best chance to reject the virus and save billions of dollars in computer debugging costs.

To achieve their goal, this highly trained group of viral professionals must physically touch all 30 gym spots in numbered sequence as quickly as possible.

All limbered up? Let's banish that virus!

Rules and Considerations

- The entire group must begin and finish behind the start line. The stopwatch starts as soon as the first person steps over the line. The watch stops when the last person crosses back over the line.

- Only one person can be on the keyboard at a time. That is, only one participant can be inside the boundary rope. If two people are inside the rope simultaneously, a glitch occurs and a penalty time is added to the score.

- If any number is touched out of sequence (for example, 3 then 5), this infraction causes the computer to crash and a penalty time is added to the score. Remember: Speed typing only works if the end product maintains high quality.

- Any part of the body may be used to touch each numbered gym spot in sequence.

- The team cannot walk back to the computer area between attempts in order to study the number set up. All planning must occur behind the line where the group starts each round. Any time the group or a player crosses this line, it is considered an attempt.

- Tell the group that they have 30 minutes or five attempts, whichever comes first. If they use five attempts in 18 minutes, they're

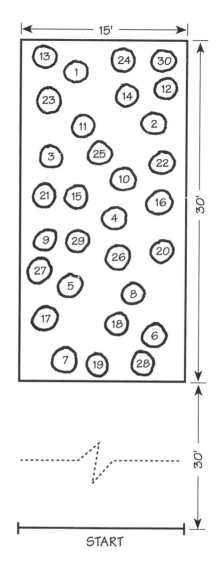

done; if they tried only three attempts in 30 minutes, they're done.

- If you don't have or can't afford 30 gym spots, use smaller plastic, circle-shaped, flexible container caps; like those covering a tennis can. Don't forget to number the caps; it's a bit confusing otherwise.

- **Penalties:** Something suitably devastating is appropriate so that the group will want to avoid errors. Ten seconds per infraction seems to have a reasonable effect; besides, it's easy to add the penalty seconds and then adjust the time.

During the aprés-debrief, ascertain if the group had discovered and used the odd/even, zig-zag configuration of the gym spots.

Keypunch — Take II

Alternative scenarios and rules for your consideration:

At the start, give the group a target time to shoot for. It's best if you know from experience that the "goal" is realistically attainable, or the group may feel disappointed that they did not reach or exceed your mark.

Distribute the numbers inside the boundary totally at random; i.e., there is no pattern *per se*. The group may still attempt to "map" the spots to assist their effort.

Allow *only one* player to touch the spots in a given round. The remaining players need to discover ways to assist the KPO (Key Punch Operator) in performing the task.

Vary the distance between the start line and the keyboard area. This distance can change the group's time considerably. It is recommended that the distance be far enough that the group cannot see the numbers on the spots from the planning area (from behind the starting line).

And finally, an untried, but appealing —

Variation

Try substituting the letters of the alphabet for the numbers. Ask the group to touch all the letters in sequence, to spell words, to write a sentence, etc. Misspellings, improper grammar, poor punctuation, etc., all result in an added time penalty. Thank heavens for spell check!!

Key Punch seems to have a great appeal every time it is used. It's portable, challenging, mental and physical, most everything you look for in an Initiative. The potential variations for use in classroom settings to teach math, spelling, foreign languages, geography, etc., lead me to think *Key Punch* is a keeper.

Mastermind Relay

The *Mastermind Relay* is a concept that I think Steve and Nicki Hall developed. It is essentially a micro Initiative run, and in this reduced form offers a series of conceptually oriented Initiative problems that can be accomplished "on the run" by a high performance team working efficiently together. Or, these engaging tasks can present a series of confounding, frustrating puzzles to a bored, turned off group of employees that actively dislike one another.

Grouping and who you work with is up to the reader, but the following micro-problems fit well into the *Mastermind Relay* format for whatever moderately motivated group you have in tow.

The following ideas were borrowed, changed, made up, embellished, pilfered and purloined from a variety of sources that would not benefit nor care about credit being offered, …but thanks anyway.

- **Rearrange six wooden match sticks to make "nothing". The match sticks may not be bent, broken, or placed over one another.**

  There are two answers that seem worthy of consideration. Take the match sticks and rearrange them into a circle (zero), thus symbolic of nothing. Or, reposition the match sticks to spell the word NIL, which means nothing.

- **If today is Monday, what is the day after the day before the day before tomorrow?**

  Dismissing the time warp factor, the answer is Monday.

- **Why are 1980 pennies worth more that 1979 pennies?**

  One thousand nine-hundred and eighty, one cent coins are worth one penny more than one thousand nine-hundred and seventy nine one cent coins.

- **You are a female. What relationship to you is your father's only son-in-law's mother-in-law's only daughter?**

The answer is in the mirror — You!

- **Arrange nine match sticks to make one equilateral triangle. Rearrange five of the nine match sticks to make five triangles.**

See illustration-

- **If you fire a .222 caliber varmint rifle with a necked down center fire cartridge and 2lb. trigger pull in contrast to a .22 caliber single shot rifle with a magnum long rifle cartridge and a 4lb. trigger pull, which slug will travel faster out of the muzzle?**

Trigger pull has nothing to do with slug velocity so the more powerful .222 cartridge will propel the faster slug.

- **Making only three lines, divide the circle into eight sections**

There are several possible solutions. One line can be curved

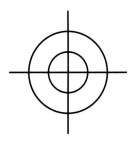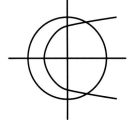

- **How many triangles or squares respectively are in the following illustrations?**

Each puzzle has a separate answer that is printed below the illustration.

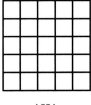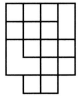

(55)   (21)

(17)   (13)

(20)

- **Add five lines to the six below and make a total of nine.**

Answer

170   *Activities*

- **Drawing only two straight lines, make a box out of the number below.**

301

Answer

301

- **Excluding this question, how many F's are in this sentence?**

FEATURE FILMS ARE THE RESULT OF YEARS OF SCIENTIFIC STUDY COMBINED WITH THE EXPERIENCE OF YEARS.

The answer is six

- **Draw only one line below, adding it to the Roman Numeral IX (9), and make the number six.**

IX

Answer

SIX

We never promised that you would like the answers, but I think you do have to appreciate the creativity. If you know of some more of these problems, please send them to us. We don't like to solve them anymore than you, but we do love to collect them.

PLEASE
NO PUZZLES WITHOUT SOLUTIONS!
WE'VE GOT ENOUGH TO DO ALREADY.

For other activity ideas for *Mastermind,* refer to (or read on):

Mergers (a.k.a. Star Wars)

Outrageous!

Set-Up

You will need one rope (nylon cord or clothesline is more than adequate) per participant. If your group is very large, this problem can be done with fewer than one rope per person. How many exactly? Adventure Axiom #6 — The answer is always, "Yes."

To begin the task, ask the players to each take a rope and tie it into a loop. (Here's a good time to practice your granny knot.) Ask them to lay the loop anywhere on the ground and then to stand inside it so that both of their feet are inside the loop. No portion of their feet may extend over or under or beyond the loop.

Once everyone is inside a loop, they are safe and the problem can begin. Explain that people are safe only when they have both feet inside a loop. The loops cannot be moved from their present location and they cannot be retied into larger loops — the loops are what they are and ain't what the participants want them to be.

Play

When you give the command, "Change!" everyone must find a new loop to occupy (assuming that there is an open loop). Participants may take as much time as they need going from one loop to another and they may walk on the ground to get to a new loop.

After two or three changes, surreptitiously sneak one of the loops away (be sure you are seen) while the participants are making the next change. Allow the group to concoct a plan to include the person who is left out. You may notice some hesitation before a volunteer offers to share a loop. Once everyone is safe, give the next "Change!" command and purloin another loop.

Depending upon the number of participants and how much time you want the problem to take, continue to remove one loop at a time, or designate a number of loops that will be removed at one time. The crunch, literally as well as figuratively, comes as the number of feet increases as the space inside the loops decreases. Now what does the group do to create a safe "space" for everyone? Do not allow the activity to proceed until everyone is safe at the end of each change.

The final result is to try and include everyone safely inside one loop.

As the leader, you will need either loops of different sizes (with one loop that can fit all of the participants' feet), or you will have to retie some of the smaller loops into a larger one. After doing the activity a few times, you will gain a greater loop awareness and be able to accurately predict the correct loop size needed for the final loop.

A word from experience: The group can fit into a smaller loop than they think they can — don't make it easy for them! Challenge in this case translates into fun.

Variations

- To increase the challenge level, specify that people must have both feet on the ground inside a loop. This variation requires more physical space inside the loop, so you will have to gauge how much space the group will need to complete the task and provide them with an appropriate sized loop.

- To allow more brainstorming and flexibility, don't restrict the group from moving the loops or retying them. Don't tell them to move the loops or to retie them, but allow it if someone comes up with that idea.

- Advanced leadership technique (or how to have a wee bit of extra fun): As the group is feeling the pressure of combining into smaller and smaller loops, dangle a large loop tantalizingly in front of them. As they begin to covet the loop in your hands, offer to make a trade. Obviously, the barter is on your terms — perhaps one large loop for three, four, five or more loops. OUTRAGEOUS! they say, as you then reduce the size of the loop and offer it to them again. This give and take can present the group with a decision or series of decisions that focuses them on making appropriate choices and can fuel an interesting debrief. It also can create a feeling that you're being awfully hard on them, so do it as you would in any other activity — with an overt emphasis on fun and humor.

Mirage

A great exercise for communication skills...

• •

This idea has been around for a long time. It's a great exercise for communication skills, creativity, accurate listening and understanding vocabulary. It could also be a terrific way to teach some basic geometry, math and maybe even some foreign language skills if the leaders had to speak in a specific language. Wait a minute, let's not make grandiose claims before you start reading.

The leaders of the exercise need to start by communicating; i.e., talking and listening. If listeners are actively participating, the leader/communicator's task is much easier. For the listeners, the goal is to hear precisely what is said and interpret the words correctly. Again, communication is clearest when it moves in two directions; the listeners can improve the ability of the leader by asking appropriate questions and/or providing feedback to let the communicator know if the message is getting through.

Play

One participant is chosen from the group and is given a piece of paper with a design on it. That person must communicate the image to the rest of the group so that players can duplicate it on their own paper. You may ask that people concentrate on their own work, or you may say nothing and allow the group to collaborate if they think it will help. However, for the first couple times I suggest that people operate solo. The versions below are samples that have worked well. Invent your own variations that highlight any specific issue you want to address with your group.

For the first couple of versions, I prohibit illustrators from showing their design to the leader to check its accuracy. In Version #4, I will allow it if the group comes up with the idea on its own.

This exercise should be done more than once, with each variation allowing different forms of communication between the "leader" and the "drawers." Each version should be led by a new leader.

Version #1

- The leader can say anything, may make no gestures, and must face away from the group. Drawers may not speak or ask questions.

Version #2

- The leader may only make gestures, no speaking. Drawers may ask as many questions as they want.

Version #3

- The leader may speak and gesture. Drawers may ask one question each.

Version #4

- The leader may speak and gesture. Drawers are divided into groups of three, each group to complete one drawing. Groups are told that any team producing the best duplication of the original drawing will receive the award — the closest copy to the original is the winner. Each group may ask a total of three questions.

This version tends to produce a competitive atmosphere, but the scenario should not prohibit sharing information or working cooperatively to produce one design from all of the groups. If the group produces one design, it wins, since it is automatically the best copy. If the groups collaborate and share information, they usually do better.

I've seen groups get so competitive that they hoard their questions, trying to insure that by asking a question they don't inadvertently help another group. This version points out that people can help each other meet both individual and team goals at the same time and encourages people to seek out all the options before attacking a problem.

Debrief

In addition to the usual topics, I try to frame the debrief in terms of not judging whether a particular leader was successful, but rather what can we learn from the experience. How could we as individuals and as a group better facilitate our own communication? Often, leaders will feel bad about themselves because they did not do a good enough job in their own minds. I feel it's important for people to end the activity feeling good about what happened. True, they may have not communicated as clearly as desired or they may not have listened effectively, but those experiences represent effective learning. Encourage students to see their mistakes as learning opportunities for the next class or problem.

To paraphrase Tom Watson, head of IBM (at one time): "The best way to improve our ratio of successes is to increase our number of failures."

Below are a few sample drawings I've used for *Mirage* to help get you started on your own collection.

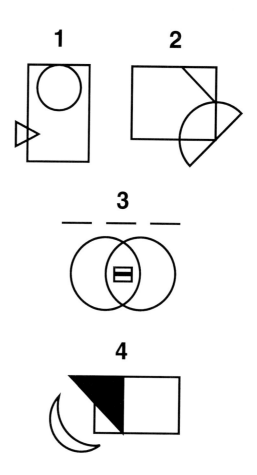

Moonball —
Level II and Level III

sb

How can anyone not like hitting a beach ball up in the air?

. . . .

OK, so high school students think it's silly and pointless, elementary kids want more competition and action, some adults think it's frivolous... we can go on and on. To paraphrase the old campaign slogan, "Where's the FUN?"

To me, *Moonball* has always been a gem. It's simple, minimal prop = minimal expense, adaptable to group size, space limitations, etc., and an engaging enough challenge to get most audiences intently involved in the action. The only real drawback has been playing outside on a windy day. Moonballs and wind don't mix.

So why write about it again? Over the years, *Moonball* has been adapted into many forms. (See *Silver Bullets,* pg. 31 for the basic rules.) But the game's ability to mutate into something new and exciting almost at your whim makes it a great game to know, because it can simultaneously serve so many needs.

Variations

Here are a few more ways to play.

All Hit Moonball

Some folks complain that the basic game leaves them feeling left out. There are too many players so not everyone can get an equal opportunity to hit the ball; or the more athletic, energetic players pursue the ball and prevent others from ever touching it; or, heaven forbid,

someone is nervous about making a mistake and consciously avoids getting near the ball and so never has any fun.

Change one rule and most of the above disappear. *All Hit Moonball* requires every player to hit the ball at least once or the group score doesn't count. Now the group not only has to track who's hit and who's not, they must devise a slightly more sophisticated plan to accomplish the goal. *All Hit* begins to focus on the benefit of teamwork whereas *Moonball* can score points even with an individualistic game plan.

Still, what if someone only hits it once and wants to hit it more, but can't? Change one more rule. Require that all players can hit the ball only once until every player has had a hit; then and only then, can a player hit it a second time. A point is scored only after everyone has made a hit.

After the last person in the group hits it, all the players can try to complete a second, third, fourth, etc., round. This activity is a significantly higher challenge. The players must work together, try to help each other by keeping the ball from flying randomly about the ozone layer, and they must be ready to re-start and go for the extra rounds after each sequence is finished. A highly structured and coordinated strategy is not required; in fact, in my observation it often lessens the effectiveness of the group. But commitment and concentration, and a willingness to try ideas repeatedly are helpful attributes to achieve success.

Knowing these variations can present you with options as you design a curriculum or program. Adjusting the challenge of the activity to meet the needs of the group is an essential role of a good Adventure facilitator. In fact, you will find a lengthy (not too lengthy, mind you) discussion of changing games and creativity at the beginning of this book. For other variations on this theme, you may want to read that section to understand the advantages of thinking creatively.

This type of approach has served us very well over the years, and so these rules are intended to impel you on your own way to tinkering with rules and activities to make them better.

PLAY BALL... PLAY MOONBALL.

Object Retrieval or Toxic Waste

ker

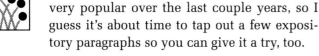

This unique Initiative problem has become very popular over the last couple years, so I guess it's about time to tap out a few expository paragraphs so you can give it a try, too.

Objective

To retrieve a desirable substance (life-saving serum?) from within a circular, toxic no-touch zone, using only those props made available.

Set-Up

You will need a bicycle inner tube cut in half, (slice off the valve area). Four sections of rope 20' long. One section of rope 40' long.

Outline a 30' diameter circular area using a section of work rope: Rope diameter is not important. In the center of that circle, place a #10 tin can, 1/3 filled with water.

Rules

- Any and as many knots as desired can be tied in the ropes or rubber sections.

- The ropes or inner tube lengths cannot be cut.

- No one may enter or make contact within the area outlined by the circumference rope. If ground contact is made, all progress stops, and the problem begins again from the start.

- If any of the water is spilled (even a drop), it's back to the beginning again.

Variation

Place a second #10 tin can (empty) next to the partially-filled can. Recognizing that the substance in the first can is extremely toxic, transfer must be made of that miasmic liquid to the second can for proper disposal. Effective and safe disposal includes not only perfect transfer of the HCF-X liquid, but also moving the second can into the center of a separate but identical circle.

If any fluid is spilled or contact made within or without either circle, it's back to the drawing board for another attempt. The can, because of its highly contaminated nature, cannot be approached, even though physical contact is possible during transfer from circle to circle. Refer to **RULES** (**R**estrictive **U**nderstandings **L**est **E**veryone's **S**neaky) above for other limitations.

Paperchute

A paper recycling game...

• •

You don't need to know a thing about origami to achieve a high-performance level while attempting this paper recycling game ...but it helps.

Do the people at your school or place of business discard used paper somewhere for recycling? If not, they should, because you need some sheets of uncrumpled paper, and it seems a waste to use new sheets. Any color is fine, but I like blue, particularly the lighter shades.

Play

Give a sheet of paper (any color) to all the participants and offer the following challenge that each person can either try to accomplish by their lonesome or work cooperatively with one or two others to come up with the most functional and/or creative solution.

Here's the challenge: From a height of approximately ten feet (ten feet is realistic, but if you can arrange a safe launch from 50+ feet, go for it) each participant or team drops their piece of recycled paper so that it ends up as close to a designated target as possible. A target can be easily fabricated on the floor with two crossed pieces of colored tape to form a large **X**. The drop can be accomplished from a stepladder, a balcony or a hot air balloon.

An additional rule states that no more than 1/3 of the sheet can be removed prior to the drop. This prevents tearing off a teensy weensy corner of the paper and rolling it up between your thumb and index finger to form a roundish object smaller than a booger. I know, that's chock full of initiative, but...

If a team tries to simply release their piece of paper without doing anything to it, they will quickly find that the laws of aerodynamics as applied to a flat flexing sheet of paper are fluky and infinitely unworkable; the paper will glide to and fro (Did you ever wonder what *fro* means? Me too. It means back: I just looked it up. Using this new lexographic bit of ammunition is easy; if an antagonistic dog approaches you, just yell, GET FRO!) and, chances are, end up quite a distance from the DZ (Drop Zone). So, just dropping the paper wasn't a good idea, but since this is an exercise in experiential education, the attempt itself was OK. Remember, the idea is to improve on the result of whatever trial and error was initiated.

Crumple up the paper. That will definitely cause the paper to fall more on the plumb, as they say. True enough, the paper will hit very close to the center of the crossed tape if you aim well from above, but the crumpled paper ball will then bounce away from the contact point, and since the criteria for success is minimum distance that the object ends up from the target, this also is not a great idea — better, but not great. Crumple up the paper so that it ends up looking like a snake. Good, but not great yet.

Remember how to make a Cootie Catcher (*Bottomless Baggie*, pgs. 72–73)? This simplistic piece of origami is not only good for catching symbolic cooties, but because of its symmetrical configuration makes an excellent ersatz parachute; i.e., *Paperchute.* I don't have the space here to explain how to fold the paper, so if you don't have a copy of the *Baggie,* just start folding to try and produce an aerodynamically stable falling origami.

Remember, the final result is not nearly as important as what the student(s) experience on the way to the result.

I should mention one other technique that you may want to limit or eliminate; wetting of the paper. A sodden chunk of paper (macro spitball) has predicable hit-and-stay properties.

CANNONBALL   MUSKETBALL   SWISS

ROCKET   COMB   DOUBLE COMB

FLOATER   SPINNER

BOWTIE   BUZZER

Ping Pong Pyramids

Solution

Twenty ping pong balls, held together by hot glue in five distinct ping pong segments, can be arranged with minimum manipulation to form a four-sided, symmetrical pyramid (see photos). Programmatic value of correctly arranging these five segments occurs within the team manipulation, discussion, decision-making, etc. Debriefing can include comments concerning resource utilization and group efficiency.

1. Lay the 4-ball linear piece on the floor.

2. Lean one of the 6-ball pieces against this 4-ball piece so that their lengths run parallel to one another.

3. Lean the second 6-ball piece against the two established pieces, so that the two 6-ball pieces are set perpendicular to one another.

4. Lean the two sets of 2-ball pieces (thinking of them as one long 4-ball piece) vertically against the three set pieces. Done.

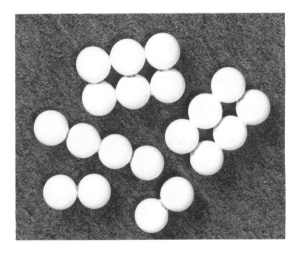

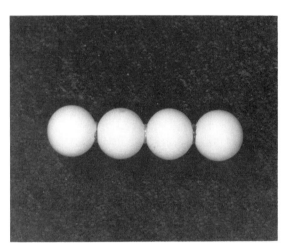

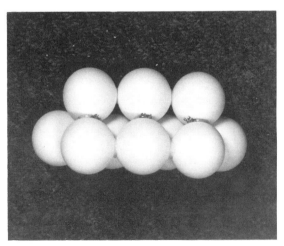

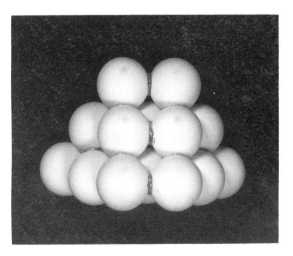

conceptually figure out the necessary spatial relationship of the pieces to produce the desired pyramid. Allow hands on only after the group has decided what needs to be attempted. This is tough.

- Offer the pyramid pieces to a larger group, as part of *Mastermind Relay* and observe the group dynamics that follow: Leadership roles, discussion skills, utilization of personnel, etc. Write down notes concerning your observations for later discussion (debriefing).

- Say, "Here's the problem," and let the group work on it at their leisure. This approach is particularly useful when the group is together for more than one day and has occasional free time. Try to have numerous sets of five pieces available to allow maximum hands-on manipulation by the group or sub-groups.

I just re-read my attempt at writing the solution and it makes sense to me. If you don't come up with a solution, just keep messing around with the pieces trying to make the words and balls fit. Reading, photo scrutiny, manipulating and T&E will eventually result in the symmetrical answer. If not, the balls break apart and discard easily. Next!

Presentation Variations

- Offer the five pieces to a group of five participants, indicating that each person is responsible for the placement of his or her piece.
- Set the five pieces separately on the floor or table and ask a small group to try and

 # Quick Line-Up

Use this run-around, willy-nilly activity to break some ice and provide a low risk, low skill sense of team affiliation.

Set-Up

First, however, you have to get the group to split themselves into four approximately equal groups. (Not to wander from the subject, but as I was sitting here six-finger tapping the old Mac Classic, I wondered why the word ABBREVIATION is soo loong. How do you abbreviate the word abbreviation, a five syllable word? I

started thinking about shortening words as I tapped out APPROXIMATELY above. Just a thought to share.) Quad grouping is easily accomplished by having everyone line up and then counting off 1234, 1234, etc., and if that sounds like fun, you need help.

Try this: Ask each person in the group to pick which number (1–4) that they would like to be, but not to say or indicate what that number is. To discover which other participants are sharing your Zen and number, walk up to someone and shake hands the number of times representing the 1–4 number that you picked.

If your number is 2, and someone tries to shake your hand 3 times, excuse yourself politely and continue your search. When you find a hand moving up and down congruently with yours, and if that hand stops at the appropriate number (jives with your karma), keep that soul buddy with you and, operating as a harmonic dyad, try to find another free spirit vibrating on your joint frequency.

Continue linking until everyone has established their affiliation with a numerical group. If you are lucky, the groups will be approx. (note the abbr. of approx.) equal in number. If not, ask a few noncommitted people to change groups to equal things up: I didn't say this grouping ploy worked perfectly. Be loose, be flexible. People usually don't care what group they are in as long as they are having fun.

Now here's your role. Stand in the middle (a bit off-center is OK) of the gym or field and hold out both your arms so that your hands are pointing east and west. If you don't know which direction is east and west, any which way is fine, just so that you are pointing in opposite directions.

Play

Ask the four groups to orient themselves around you so that group 1 is north, group 2 is east, group 3 is south, and group 4 is west. Having groups orient themselves as to the points of the compass is interesting and entertaining, but, most significantly, causes strangers to have to talk to one another and share ideas and opinions. However, if you are pressed for time or compass headings give you a headache, just ask the four groups to arrange themselves equally around where you are standing. Whichever position they pick must become part of the group's memory, because as you move and reorient yourself as to the compass points or geographically in another part of the room/ field, the groups, at your shouted signal of "DO IT," must all run to reorient themselves around you exactly as they were before you moved. The last group to achieve its proper position loses, and the three other groups get to hoot and howl and point fingers.

There is no way to win this game, only lose, and losing in this context is not so bad, so who cares?

Make your first couple of moves simple; north to south, east to west type of thing. Then run to another part of the room or field before you shout, "DO IT," or stand on your head, or stand next to a pool... Continue to play until you have achieved some ice breaking or you notice that the level of enjoyment needs more joy.

Variation

Provide each of the four groups a hula hoop. As the group moves from one position to another, players must pass the hoop over their bodies before reaching their destination — providing yet another dandy way to lose.

Scrabble Babble

Come up with a 5-letter word every 30 seconds.

• •

The following is a variation of *Four Letter Word* that Garth Baker of New Zealand developed.

Play

"I have marked the game letters on 3"x5" cards and decided on the number of letters as to the distribution of letters in a Scrabble game. The cards are divided evenly between two groups. Both groups have 2 minutes planning time after which they have to come up with a 5-letter word every 30 seconds until they or their letters are exhausted. I allow English or Maori words."

(Ed. Note — I'm not sure of the scoring here, but the action sounds like fun, so just do it. The words used and their origin depend upon your student's linguistic knowledge and their level of travel sophistication. The local Boston patois is not technically a second language, but for this game could certainly be allowed; i.e., garbage = gaabidge.)

"Groups have developed different strategies: Separating vowels, using difficult letters first,

just going for it. There is also good potential for discussing group process in the debrief, as different abilities come to the fore.

A variation consists of having a race with groups, allowing any size words to be used. The criteria is to use up all the letters as quickly as possible.

Having particular sorts of words; e.g., adjectives, feelings, colors, animals, jargon is another variation that will make this game suited to the classroom.

Or, instead of simply making a list of the words, the students find that the words can be linked to resemble a Scrabble game or crossword puzzle. This means they use some of the letters several times... a cunning development.

It would probably be best to play this variation with a simple time limit —- say five minutes — to use up all the letters.

	SCRABBLE
	A
Perhaps this variation	B
could be called:	B
	L
	E

The letter cards are also useful in an icebreaker/ name-reinforcer game. Issue several letters to each person, then allow the players to mingle for five minutes and form into as many words with as many other letters as they can find.

People hold out their cards to make one word, name everybody in the word, then move to a new combination."

Dear Garth,

There are a couple fine points associated with the variations that I don't quite understand. I think it might be necessary for me to come over (say late February) and discuss the intricacies of Scrabble Babble. Perhaps Piha beach would be a good place to meet.

— Karl

The Shoe Sort (or Le Problem des Pieds)

This is a quick problem to explain (hence, a good one for your back pocket), involves no props, but is tricky to solve.

Play

Start by asking people to line up, standing shoulder-to-shoulder. Hand out blindfolds, or ask people to close their eyes. Tell them they have suddenly become speechless. In order to prepare the group for its voyage to Pluto, the group must line up by shoe size, from smallest to largest. Obviously, they must line up this way to be outfitted for space boots before entering the rocket ship.

Since the group cannot see or speak, you may need to spot occasionally to prevent people from bumping heads.

You may read this and think:

a) Now these two have gone off the deep end;

b) how did they get me to pay money for such a simple-minded idea;

c) no one will ever like this activity; or

d) all of the above.

Try it first, then decide. Sometimes the simplest problems are the most fun. And besides, you may just find yourself with fifteen minutes some day, no activity planned, no props available and *Shoe Sort* will be the perfect filler.

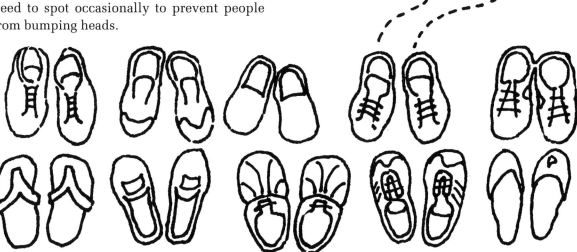

Stepping Stones

sb

This seemingly simple activity is fast becoming one of my favorites. It is a deceivingly complex problem, requires a goodly amount of thinking and cooperation, has several possible scenarios and solutions, and generally is received well by participants. What more can you ask for? No, Karl and Steve will not come to lead this activity for you just because we like it so much.

Stuff You'll Need

One prop per person and two ropes or another suitable method for identifying the Take-Off (Point A) and the Safe Zone (Point B).

Props can be:

- **rug pads** — 12" squares work well or odd-shaped pieces big enough for 2–4 feet — people feet that is — to squish onto a pad;

- (12) 18" lengths of 4"x 4" lumber;

- **rubber deck spots** — available from the PA equipment catalog; or any other type of material suitable for standing on;

- **Extras:** One suitable safety or rescue kit to be carried along by the group in the event of a catastrophe.

Set-Up

The basic set-up here is the old "get from Point A to Point B without touching the ground in between" routine. People are assembled at Point A, given one prop less than their number; i.e., nine people get eight props and told to arrive safely with the entire group at Point B before time runs out. If this sounds too much like the same old thing, here's the fun way.

People are on Planet Lrak-Dna-Evets — a marvelous world of beauty, peace and fecundity. The people there want to spread their chromosomal bounty throughout the universe so they are embarking on a space voyage to another world. To leave the planet they will need special life-support vehicles to carry them safely through space and shield their genetic treasure. Their life-support vehicles are the props. Any life-support system can support as many people as can stand on it.

Rules

1) Anyone touching the ground in space; i.e., between the boundaries, must return to the home planet for decontamination and spiritual healing. Rescuing these fertile travelers is recommended, since all people are expected to arrive safely at the new planet.

2) For a life-support vehicle/system to function, someone must be touching it at all times when it is in space to maintain the 98.6° temperature necessary to maintain DNA viability. If a life-support is untouched for even an instant, it ceases to function and it is immediately removed from the activity. Example: A person tosses the support onto the ground, and then steps onto it. Because it left that person's grasp when it was tossed, it is lost forever. A correct use would be to place it on the ground and step onto it while having constant touch with the prop by hand. Call the Intergalactic Life-Support Regulatory Administration for further clarification (ILSRA @ 800-GET-HELP).

3) Generally, life-support vehicles only move in a forward direction. If you supply this information, you may eliminate the possibility of a rescue should someone fall into space. Sometimes, only a few props are allowed to go in reverse, or props can only cross the universe one time. This rule attempts to prohibit the solution of having people "shuffle" across space using two props as skates and sending them back for another person to use. It's a creative solution, but doesn't require much teamwork or cooperation. It may, however, be a very effective technique for younger audiences.

4) Be extremely watchful for untouched life-supports. People try to hide the fact that they make a mistake. Don't let a untouched prop remain in use (unless the group really needs to succeed — read the "Enforcement" section of this book).

5) Setting boundaries: Generally, it makes sense to set the boundaries far enough apart so that the group will need to recycle some of their props in order to cross the gap. I usually lay the props out in a straight line from boundary A, then add 3–5 feet of open space before placing boundary B. This spacing requires the group to work together to use their props, using some of the materials two times to be successful.

Considerations

I have mixed feelings about the shuffle solution — where one person takes two props and skates across the gap and then somehow returns the props to the start for others to do the same. As stated above, it is a creative solution. But my observation is that it is also an individualistic approach, not a team solution. Usually groups employ this idea because they are stuck and can't think of anything else that will work. It's important for the group to pursue creative alternatives whenever possible, but on balance, I recommend that you limit the number of times props can cross the gap or prohibit them from going in reverse.

Variation

• Divide the group in half. Each group starts on a different planet — half at Point A and half at Point B. They must exchange places. Each group gets one less prop than people. Do not state it explicitly, but the groups may share their resources (props) if they choose to. The focus of the problem suddenly becomes one of identifying whether two different goals can be pursued simultaneously for a common good, or will the two groups operate independently and/ or competitively.

Sticky Steps

A very portable variation of *The Trolley*...

• •

There's a useful handsaw on the market called a Stanley Short Cut. It's a toolbox saw that's about 15 inches long and is advertised to cut 50% faster, because of aggressive tooth design, than conventional saws. I'm not sure what a conventional saw is, but I guess it's one that cuts 50% slower than Stanley's. I've said all this to indicate you need a saw to cut some sections of 4x4, and since I just bought the one above and like it, I thought you would too... But, any ole saw will do really.

You might want to read to the end of this handy little discourse to find out what I'm leading up to and before you start cutting up your 4x4s. But even though I'm out of sequence here, I'll just keep going if you don't mind.

Set-Up

Measure off 12" sections, and zip through that try-square scribe line with your shark-toothed, short-cut saw. Collect all those one-foot sections (one section for every participant) and countersink (use a 1-1/2" bit) one third of the blocks to look like illustration #1. Countersink the second third to look like illustration #2, and finally for the third third to look like illustration #3. With a 5/8" diameter bit, and starting in the center of each countersunk hole, drill all the way through each 4x4.

Cosmetic hint — stop drilling when the point of the bit just breaks through the far side of the 4x4. Turn the board over and begin drilling where that pin prick hole is located. Doing this prevents the wood from splintering as the drill bit eats through the final 1/4" of wood. Just a common wood-working trick, but it may impress somebody, and it does produce a neater hole.

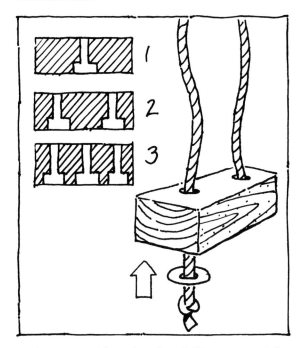

Cut some 6' lengths of multiline to equal the number of holes drilled, less seven. Back splice one end of each rope and tie an overhand knot in the other end. Place all of these accumulated props in a hodgepodge pile and offer the following challenge... finally the crux.

Play

Using these assembled props and none others, attempt to move your group from point A to point B in the quickest, most efficient manner without touching the ground. Sound familiar? I'd guess so, but the solution(s) are unique, interesting to both participant and facilitator.

Rules

- Players may not touch the ground (floor) with any part of their body. If ground contact is made, that person must either return to the start or receive a time penalty — depends upon your presentation.

- No one may operate independently, but must maintain physical contact with at least one other person.

- The blocks may not be used as simple "stepping stones."

- You may use as few or as many of the props as desired during the crossing.

- The props do not have to be returned to the start, but may be used for more than one crossing.

As a result of the rules format, you are trying to get the participants to make some decisions as how to best use the props.

Example 1 — If you put a rope through the middle hole, then stand on the block with rope in both hands, you have essentially fabricated a no-springs pogo stick. Then by initiating a controlled hop, surprisingly easy forward progress can be made, and, to abide by the rules, this hopping must be done in tandem.

Example 2 — Insert two ropes, one each, into the two outside holes. Use a block per foot and grab a partner.

Example 3 — Have two people stand side-by-side with a single rope block for their inside feet and a double roped block for each outside foot. Variations and decision-making go foot-in-foot.

Considerations

- Remember to remove the ropes from the blocks before you allow another group to make an attempt.

- Turned ankles are a possibility, so do not allow running attempts.

- Rout the edges of the 4x4s before cutting into sections.

- Transport these short boards in a duffel bag, sardonically smiling as you remember what it was like trying to tie 12' 4x4 sections to your Honda Civic.

Tinkering Around

ker

You can still be a kid at any age.

. . . .

Project Adventure trainer Carol Call has been playing around in Georgia for a number of years, and one of her at-school play situations is detailed below.

It's based on the use of Tinker Toys, which are still manufactured, bye-the-bye. I'll bet some of you owned a set of Tinker Toys when you were a real kid (you can still be a kid at any age, but there's only one span of chronologic time when you were a real kid) but thought that they were no longer made — they are, but because they don't whiz, flash or look like something Rambo would use, their sales are somewhat limited. Too bad, 'cause I can still joyfully remember taking the metal cover off the cylindrical cardboard container (I even re-call the smell!) pouring out the crafted wooden contents, and fabricating another imagination-generated fantasy structure. There should be more Tinker (do-it-yourself type) Toys and fewer expensive do-nothing plastic goodies that serve only to assuage parental guilt and fulfill a child's whimsical (and fleeting) TV-generated consumerism. There! ...so much for non-biased game reporting.

You can also use Legos for the following activity, but they are comparatively expensive, and their use doesn't fit with Carol's rubric for this description. Additionally, Tinker Toy sections allow a larger structure to be set up in a shorter period of time.

Carol's suggested activity, Build a Tower, couldn't be simpler; the idea is for a team to build the highest possible tower within a set time limit.

Rules

- Each group must build on a similar base (desk top, set of floor tiles, etc.).

- Tinker Toy sections that roll off the base or out of the base area may not be used after the start.

- Group members may or may not talk while assembling their tower; a perfect example of the waffle rule.

- Whichever group builds the highest tower — because of their high level of cooperation, effective utilization of resources, and dynamic time management — get to knock the tower over with fleece balls from ten paces.

Up Chuck or Barf Ball

ker

Make sure each player has a ball. The ball needs to be the type that you don't mind getting hit by; like fleece, Nerf, etc.

Play

Standing in a circle or cluster, or however the group wants to arrange themselves, ask everyone to toss their balls aloft to a height of at least 10 feet, and then attempt to catch a ball that they did not throw. Count the number of balls that are missed (not caught); that's the group's negative score for that round.

After some discussion, ask the group to make as many attempts as they would like, toward achieving the result of no balls missed. As this task is eventually achieved, see how many all-catch rounds can be made before a miss occurs.

To make the team effort initially more difficult, start with one ball being thrown aloft (the first person who throws a ball up should be named Chuck). After one ball is successfully caught, try two, and so on until all the balls are thrown simultaneously and caught. If a ball is missed, the group starts over with one ball being lofted.

Whale Watch

The Teeter-Totter...

• •

We (Project Adventure) used to build a ropes course event called *The Weimea* or more accurately the *Teeter-Totter*. It was just a 20' utility pole balanced on a fulcrum. The object was to get the entire group balanced on the log before either end touched the ground, and the results were pretty much what you remember from your playground days — slip/slam/bang.

If one person fell off, the remainder of the participants found themselves on (occasionally off) an out of control log that was due to make ground contact in about .17 seconds. On contact, the remainder of the log riders dismounted like shrapnel from an exploding grenade. Perhaps I'm somewhat given to hyperbole here, but *The Teeter-Totter* was a safety disaster, and is no longer offered as a low ropes course element.

Recently, PA ropes course builder John Lazarus came up with the idea of doing the *Teeter-Totter* thing for physically disadvantaged people, specifically those folks (for whatever reason) in wheelchairs. John designed and Don White built the first *Whale Watch* (*Tetter-Totter*) platform. Like most good ideas, The *Whale Watch* is a simple variation of the classic original. Rather than trying to balance on a narrow pole, John designed an 8'x13' platform that was balanced on a 6"x6" fulcrum. When balanced, the beveled ends of the platform are approximately 12" from the ground.

So far, this event has been very popular with physically disadvantaged and able-bodied folks alike. It is one of those rare ropes course events that can be used and enjoyed by practically any group.

Play Variations

There is more than one objective than simply balancing the group on the platform.

The Basic Version: Split the group in half and position each half at opposite ends of the platform. Entering only from the ends (you may

not board the *Whale Watch* from the side of the boat, silly), the group must all board the ship without allowing any ground touches. In a fanciful scenario, a ground touch means hitting a reef with whatever appropriate consequence your leadership skill deems necessary. The goal is to have all the passengers board the ship and then maintain a balanced boat for at least 10 seconds.

The WHOA (The Whale's on the Starboard Side) Version: A 50/50 divided group standing on opposite ends attempts to change ends without letting the platform make contact with the ground.

The, "Hey, Where's the Whales?" Version: A group standing all the way around the periphery of the platform attempts to make a 360° rotation without letting the platform touch the ground.

The Ballast Beam Version: With a group standing on the ground at each end of the platform, the participants try to exchange ends with the least number of platform ground touches.

A platform end is not allowed to be held on the ground at any time.

The Walking the Plank Version: With the entire group balanced in the center of the platform, the players attempt to move to the ends of the platform so that everyone is located within 18" of the ends of the platform. This is attempted, of course, with the least number of platform ground touches.

The Abandon Ship Version: With the entire group balanced on the platform, everyone must abandon ship without allowing the platform to touch the ground. NOTE: If people leap off the platform, you may encounter sudden movements of the platform resulting in hard impacts with the ground. Advise people of the risks and dangers of the impact and of the potential for being knocked off the platform. Be certain you and the group have an appropriate procedure for monitoring safety.

Contact Project Adventure, at any of our offices for information about how to have one of these platforms constructed at your site.

Variations

The Confused Meuse

Here's an, "idea from down under," Kiwi-style that is.

• •

Ross Merrett, former PA intern and current PA International Trainer (New Zealand), sent along this variation of *The Meuse* Initiative problem. I have to admit that *The Meuse* is not one of my favorite Initiative activities, and I'm not sure why — perhaps because of its slooow pace. Nonetheless, I was intrigued by the way Ross had designed *The Confused Meuse* to handle larger groups. Much of the following text is quoted directly from Ross' letter. I'll use the italic font for directly quoted text.

See *Cowstails & Cobras 11*, pgs. 87–88 for the framing, props, rules, illustration and processing tips associated with *The Meuse*.

"The Meuse has been a favorite activity of mine for some time, but tends to have diminishing returns for groups larger than about 10 or 12. To increase the potential usability of this Initiative for larger groups, I experimented by having two groups attempt the activity simultaneously, converging from different directions towards two strategically positioned 3'x3' platforms in the middle.

Groups that I have used this activity with initially begin separate and competitive, taking some time to discover the strength of working together — though both groups must stay on their separate sides.

Recently, I was working with a group of 42 peer leaders from a local high school in Auckland. Having worked as four smaller groups, we needed to bring the whole group

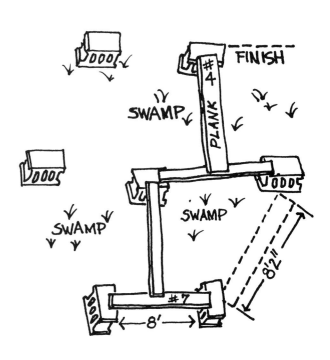

back together as one large group, while also allowing a continuation of the skills developed in the smaller groups. I used The Confused Meuse; here's what to do.

Set-Up

Set out four separate sets of Meuse props so that all four groups converge from four different sides (N.E.S.W.) working toward four different platforms in the middle. (See illustration.) Space these platforms about three feet apart from one another, forming an empty square shape between them. As before, have each group start from the outside, and using only The Meuse props provided, embark upon a journey to "unity."

Play

I briefed the activity so that the start area represented the culture of the student's school that they wished to leave behind. Their journey towards the center platforms was their opportunity to develop those skills and behaviors that they wished to incorporate into their new school culture.

Though not initially apparent, the likely outcome is that one, or even several, of the smaller groups will abandon their station and travel around the perimeter to another group, taking their props with them. This cooperative behavior allows for quicker and easier construction of a bridge to the central platforms. Some groups may even consider taking their planks with them to the center, using them as a bridge between platforms, thereby increasing the surface area for other folks to stand on.

I haven't tried this variation Ross, but I suspect that the "likely outcome" mentioned in the paragraph above would be *very* likely, as the students quickly find that the collected boards make the crossing relatively easy. But, hey ...that's life, and the collected mass-board outcome is a neat cooperative solution that can't be denied; go with it.

A Minor Meuse Variation with Major Results

Peter Aubrey (PA Trainer) passed along "...a minor change to *The Meuse* that worked out well with a group that had done *The Meuse* before." And the change *is* simple, as explained by Peter.

"Change the distance of row-three blocks (islands) so that they can be reached on a diagonal with the boards, but maintain the traditional spacing of the other blocks." ...so that they cannot be reached on the diagonal.

Rearranging the Meuse blocks, "...met the needs of the group, met my needs for providing a unique challenge, kept the group off balance (some participants had been involved in the traditional Initiative before), and reduced the time it took to complete the problem, thus helping with our workshop time management."

Once again an example of a little change yielding big benefits... also challenging the notion that things can only be done one way."

Dangle Duo Double Use

If your Ropes Course *Dangle Duo* is hanging in an open spot; i.e., no trees, rocks, or bushes to run into, try combining the activity *Bottom Line* (*Bottomless Bag*, pg. 15) with your dangling 4'x4's.

The idea of the game *Bottom Line* is to hit a Moon Ball over a line strung at about 15' a predetermined number of times, scoring one point for each hit over the line, and losing all accumulated points if the ball touches the ground. Now do the same thing, except use the open areas between rungs on the *Dangle Duo* for scoring points, and increase the potential points scored as the ball passes through a higher open area.

Should you consistently hit for the easy one point opening, or go for the highest and most difficult five-point entry, recognizing that the "bottom line" phenomena becomes manifest as the angle of the struck ball becomes more acute? If you don't understand the geometry of that last sentence, you have to be there. If you don't like geometry, forget what I just wrote ...hit the ball and have some fun.

Fire In The Hole — Movement At Risk

An off-the-wall means of eliminating balloon storage problems...

• •

I mentioned in a previous publication that alternating players in a balloon-people-balloon queue could result in a firecracker-like series of boomers. To initiate this aerotecnic blast, just have folks stand front to back and include an inflated balloon between themselves and the person distal to their anterior (balloon at their belly button). Then everyone simultaneously pulls at one another to initiate the expand-to-burst scenario: Good fun and provides an off-the-wall means of eliminating balloon storage problems.

To stimulate a variation, arrange the group as above, but this time encourage moving en masse from A to B without bursting or losing contact with a balloon. (Only body pressure is allowed; i.e., no hands.) If a balloon is inadvertently burst, have another one available so that the journey can continue. When the goal is reached, the patient player's reward for being so careful is — *Fire In The Hole.* Go for it!

Hansel and Gretel

A Variation of the Compass Walk...

• •

Mark Collard (PA trainer and full time Project Adventure Australia employee) showed me this visual *Hansel & Gretel* addition to an old workshop classic, *The Compass Walk*.

I had already asked the participants to try walking individually toward a chosen destination with their eyes closed (large paddock or footy pitch), and I was now priming them for a full group attempt at the same thing.

Rules

• The group had to move en masse with physical contact maintained between all walkers.

• The group had to choose a contact person; i.e., a person within the group who was to make contact with the chosen destination.

• Eyes closed for the entire walk. I asked that they all keep their eyes closed, even after stopping, so that each person had a opportunity to demonstrate the usefulness of their own internal compass, and point toward where they *thought* the goal was located. Considering that all 360° are predictably used, for safety's sake I asked that they point slowly to prevent sticking each other in the eye (or cheek, or nose, or whatever...)

As the group moved toward their ultimate goal, and as I watched out for their safety, Mark (Hansel in this case) followed directly behind the group and dropped a fleece ball every 3–4 steps to mark the flow of their directional movements. At the stopping point, after most had enjoyed the futility of their final pointing effort, it was satisfying for all to look back and reflect on the often meandering path marked by the balls.

Obviously, any type of ball can be used for path marking. Brightly colored, plastic sensory balls also work well.

Group Juggle Variations

The activity *Group Juggle* has been around for a number of years and is usually played in association with the Initiative problem *Warp Speed*. Both of those activities are detailed in *Cowstails II*.

Variations

Try these:

- Each person adopts a sound, then, whenever they throw a ball in the juggle sequence, they loudly proclaim that sound.

- Starting with one ball per person, try calling out *reverse* as soon as most balls are in play.

- Using only 2–4 balls (per group of 12), try starting 2 balls in one direction and 2 balls in the reverse direction. It's difficult to complete even one round, but it can be done.

- Add a ball as a "rumor," which as you know can move anywhere and usually at blinding speed.

- Substitute small water balloons for balls — on a warm day!

- Add a tumbler (plastic) of water to the established sequence — also on a warm day.

- Try completing this exercise using *Iky-Poo* balls.

- Play this game with a **hot** potato.

- A raw egg as the throwable lends a sense of immediacy and benign consequence.

Hog Call Help

ker

What is the most fun you have ever had?

• •

The introductory game *Hog Call* (*Silver Bullets*, pgs. 98–99) fulfills a number of workshop goals including acting as a vehicle to allow just-met people to get to know one another better. The latter part of the game is structured so that paired participants ask each other questions in anticipation of introducing one another to the entire group.

Here are a few questions that are interesting to think about and provide a conversational jump start. Use only one of these questions per participant.

• What is your greatest personal achievement?

• What is the most fun you have ever had?

• If you were to print something on a T-shirt, what would it say?

• What possession do you prize the most?

• If you discovered that you had six months of healthy living left before a rapid demise, what would you do differently?

• What books would you like to have if you were alone on a desert island (all your survival needs are met)?

• What is the most embarrassing thing that has happened to you?

An interesting and challenging variation to the interview process above is to ask the two people involved to attempt to find out as much as they can about their partner without saying a word — right, non-verbal all the way. Gesticulate, mime, jump around, use facial contortions — but no talk. As always, spontaneous laughter is appropriate and welcome.

Maze

Blindfolded, the players try to make their way out of the Maze.

• •

All of the *Mazes* I have used over the years have required that the participants be restricted to the inside of a rope/bungee enclosed area. Blindfolded, the players try to make their way out of the *Maze* via a small exit space. Once out, they are tapped on the shoulder (a signal to remove their blindfold) and they are then free to quietly observe what's going on.

I take the time at the beginning to blindfold my group some distance from the *Maze*, precluding any pre-event orientation. I walk the blindfolded group in a circuitous manner toward the *Maze*, including side trips through thickets, over logs, near water, and down inclines. It's interesting to bring the group back after the *Maze* experience to this preliminary "blind walk," so that individuals can relate what they felt at the time (huge logs, thick brush, steep drop offs) as compared to the reality (small logs, sparse brush, gentle inclines) of the situation.

In the past, when I arrived with the group at the *Maze* site, I would explain the necessity of placing each person within the *Maze*. I'd do this to make sure each player was separated from the other participants and to increase individual disorientation.

Stating that communication and teamwork were allowed, I'd say GO and wait for the group to eventually make its way out of the *Maze*. During this time I'd look for examples of working together, how individuals handled frustration, communication attempts, individual heroics, etc. to use afterwards in the debrief.

Not a bad Initiative situation all in all, but here's another approach that works just as well and perhaps better. I picked up this variation from Tony Haun at the Polding Center in New South Wales.

Set-Up

While constructing your *Maze*, don't bother weaving a peripheral boundary, just link a number of trees or stakes together with 1/4" bungee cord. Connect some low, some high (not out of reach — be fair!) and somewhere in the midst of all this amazable cord (see next page) hang some type of small symbolic figurine at about head level. Making contact with this figurine is the group's goal. Considering the current popularity of dinosaurs and their availability in toy stores, try suspending a friendly and soft Brontosaurus.

Play

Start the group all together and leave it up to them whether they think it's best to separate or quest as a group. When somebody finally fingers the figurine, amidst shouts of, "Over here! over here!" (which doesn't mean much to a blindfolded person) the rapidly collecting players perform a choreographed group grope of the poor plastic dinosaur and get to open their eyes.

Notice in the illustration that pieces of nylon cord extend from a couple of the dead end stakes. Holding onto these cords allows the group a sense of continued connected safety and the ability to do a pendulum sweep.

Consideration

I allow participants to separate from the bungee or nylon and wander — chance taking at its best. But if you plan to allow this freeform questing in the dark, make sure that there are other people with their eyes open (other than just yourself) to make sure these adventurers don't wander off into a ditch or into a tree trunk.

As in any blindfolded situation, make sure that there are no punji-type stumps (protruding at eye level or sticking up from the ground) that can cause injury.

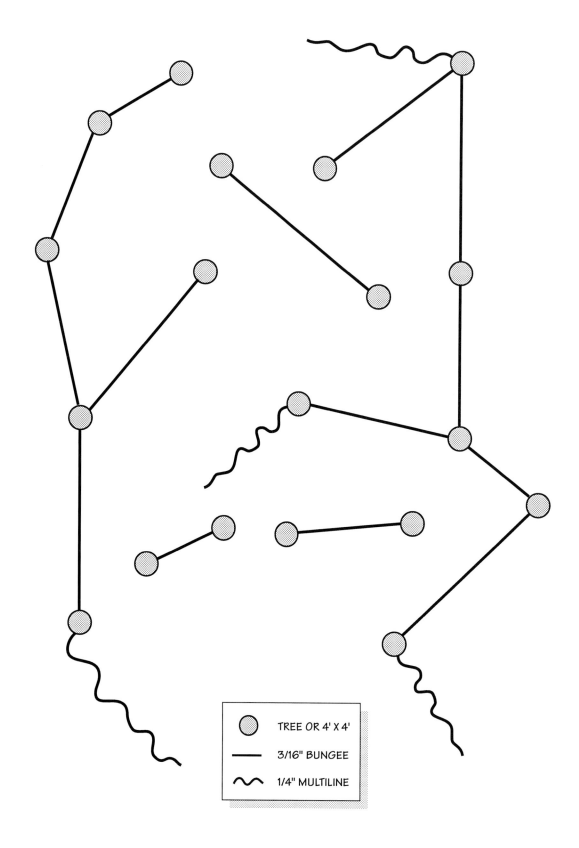

TREE OR 4' X 4'

3/16" BUNGEE

1/4" MULTILINE

Mine Field in a Circle

A Variation in the Round...

Remember *Mine Field*? (*Silver Bullets*, pg. 24) That's where you dump your game bag out on the floor and rearrange the contents so that everything is evenly distributed within an outlined rectangular area. Then split up into pairs and try to lead one another through the *Mine Field.* Remember, one of the members of the pair is blindfolded (eyes closed) and the other is simply giving verbal directions; i.e., no touch. This is an all-time favorite activity of Adventure Programming workshop participants. See pg. 51, *The Bottomless Bag* for other set ups and variations.

This variation involves simply setting up the *Mine Field* within a large outlined circular area; use a rope for the boundary. In the center of the circle (target area), place an appropriately bizarre squeaky toy so that an audible reward is there for the successful pair to step on.

Mohawk Walk

Split the group in half. Ask each smaller group to start from opposite ends of the *Walk.* Give each *team* a rubber ring, and indicate that both rings must be carried to their respective far ends for the whole group to be successful.

Rules

- If a person carrying the ring falls off, that player must return to that group's beginning point.

- If any other person falls off, that person must return only to the support from which she just left.

- The ring can only be transferred to another team member at the start of the traverse.

- The ring can only be passed hand-to-hand to the other *team*; it cannot be thrown.

- An offered crutch (use any 4-foot section of dowel, rod, or stick — but a *real* crutch is best) can be used to make ground contact anywhere on the traverse, but it must always move forward, any movement in reverse (as per ground contact) results in loss of the crutch. Pivoting movements forward and/or backward are allowed. The crutch cannot be passed person-to-person in reverse. A crutch is offered to both halves of the group.

Debrief Questions to Ponder

Why does the crutch get such inordinate attention?

Is the crutch useful or does it prove to be a handicap?

Do the two groups see themselves as part of a single larger group or as two competing teams?

At what point do the two groups seem to recognize that they can use each other?

What happens if the two groups continue to operate as *two teams*?

Is initial emphasis given to movement of the groups or positioning of the rings?

Micro Pick and Choose

If it works BIG, it will probably work SMALL.

• •

Kim Marshall and Lorna Controy of the U.S. Forest Service have come up with an adaptation of the Initiative game *Pick & Choose* (*Silver Bullets*, pg. 77) that looks like a winner.

"The basis for this event is simple. Follow basic *P&C* rules adapted to a small area, using marbles rather than balls." Make three string or tape circles or squares on the playing surface (a large desk or table), locating the outlined areas as you would the plastic milk cartons in a regular game of *P&C*, proportionally speaking of course.

Split the players into shooters and retrievers and have them shoot marbles at the circles or squares awarding points following the MORE rule; more distance from the shooters, more points are awarded. The farthest circle should net 5 points for each marble that remains entirely within the taped boundary. The other two circles allow 3 and 1 point respectively.

Another variation is to add "boulders" (outsized marbles) and count them as double or triple points."

Kim and Lorna suggest a 1-1/2 minute time limit per attempt.

Moon Ball

Moon Ball games display and deliver all the good learning stuff that is regularly touted as valid and useful in educational texts, but these basic beach ball games are admittedly more involvement oriented than aerobic. Smacking a beach ball a predetermined number of times as a group challenge won't cause your carotid pulse to go much over 100 bpm (I know... I know, "Speak for yourself, Karl."), but the game *Moon Ball* was developed to develop cooperation, a sense of comfortable participation, appreciation of fun, etc. — not C/V fitness.

This *MB* variation will generate some hard breathing, powerful ventricular responses, and, depending on the day, perhaps a surface moistening of the skin.

In keeping with the simplistic set-up of other *Moon Ball* variations, here's a minimum set of rules to maintain that minimalist consistency. The group (everybody — there are no separate teams) tries to strike, slap, head, or elbow a beach ball the length of a field (distance is up to your need for push or pleasure) in the *least possible elapsed time*. The ball must be struck sequentially by team members; i.e., players cannot hit the ball after their first strike until everyone on the team has made contact with the ball. Since this is a timed event (the number of hits is irrelevant), more than one attempt should be announced so that the group is anticipating and planning for (thinking about) a second try.

Is that simple? Usable? Functionally efficient? How come you didn't think of it? Think about other possible *Moon Ball* variations. This is not the end.

Name Tag

This is a name-reminder game.

• •

I just tried looking up the game *Name Tag* so I could refer to it as previously presented in *BOT's*, or in a Project Adventure publication, but I can't find it. Did I ever write about it? I'm not sure, but after just spending longer than I wanted to looking through electronic files for whatever it was that I think I said (wrote — same thing), I figure that I'm better off just writing what's currently on my mind and hope you know what I'm referring to. Maybe I'll find *Name Tag* later on, and if so, you will never read this — but you are, so I didn't.

Rather than continuing my *mouse hunt*, here are the basic rules — so I can tell you about a variation that Lee Gillis passed along. It all seems a bit circuitous, but the game and the variation are worthwhile.

This is a name-reminder game, so the group would have had to previously played one of the other name games that associates faces and names.

Play

Ask the group to close their eyes and with "bumpers up" (hands protecting faces) to slowly mill around until you say, "Stop." When the group is nicely separated and disoriented, tell them that you are going to tap somebody's shoulder and say aloud that person's name. The tapped person immediately opens her or his eyes and quickly finds someone nearby to tap and name. This procedure continues until everyone has had a turn.

Tell the group before you begin that their attempt from start to finish will be timed. Try this activity at least twice so that the group gets the opportunity to best their previous time, and forgetful folks (like me) get to wet-cement a couple more names in place.

As a convenience to the tapped and often frantically searching player, each person who has had a turn should kneel or sit down to indicate that their tag turn is complete.

It's embarrassingly interesting to watch tapped players open their eyes, look directly at the person in front of them, then dash off to tag someone at a distance. It's painfully obvious why the vis-a-vis person is ignored, but the forgetting and enjoyment of the consequence is shared, as names eventually become people.

Variation (Finally)

When a person taps someone and says their name, they must join hands with that person and move as a pair to tap and name a third person, etc., etc. The game ends (stop the watch) when everyone has joined hands.

Was it worth it? Well, I guess! **NAME TAG! NAME TAG! — YES! YES!! YES!!!**

— SEGIEN

Nuclear Fence

I might as well tell you right up front...

• •

Nuclear Fence is just another name for *The Electric Fence*. **WHAT?** You're writing about *the electric fence?* Why... I knew someone who jeopardized their tenure by simply telling an electric fence joke! Nonetheless, it's true, this brief but poignant essay offers a contraband variation of the electric fence Initiative problem.

The Electric Fence????????

Aaaaargh! Heresy! Retributional Rubric! You shall incur the wrath of the AEE, AAHPERD, NEA and PA — family, home, fortune and friends are surely forfeit.

Hysteria aside, here's the skinny on how to do the *Electric Fence* sans trauma, as passed along by Brahm Schatia.

Tie or hold a section of 3/16" bungee cord at approximately crotch height between two normally elevated crotches, then ask your group to cross from one side of the cord to the other without touching the cord. The group must travel en masse; i.e., there must be a *constant* electrical (physical) connection between *all* participants. If this connection breaks down at any juncture, the group must restart. If anyone touches the cord or breaks the "force field" under the cord, the same consequence is experienced.

This simple people-to-people rule removes the body-launch technique that has injured so many people in the past, and revives the best of a much maligned Initiative problem. Welcome back.

Pile Up

A *Have You Ever...?* variation.

• •

Since *Have You Ever...?* is written up in this edition, we thought we'd give you a new twist on it at the same time. Why wait till the next book?

This version allows for a definite end point to the game, which may be a good idea in that people can often keep asking *Have You Ever...?* forever. Of course it also means that the game may go on longer than you want it to. But all good facilitators know that they can end an activity whenever it seems appropriate.

Play

Anyway, with people seated in a circle, questions are asked by one person (who is not playing) or randomly by any member of the group. The action involves moving one position to the right if you respond yes to a question, or staying put if you answer no.

The goal is to move yourself completely around the circle and return to your starting position before anyone else in the circle has done the same. Obviously, the more you answer yes the faster you move.

It is possible, in fact highly probable, that two or more people can end up occupying the same space in the circle at the same time. Therefore, it's important to have people in comfortable chairs so people sitting on other laps (knees) won't cause any major discomfort; or have everyone sit on the floor where they can sit in front of each other instead of on each other.

Don't be turned off by the potential lap contact involved here. The game is fun and the mildly competitive aspect merely adds a bit more concentration.

Spider Web Variation

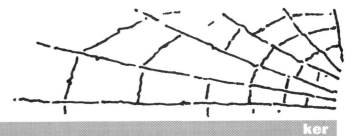

A classic Initiative problem...

• •

Another variation ...there doesn't seem to be a limit on imagination concerning this Initiative problem. I still haven't come up with the name of the individual who sent me the *Spider Web* Initiative idea many years ago. The letter arrived with two photographs showing students smiling and crawling through a very ragged looking *Web* made of string. If anyone reading this paragraph recognizes their own largess, let me know who you are, I'd like to extend credit for what has become a classic Initiative problem.

This time the variation comes from Kevin Shaffstall of Adventure Woods in Kansas City, MO.

When you build the frame for the *Web*, rather than reeving and tightening a rope try the following: Cut two good sized saplings (2" diameter min. and 12' long) and trim them to fit into 4 **U** brackets bolted onto the tree at 6" and 72" off the ground; i.e., so they are parallel to the ground and one another (about 5-1/2' apart).

Evenly space five type-O eye screws (3/8" diameter) into each sapling and 4 of the same eye screws into the vertical supports (trees or poles). These eye screws are all interior facing and provide the attachment points for the bungee *Web* sections.

The bungee sections that fit between these eye screws are provided with inexpensive snap links attached to each end, (use figure eight loops). Kevin suggests the following bungee lengths: nine, 4' red cords; two, 4' white cords; two, 9' blue cords.

When the students show up to attempt the problem, they are briefed as to the rules (including whatever fantasy you deem appro-priate) then given the bungee cords to construct their own challenge. Not bad — by setting their own task, they necessarily buy into the challenge. Being able to take the cords down after the problem is finished also precludes casual vandalism.

Kevin also included the following ideas:

- Have the group transport a cup of water (a life saving serum?) through the *Web*. Any spillage — start over.

- Specify at the beginning how many times the *Web* can be touched before the entire group has to return to the start.

Traffic Jam

While we're talking about *The Traffic Jam* Initiative problem (*Silver Bullets*, pg. 122), let me pass along a simple variation that I have been using with corporate groups, and one I think will work with any group that has been imbued with our society's competitive, win-or-else mentality.

Set up the problem so that you have two groups performing the same task concurrently. Present the rules to the group as a whole; i.e., before you ask them to separate into two smaller groups. Emphasize that you are *not* splitting the group into two competing teams, and encourage each sub-group to *share*

whatever they learn toward completion of the problem.

The performance results are predictable. Each group becomes very solicitous of whatever progress *they* have achieved, and become reluctant to share any acquired knowledge. The group that initially reaches a solution is usually glad to share their good fortune, however, the still-struggling group wants nothing to do with their largesse, preferring to "...come up with the answer ourselves." The various and sometimes unpredictable dynamics of this variation lend themselves to revealing and often heated discussions.

TP Shuffle

If a devious group figures out that taking the penalty is more efficient than playing it straight, invoke the travesty rule.

• •

See *Silver Bullets*, pg. 110, for the original presentation.

Rather than splitting the group in half and asking the log-mounted individuals to change ends without touching the ground, add some variety by asking the log riders to:

• Choose a standing place on the log as to their respective ages, youngest to oldest, etc. Then ask the players to reverse their positions on the log as to their chronologic ages. The answer to any question you or the students have about this is *yes*.

• Ask the students to line up on the log so that the most height impaired person is at one end and the tallest individual is at the other end. Switch!

TP Sprint

• Don't forget *The TP Sprint*! You forgot? It's on page 91 in *The Bottomless Baggie*. You don't have the book? Whose mouse are you? OK …ok, here's the rules. Place four volunteer "facilitators" on the TP log. During the course of the problem they are not allowed to step off the log.

Split the remainder of the team in half. Each half moves separately to either end of the log; i.e., just walk as a group, on the grass, to the end of the log. The object is to trade ends of the log as quickly and efficiently as possible, recognizing that the starting and ending positions for each team (same team really) is on the ground at the ends of the log. Place a short length of slash rope perpendicular to each end of the log. That's the start and finish line you are not allowed to step over and/or into the toxic material — which looks like dirt and grass to most people.

Rules and Penalties

- The four facilitators must maintain separate contact with the log. If any of the four inadvertently or purposefully slip off the log each ground touch receives a 30-second penalty.

- This 30-second penalty for each trip to the turf also holds for all other participants.

- No props are allowed to be used.

- If a devious group figures out that touching the ground and taking the penalty is more efficient than playing it straight, invoke the **travesty rule,** which in part states, *"To maintain the integrity of the game as stated in the initial rules, and to protect against outlandish (sneaky) initiative machinations, the instructor may, without warning, change the extent and/or duration of incurred penalties as to best maintain the original intent of the game situation."*

There are a couple beautiful solutions to this variation, and I'm not going to tell you what they are because your groups will eventually show you. After seven months or so, if you really, *really* want to know, send me a card and I will respond as ambiguously as possible.

Trolley

Don't give any indication how the problem "should" be done.

• •

I don't use *The Trolley* much anymore, partly because I've over-used it in the past, but also because it seems inevitable that unloading two lengths of rope-festooned boards is a sure-fire give-a-way of how to solve the problem. But, if you unloaded the boards with no ropes attached, then threw a bunch of different length ropes on the ground explaining, *Here's some props to help you cross this morass of poisoned peanut butter* — thinking, idea sharing, decision making, and hands-on experimenting is going to take place.

Tips

• Screw Type-0 eye screws (3/8" diameter) into a selected top section of board. Space the screws about 12" apart, but varying the distance twixt screws by a couple inches is okay, too. Countersink where you are going to place an eye screw so that you can screw the eye partially below the board's surface, (but not so far that you can't reeve a section of 3/8" rope through the eye).

• Cut lengths of 3/8" multiline and just tape both ends, no splicing or knot tying necessary, let the participants do that. The ropes lengths do not necessarily have to be the same — say somewhere in the 5–7 foot range.

• Use short (4') sections of 4x4 with a 5/8" shoulder lag eye screw (SLES), screwed into each end of the boards. Have 1/2" rapid links available to connect the SLES eyes. This foreshortened variation isn't necessary (none of this is necessary), but it makes transporting the boards a lot easier in your Honda Civic.

• Don't give any indication how the problem "should" be done. Let the group *decide* how they want to attach the ropes, arrange the boards, move over the "poison peanut butter," etc., all you need to suggest is that they make the passage from A to B as quickly and efficiently as possible.

Another Trolley Variation...

When you make your next *Trolley,* only attach ropes for two people, the leader and the caboose. The remainder of the riders, to maintain their balance, must make contact with one another somehow as they respond with alacrity to the commands of the leader.

This makes so much sense it makes me feel like all those drilled 4x4s and spliced lengths of rope were a waste of time. People cooperating, balancing, touching, laughing — if it wasn't snowing out I'd take a *Trolley* trip right now.

Two Woosey Variations

A useful balance/trust/communication exercise...

• •

The *Wild Woosey* has been around for almost twenty years and has become part of many low challenge ropes courses, and rightly so, it's a useful balance/trust/communication exercise. But the *Wild Woosey* is the *Wild Woosey*, and there's not much that can be done with the diverging cables except trying to make it from A to B. Here's a couple variations in construction and implementation.

Variation Ideas

• Make a 1-1/4"x 3' dowel available to the two people starting on the event. Don't give any indication as to potential use, just mention that this prop can be handled as best fits their imagination, but that it cannot touch the ground.

If they try to use the dowel as a counterforce object; i.e., leaning back against one another while holding onto opposite ends of the dowel, they will soon discover the meaning of "white elephant." However, if they use the dowel as an object to grip and lean in toward one another (orientation of the dowel is perpendicular to pressure being applied), they will have found a comfortable and safe way to apply a considerable amount of pressure onto one another's hands, wrists and arms. Paint the dowel a bright color to make it appear to be something it isn't, and to add to the festive aire of funambulistic Adventure.

- I can't tell you the number of *Wild Wooseys* I have seen (inspected) that are ill proportioned — a combination of too short, long, narrow and wide. It's as if someone walked into the woods looking for *Wild Woosey* supports and choose the first three trees they tripped over. One of the most common construction mistakes is to design such an obtuse angle between the cables that no participant pair can complete the traverse. The rationale (rationalization) is that then "everybody fails," so no one feels badly. Sounds like you're blowin' wind to me, and I've blown enough to recognize when it's comin' my way.

Here's how to adapt your *Woosey* so that you can change the angle orientation of the two diverging cables and let everyone have the chance of failing-forward.

Considering that your *Wild Woosey* resembles (should resemble) an isosceles triangle, connect the two base support trees or poles, (at the same height as the cables) with an equal diameter section of tree or pole; i.e., suspend a log there. Drill (11/16" bit) through the support tree at the height of the *Woosey* cables and continue drilling directly into and through a 6"–8" cut log that is supported parallel to the cables and perpendicular to the ground on the far side of the support trees. With dispatch, bang a proper length 5/8" machine bolt (usually at least 20" long) through both sections and nut down tightly — don't forget to use fish plate washers.

Measure out 12" on this horizontal log from one of the vertical supports and drill through so that the finished hole points directly at the apex support tree, (remember the isosceles triangle?). Put a 5/8" nut eye bolt into the hole with the eye facing the apex support tree. Measure out another 12" from this bolt, drill a similar hole and establish another eye bolt oriented in the same way. Place a third bolt just like the second, and as many as you want along the log considering how many variable challenges you want or need. Getting the picture yet?

Eye swage or cable clamp one of your *Woosey* cables short enough so that you can make use of a turnbuckle (PA Equipment catalog, pg. 10) at the end of the eye swaged cable to adjust its positioning.

If your group members all have comparatively short legs (elementary students), you can now adjust the acuteness of your cables to allow completion for those height challenged students. Isn't that the way it's *suppozed* to be?

Trust

Buddy Ropes

If squeals, yucks
and sweaty palms are
too hard to handle.

• •

Ever had a hard time getting a group of junior high-aged students to hold hands for a game or Initiative problem? Maybe not. After all, developing a sense of unselfconscious touch is one of the "group" goals that we work toward in an Adventure curriculum approach, but try *Buddy Ropes* if the squeals, yucks

and sweaty palms are too hard to handle on a Monday morning.

Set-Up

Cut a series of rope lengths that measure about 5' long, and tie an overhand knot in each end. Give each student one length just before the chosen activity begins. If provided the ropes (whips) too soon, your dispassionate charges will use them for everything that your instinct says not to use them for.

Remember the old Initiative problem called *Knots*, AKA *Tangle* or *Hands*? Can't remember?

Look on page 117 of *Silver Bullets*. Haven't got a copy handy? No worries — that's the people poser where you ask 8–10 players to stand in a cluster, face-to-face. Each person then reaches across the small circle and grabs someone's hand (like shaking hands), and again reaches across the circle and grabs someone else's hand. If your group is mature enough to hold hands for a few minutes, a grand tangle of hands and arms will result. The objective is to untangle the group without letting go of the various grips. Remember now? Not a bad activity, but one that is functionally limited to 10–12 participants.

Play

Now, try *Tangle* using the *Buddy Ropes*. Rather than grasping a hand, grasp the end of a rope. Each person is assigned one rope and is genetically allotted at birth two digital graspers, so when all the grasping is done, this hand-in-hand scenario should come out even. Make sure, as in the hand-holding classic, that you don't grab two ropes coming from the same person, otherwise this vis-á-vis close encounter will severely limit your group involvement.

Notice how the tangled ropes allow a better view of what needs to be accomplished. Ordinarily, when you begin this problem (hands only), a participant's initial view is usually of someone's armpit or the back of a head. It also becomes quickly obvious that the ropes allow more people to be involved. Fifteen participants sharing tangled ropes is no problem. Fifteen tangled people holding hands might result in separated shoulders.

Some Other Ideas

Tangle is just one example of how *Buddy Ropes* can be used. Think about other games or Initiative problems that involve two people operating as a connected pair. *The Clock*? (*Silver Bullets*, pg. 116). I tried *The Clock* using *Buddy Ropes* last week with enthusiastic participant feedback. The centrifugal feeling that develops as a result of trying to beat the clock is more in evidence.

Ask a line of "roped" (*Buddy Ropes* held hand-in-hand) participants to tie an overhand knot, thinking of themselves as a single rope length. When finished, the knot will appear in one of the centrally held ropes. Considering the shortness of the ropes, substitute one longer rope (8 ft.) in the center of the line of people. The overhand knot will be easier to establish in this longer rope. This simple sounding Initiative problem will often confound the most together group.

Yurt Circle? Pairs Frantic? Paul's Balls? Off the Wall? Moonball? Circle the Circle? Sherpa Walk? Any of these activities and more can be varied by the use of *Buddy Ropes*.

Consideration

A caveat. Don't use *Buddy Ropes* for a game if there is a chance, because of rapid pairs movements, that someone will get "clotheslined" with a rope.

P.S. — I used 5' sections of retired kernmantle ropes with a knot in either end, but I think whatever cordage you have on hand will do.

Come To Me

I like this activity because it can serve two purposes.

• •

You need to have people work in purposeful pairs, though I imagine threes or fours could work just as purposefully.

One partner wears a blindfold, or simply closes his or her eyes; the other partner remains sighted and begins the game by standing approximately 10–15 feet away. As soon as the blindfolded players have closed their eyes, the sighted partners begin to walk towards their sightless partner until that person holds up her hands (palms out, of course) and says, "Stop!"

As a trust activity, it is a revealing exercise to explore one's comfort level as another person enters your *personal space* and mentally measure what level of discomfort is experienced by that person's approach. Some people enjoy allowing a partner to get close enough to touch; others stop them at a distance of several feet. It can produce some lively discussion about why the sightless person said, "Stop."

Variation

A slightly different focus to the activity changes the dynamic, making this into more of a game. When the sighted players approach their partners, the intent is to be as quiet as possible and to get as close as possible before the sightless player stops them. Circling around behind partners, standing still and other strategies, enliven this variation as the sightless players attempt to determine where their partners are. Depending on the styles of the players and the safety level of the group, this version may cause more or less nervousness for the participants.

As with any trust or sightless activity, knowing your group and judging what they are ready for is crucial. People have responded well to these ideas, both as trust builders and just for the fun of trying to sneak up on the other person. Encouraging people to be silent, outlining what types of sneaking are appropriate, and identifying any behaviors that are inappropriate (no tickling or making fun of the sightless people, for example) may help create a suitable environment for trying this activity.

If the action sounds too simple to be good, try it for yourself. When I did, I changed my mind.

DOAF — Decide On A Face

The choice of gesture should be compassionately chosen.

• •

Jim Schoel asked me this morning if I had heard of *Passing A Gesture*, and I responded that I had not. So fill me in...

After you have been with a group for a couple days in a workshop setting, or with a school group during a semester together, ask everyone to decide on a gesture or idiosyncrasy that they think kinetically represents one of their friends; perhaps a typical facial expression, a habitual movement of the hands, characteristic body language, something that might be recognized as associated with a specific person or persons. Emphasize before starting that you are not trying to embarrass anyone, so the choice of gesture should be compassionately chosen.

Play

Standing in a circle, one person initiates a gesture and it is then copied (mimed) by everyone else in sequence around the circle. After all this posturing and gesticulation, everyone should attempt a guess as to who the gesture is associated with. Then someone else volunteers a gesture, etc., etc. Note: As in all potentially embarrassing "volunteer attempt" situations, do not require a gesture from everyone, and if you think that a particular gesture could be character-threatening, kill it.

A less threatening and more spontaneous approach is asking each person to volunteer a gesture or facial expression that "...just comes to mind." It does not have to be associated with anyone or any particular situation. The chosen gesture is then passed around the circle quickly, then it's on to the next person. Try to keep the activity low key and fun, remembering that passing must always remain an option.

Have You Ever...

The game format allows people to say something about themselves without bragging.

● ●

Playing *Have You Ever...* is one of my favorite workshop activities. I don't know of any other game that allows you to learn so much about people, in a short period of time, in such an unselfconscious way.

Play

There are a number of ways to play the game, but try this one to get started. Sitting in a circle, indicate to the members of the group that as a means of finding out more about the circle sitters, anyone may ask a question of the group that is prefaced by the words, *Have you ever...?* To ask the question, the person asking must be able to answer yes to his own question. If your answer is YES, raise your hand, if NO, just sit there enjoying the other players' responses.

As facilitator, you may, from time to time, ask if someone in the group who answered YES would like to tell the story behind that affirmative response. For example, if I answered YES to the question, "Have you ever parachuted from a plane?" then someone in the group might be interested in hearing the entire scenario surrounding the jump. The game format allows people to say something about themselves without bragging. The game also allows a more reticent player to say nothing without fear of censure.

Other ways to play the *Have You Ever...* can be read about in the books, *The Bottomless Bag Again* and *The Bottomless Baggie*. There are also extensive lists of other *Have You Ever...* questions in these two books. But don't depend upon someone else's text, develop your own questions and game formats — that's part of the larger game.

Have you Ever...

...attempted to get away from a cop car; i.e., attempted to out-run the vehicle?

...flown a stunt kite?

...been involved in stunt kite combat?

...won a medal in a master's competition?

...returned to your high school after 10 years? 20 years? 30 years? 40 years? etc.?

...eaten Haggis?

...started a fire with a magnifying glass?

...as an adult, spent New Year's Eve alone (from 9 PM – past midnight?)

...blown a dart through a blowgun?

...stuck your tongue in a stranger's ear?

...purchased a comic book for more than ten dollars?

...purchased a comic book for ten cents?

...immersed yourself at least to your waist in a golf course pond looking for balls?

...found over 500 golf balls in one day?

...had your tonsils surgically removed?

...torn a rotator cuff muscle?

...cut out the inside of a book to make a secret hiding place?

...made an origami cootie catcher?

...had the hood (bonnet) of an auto release while you were driving and fly back into the windshield?

...drilled numerous holes in something to make a pencil holder?

...smoked a full bowl of pipe tobacco?

...dug a hole in the sand at the beach until you hit water?

...done a one-arm push-up?

...performed a full flip on the ground without touching the ground with your hands (forward or backward)?

...sharpened a knife so that it was keen enough to shave the hairs off your arm (leg)?

...spent time perusing a dictionary just because you wanted to?

...sailed a bottle cap at least 20 feet with the flip of a finger?

...operated a jackhammer?

...worn steel-toed shoes or boots?

...actively looked for your car in a parking lot for over 15 minutes?

...recited from memory more than 100 words (not a song)?

...kept proper score in darts?

...plowed a field with a tractor?

...cut down your own Christmas tree?

...personally set fire to a used Christmas tree?

...rolled a snowball as tall as yourself (with help)?

...been to a prize fight in person?

...been to a rodeo in person?

...folded an American flag properly?

...driven a GO-Cart?

...read Braille; i.e., understood what you were feeling?

...killed a crow with a shotgun?

...sung along with one of your favorite groups, recorded the effort, and recognized that you are never going to make the big time?

...worn an oral prosthetic device to keep from grinding your teeth at night?

...sheered a sheep?

...been buried vertically in the sand up to your neck?

...passed out underwater?

...hung up on a telephone solicitor after having identified yourself?

...cut a golf ball open and had the liquid center spew into your face?

...tossed a caber?   ...tossed a caber correctly?   ...tossed a caber in competition?

...climbed to the top of a utility pole over 90-feet high?

...been in a shelter specifically designed to protect you from bombs?

...successfully climbed a vertical sand dune?

...seen a section of 7/16" goldline rope break?

...been shot by a slug measuring .22 caliber or more?

...driven across the American continent, paying less than $30 for petrol?

...been called to attention by a drill instructor?

...fanned a revolver using live ammunition?

...been stung by: honey bee • wasp • yellow jacket • white-faced ground hornet • scorpion • black widow spider • brown recluse • tarantula • Australian bull ant • red fire ant • sea anemone • fire coral • sting ray • stinging nettle • green head fly • black fly • centipede • cone shell • Portuguese man-o-war • jelly fish • Funnel Web Spider?

...spent an entire night in a hammock?

...chummed for sharks with human blood?

...worn a money belt?

...eaten Kim Chee?

...baked a cake or pie from scratch?

...cooked a dinner (not frozen) for 6 people or more?

...kept a batch of sourdough yeast going for more than two years?

...grown an avocado plant from a seed using toothpicks and a glass of water?

...made whipped cream using a hand beater?

...painted an entire automobile with a paint brush?

...shot whipped cream from an aerosol can into your mouth so forcefully whipped cream came out your nose?

...given yourself a haircut?

...used an in-house *ice box* to refrigerate groceries?

...eaten one peanut or potato chip when many were available?

...wondered why or how your rear view mirror can be flipped at night and still allow you to see the cars behind you?

...bungee jumped over 100 feet? ...wanted to?

...climbed and ridden a birch tree to the ground?

...taken a shower in an airport or train/bus terminal?

...spent the night in a YMCA or YWCA?

...flown without mechanical aid in one of your dreams?

...failed a college level course (not correspondence)?

...failed the same course a second time?

...failed the practical part of a driver's test?

...worked for a company that added a stipend to your paycheck to cover laundry expenses?

...tried to put a whole banana (peeled) in your mouth? (no chewing or swallowing)

...bet on a horse race? A dog race? A cock fight?

...paid more than $100 for a single taxi ride?

...banded a bird?

...owned a switchblade?

...read a 500+ page book nonstop?

...eaten a mountain oyster?

...lost more than 12 pounds (water weight) in 24 hours?

...lost your glasses and found them on your face?

...tried sand skimming at the beach?

..."totaled" a car?

...kept a goldfish (alive) for more than five years?

...chewed spruce gum?

...melted snow for drinking water out of necessity?

...done an ocean dip in New England in Dec. — Feb.?

...Cross-country skied more than five miles non-stop in a single direction?

...waited outside a mall until opening time?

...reloaded your own ammunition?

...actually sent for and received one of the "valuable" prizes that "you have already won" from one of the many commercial mail-order houses that employ this mass-mailing and border-line fraudulent advertising technique?

...maliciously let the air out someone's auto tire?

...paid a one-time fee of more than $50 for parking a vehicle? Does not include fines.

...read the entire Bible?

...worn a skirt without underwear?

...had a beer for breakfast?

...flown on the Concorde?

...collected something avidly for over 10 years that is extrinsically worthless?

...been able to count to ten in three languages other than your own?

...taken a dose of liquid cod liver oil from a spoon?

...had a full-sized accordion hanging from your shoulders and tried to play a few notes?

...smoked an entire cigar?

...stood in front of a judge in criminal court in order to say, "guilty" or "not guilty?"

...swallowed something valuable and had to look for the object at the other end of the alimentary canal? Did you find it?

...given a dog a pill? A cat?

...urinated in the shower?

...watched a movie from the front row?

...watched a movie from a balcony?

...asked someone in a theater to stop talking (not family)?

...walked out of a movie that you paid to watch? Which one?

...been cross-examined during a jury trial?

...stayed in a motel room priced at over $200 per night?

...had a loved one die at home?

...made a call from an in-flight phone?

...saw a double feature at a movie theater (not a drive-in)?

...watched a movie at a drive-in theater?

...flown a kite in a snow storm?

...let go of an airborne kite on purpose?

...flown a kite from a canoe or kayak?

...used powdered toothpaste?

...ducked under water to hear the raindrops on a lake's surface?

...brushed a dog's teeth?

...snorkeled in water with visibility in excess of 100 feet?

...paid more than a $100 per person green fee to play 18 holes of golf?

...hit a hole-in-one (or seen one played in person) on a regulation golf course — not on a par three course?

...dug a grave for and buried a dog?

...been relieved of a job by the actual spoken words, "You're fired!"

...run a rack of pool balls?

...bowled a 300 game?

...wind surfed over one mile in the same direction?

Author's Note

I just took the test and scored 119 YES responses, finishing strong with four NOs in a row. My score indicates that I am probably over 50 years old, I have a lot of time to attempt strange things, and I have an understanding wife.

Pairs Walk

For most groups, I ask that the entire activity be accomplished in silence.

· ·

Trust exercises have never been among my favorites because of all the precautions and safety rules to remember. I like this one because the premise is simple, but the implementation requires a lot of individual initiative.

Set-Up

Before starting this activity, I recommend you set out a walking course that you feel comfortable with. By this I mean that there should be some obstacles (ups and downs, things to step over, things to go under, something to walk on top of, something small to climb up and/or down). But no obstacle should be included that will cause excessive risk to any participant. If you have any doubts when first setting a course, err on the side of caution until you observe how people manage the obstacles at hand. You may have to alter your course as you progress if you observe the group having too much trouble.

A wooded area seems best for this walk, though I'm certain an appealing course could be manufactured indoors. The best part about an outdoor trail with terrain unfamiliar to the participants is that it will create the impression of risk where little or no danger exists due to your prior selection of the route.

Lead the group to the area for the trust walk, stopping a short distance from where your trail begins. Brief the group at this point before taking them any further.

Play

Tell them they are about to embark on a journey. Working in pairs, one person will start blindfolded, one will be sighted, acting as a guide. You can also ask players to close their eyes in a *Challenge By Choice* scenario. It is the sighted players' responsibility to keep their partners totally safe. The sighted guides must do whatever is necessary to prevent injury or discomfort to their partners. Guides must have physical contact with their partners at all times when they are moving, but they can position themselves any way they want in order to most effectively lead their partners safely through the course. Holding hands, one arm around the waist, walking in front with their partner's hands on their shoulders, are just a few examples of a guide's position.

The guides should remember that they must also be sensitive to their partner's emotional and psychological safety as well.

For most groups, I ask that the entire activity be accomplished in silence. The only breach of the silence should be if there is a safety hazard that poses a significant danger or if any blindfolded partners begin to feel so uncomfortable that they want to stop. Be aware that some younger groups may need to verbally communicate in order to insure safety.

Tell the group that the journey they are embarking on has two parts. For the first section, the group will be divided in half. Ask for volunteers who want to be blindfolded first. Give these players blindfolds and ask them to put them on. When all are ready, ask the sighted guides to quietly go to their designated partners and put a hand on that person's shoulder. A hand on the shoulder assures the blindfolded players that someone is ready to guide them safely.

Explain that once they reach the halfway mark, you will indicate to the guides to put their partners in an indicated safe place, then move away. On a signal, the sightless players will remove their blindfolds, hand them to someone who was previously a guide, then step away. Once the new group has put their blindfolds in place, the new set of guides will approach and place a hand on the shoulder of

the individual they have chosen to guide — and the second half of the journey begins.

This technique adds a bit more uncertainty to the experience, since people will not know who their guide is to be. If this challenge seems too much, allow people to select their own guides.

Remind the leaders of the need to be responsible for their partners' safety. It might be helpful to offer an example of what that responsibility means.

Ask for any questions and if all the leaders are ready, tell the people that they need to follow as closely as possible in your footsteps.

They should not deviate from your path to avoid obstacles. Pairs at the back of the line should follow the pair in front of them if they lose sight of your route.

Once you begin leading the group on the trail, WALK SLOWLY. Allow ample time for the pairs to negotiate the terrain and stop if necessary to prevent the pairs at the end of the line from dropping so far behind that they lose contact. Move as quietly as you can and lead them through terrain that will challenge the guides and their partners.

If at any point you observe something that is unsafe and you fear someone may be injured, you should intervene to spot, coach or somehow assist the guide or blindfolded person.

When you reach the end, silently designate the safe area where the guides should leave their partners. Wait for everyone to finish and then ask the blindfolded people to exchange their blindfolds. Remind people that they should try to remain silent during this transfer.

While people may feel anxious before and during this activity, my experience has been that people enjoy it. Many people find it relaxing and peaceful to be guided (assuming the guide does a good job). The activity can be done just as a fun recreational experience, but there is also much to discuss afterwards.

Debrief

During a debrief, you might ask the following questions:

- What did it feel like being guided?
- What did it feel like being the guide?
- Were you frightened?
- What did your guide do to make you feel safe and comfortable?
- What, if any, communication took place between the guide and the partner?
- Have you ever experienced a situation where you felt "blinded"? What, from this experience, would help you in a future situation where you feel lost or unsure about where you're going?
- Was there any difference between the first half of the journey and the second half? Did people experience it as being easier, harder, safer, more dangerous? Why?

Don't try this activity with a group that you are not sure will protect each other. This activity can challenge the abilities of a group to take appropriate risks and to provide effective and safe leadership. But it's your task as the instructor to assess the readiness of your group before presenting this challenge.

SEGIEN

Pitfall

Describe the Pitfall as the area where all the problems exist.

· ·

Been using the activity *Minefield*? Like it? Here's a variation. Along with the 3-D version included in this edition, this idea provides an additional challenge. Since groups seem to love this activity, it's always useful to know additional ways to present it.

A word on the name: I changed it to *Pitfall* a couple of years back for two reasons: One, the term *Pitfall* fit the challenge as stated here more appropriately; and two, during the Gulf War, the image of a *Minefield* took on much more real significance for people. Use whatever title works best or make up a new one.

Set-Up

Set up your *Pitfall* area in the usual manner — either traditional ground only or 3-D. In other words, gather up armloads of stuff and distribute the don't-touch-me objects liberally in a confined area to create a suitably challenging course for people to negotiate.

Before starting, give each pair of people a pipe cleaner, or some other object that they can

use to create a symbol. Describe the *Pitfall* as the area where all the problems exist that cause them trouble at school, at work, at camp, where they live. If appropriate, ask them to identify some of those problems. Then tell the pairs that the pipe cleaner represents a support to help them through the problems. It might be a person, an object, a class, a special skill, a place they go. They need to shape the pipe cleaner so they will recognize it in the midst of the *Pitfall* zone.

Play

Before starting across the *Pitfall*, each pair places their support symbol somewhere in the area. Their task is to retrieve the support symbol without touching any of the taboo objects. Each pair consists of one blindfolded person being guided by a sighted leader.

Having to locate and pick up the symbol adds another challenge to this Initiative. People respond well to having a more defined goal, rather than just trying to avoid obstacles. Identifying all the support symbols as tools for the entire group also allows the members to work together as a team to see how many supports they can retrieve in a specified time. This focus may take some pressure off people who do not feel comfortable walking the course individually, but want to contribute to a team effort.

Trust Circle

Don't present this activity until you are sure that your students care enough about one another to make it work.

Set-Up

Ask the students to arrange themselves in a circle. Announce, "Eyes closed and bumpers up." (*Bumpers Up* is a hands-up, palms-out position that blindfolded or eyes-closed participants assume in order to protect their faces as they move slowly amongst one another.)

Play

Indicate that each person will walk slowly from one side of the circle to the other side and that everyone is to do this simultaneously. Obviously, there will be some jostling near the center of the circle, but if everyone is aware of the mass group movement, the gentle shoulder bumps and palm contact should be no problem.

If everything goes well, ask the walkers to make another sightless trip across the circle, but at a more confident rate. Careful: More speed = more contact. Encourage compassion by asking players to protect one another from the consequences of uncaring contact. Suggest one more trip across the circle at a brisker pace if the group has handled the first two crossings in a desired fashion.

Emphasize caring and compassion over and over. Remember, you are conflicting with years of training, in the schools and often at home, that emphasizes the benefits of speed, size and a win-at-any-cost competitive attitude.

(If this circle crossing scenario appears too much for your group to handle sightlessly, ask the participants to simply cross over with bumpers up, with their eyes open. If they handle a couple crossings well, ask them if they would like an additional challenge; i.e., eyes closed.)

The purpose of this apparent disaster-waiting-to-happen is to promote caring among participants by encouraging each of them to voluntarily participate in an activity punctuated with imminent and obvious consequence. The safety and satisfaction concerned with this trust crossing is entirely dependent upon your "reading" of the group's readiness for cooperative participation.

Consideration

Do not use this activity if the group has not worked together toward developing a sense of caring for one another. If there is any fooling around, chances are someone will get uncomfortably jostled or hurt, and the trust that you are trying to develop will diminish. It's much easier to lose trust than gain it; faster, too.

Trust Wave

This activity is incredibly simple. So simple, in fact, that you may decide to pass over it. Try it before you make a judgment. The challenge level is deceptively high.

Set-Up

Divide your group equally in two and form two straight lines with each player standing opposite someone from the other line. The lines should be just far enough apart so that when the player's arms are fully extended, at shoulder height and in front of them, their hands reach to approximately the wrist of the person opposite. These players are called the *spotters*.

The goal is for one player, the *runner*, to start

ten yards from the group and walk, jog or run between the two lines of people. The players in the lines raise their arms just before the runner reaches them and lower them as soon as the runner has passed by.

Ask runners to attempt to maintain the same speed throughout their runs. Slowing down is not a problem, but speeding up can be.

Safety Factors

Obviously, the spotting lines need to be extremely careful or the runner will get smacked in the face/head. Spotters need to carefully watch the runners and judge their speed. Spotters should lift their arms with sufficient time to insure that the runner is not hit. If you have doubts about your group's ability to perform the spotting role, either don't try the activity or allow walking only for the first round or until everyone seems comfortable with the task.

Allowing for a ten-yard space before the runner enters the line helps people gauge the speed and judge when to lift their arms. Don't allow players to start only 2–3 feet away, especially if they are running. The faster that runners intend to go through the lines, the farther away they should start their approach to maximize safety.

It would be appropriate to set a series of commands to indicate a runner is starting, much like with a *Trust Fall*. The runner should ask the spotting line, "Ready?" and wait for a reply before starting toward the lines.

If there are more than 10 people in the spotting lines, be sure that the spotters are all focused on the front of the line and the runner before starting. When runners have been hit, it has often been because people in the middle/end of the line did not see them coming or did not react quickly enough.

Some people experience the thrill of the *Trust Wave* to be equal to that of a *Trust Fall*. Try it and see for yourself.

Stunts

4 Sheets to the Wind

Is there a right or wrong way to fold and tear a sheet of paper?

• •

Ask your group to either put on blindfolds, or close their eyes (*Challenge By Choice*) for this exercise. The blindfolded (eyes closed) participants are not allowed to ask questions, but can talk freely among themselves.

Hand participants sheets of paper that are equal in size, and ask them to sequentially:

1) Fold the paper in half and tear off the bottom right hand corner;

2) Fold the paper in half again and tear off the upper right hand corner;

3) Fold the paper in half again and tear off the lower right hand corner.

OK, eyes open and compare the results. Just a simple exercise to emphasize how people interpret ambiguous instructions, allowing Murphy's Law full reign. Ambiguous directions produce disparate results.

If you follow the above directions, is there a right or wrong way to fold and tear the sheet of paper, Murphy notwithstanding? If you change the directions in 1, 2, and 3, above, will the results of this exercise change?

Now, line up in a circle, and face each other back-to-back…

Action/Reaction (Dollar Drop)

I forget when or where I first saw the *Dollar Drop* trick, but I was young and naive enough to bet that I could pinch the dropping dollar bill before it fell below my grasping fingers. I pinched a lot of air while trying unsuccessfully to prove I had the fastest hands alive. If you aren't familiar with this stunt, read on, because the activity itself provides good raw material for a science experiment and is also programmatically useful as a humbling experience for those who think they are soooo good.

Play

Obtain a new unfolded dollar bill (folded ones work okay, but not as well as a crisp new simolean). Ask someone to hold out his hand, palm down, so that the thumb and index finger are prehen*silly* opposed in pincer-like fashion. Then you hold a dollar bill so that it is suspended to about half its length between the volunteer's thumb and index finger. There has to be *at least* a one quarter-inch space between the catcher's thumb and finger at the start. Tell the challenged person that he may

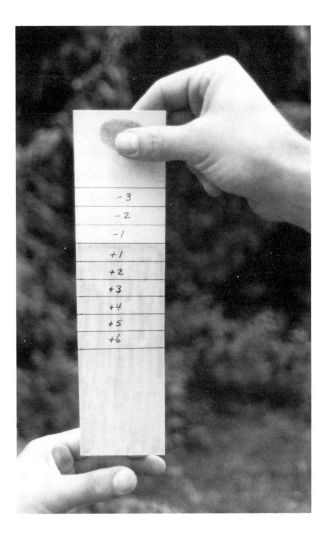

keep the dollar if he can pinch it before it falls below his fingers (just pinching — no dropping or scooping motions with the hand allowed). Not many individuals have the reaction time to make that kind of rapid psychomotor movement, but be prepared to occasionally lose a buck or two, because there's always one or two of those genetic quick-twitch, muscle-mass people around that make us all look like we're standing still.

If you would rather not risk any loss of the folding green, and make the experiment more scientific; i.e., wimpy, substitute a half sheet of paper for the dollar. Before you start the *drop-and-grab* sequence, mark the length of paper (top to bottom) in half-inch gradations so you can estimate and measure the reaction time of different people. Start with the bottom of the paper just between the fingers. Don't allow any anticipatory sounds or movements. For example, don't say, "…ready, set, GO." Have lots of measured sheets available so that players can operate in pairs or troikas.

Offer sleazy plastic trophies for the consistently faster people so that their superior and cocky demeanor is further encouraged and made less tolerable. This will alienate them from the majority of slower students, causing them to seem even more obnoxious. A milk/cream scenario finalizes, with the elite performers separating from the slower, less adept players until two separate *Dollar Drop* leagues are formed, resulting in a windfall for the trophy manufacturing cartel.

The Bends

ker

This simple activity is much like *Squat Thrust* (*Silver Bullets*, pg. 94), a competitive one-on-one contest that can be easily repeated over and over. Use this mini-contest as a means of warming up the group and of encouraging unselfconscious touch. Emphasize the fun aspect, and downplay the importance of having to win.

Play

Shake hands with your partner and hold that grip. With your free left hand, reach behind you and grab your uplifted left foot. From this somewhat encumbered, paired position, the object is to try to make your partner lose her balance and release her foot. Jousts are usually over in a hurry, allowing players to engage in multiple contests.

Do not allow these jousts to occur on concrete or any other hard, abrasive surface, as falls are possible. *Wait!* Before you stop reading, consider the programmatic usefulness and inherent safety of the handshake grip. If that grip is maintained, even if one of the players looses his balance, the more balanced partner can prevent a fall by continued support with that gripping hand; a bit of physical *noblesse oblige*, but welcomed nonetheless.

In keeping with this player-helping-player concept, use these contests to encourage the practice of *compassionate competition*; i.e., being able to play hard, but concurrently caring enough about your partner, that efforts to win are tempered by a concern for safety. For example, in the contest above, after it's obvious that you have pushed or pulled your partner off balance, it's not necessary or indicated to continue applying force until the person is thrown to the ground. The ideal win is to initiate an obvious loss of balance, then keep your contest partner from falling down by continuing to provide hand support.

An Aside

I just finished reading an editorial in *Time* magazine by a social psychologist who attempted to point out the devastating and far-reaching social aspects of excessive and gratuitous violence in the media that is available for viewing by young people, and how that relates to the increased physical mayhem in school sports — the type of coached violence that is specifically taught to increase the chances of winning. Athletes are often instructed to "take out" someone on another team, meaning injure them to the extent that they cannot continue to "play." To further compound the mixed-role message that a student receives, gender issues are used to skew young athlete's views of why they participate in sports and of their individual roles, not only in sports, but in day-to-day relationships. To change these views, a new way of relating to one another (not just in a competitive sense) must be taught in a way that is acceptable and *enjoyable* to the student audience.

Comet Ball Boccie ker

Every time I visit my *old* friend Adrian Kissler in California, I know that we will eventually play a game of *Backyard Boccie* at his place. The game simply involves tossing a golf ball (the Jack) somewhere in Ade's backyard venue, then, using two boccie balls apiece, trying to toss your two balls closer to the golf ball than anyone else. Competitive? Correct! If you're interested, the scoring goes like this:

- One point for the closest boccie ball to the golfball;

- Three points if both of your balls are closer than any other competitors;

- An additional five points if your boccie ball makes contact with the golfball, notwithstanding where it ends up.

Rules

Additional rules that make the game different:

Whoever picks the "hole" gets to suggest bizarro rules of their choice for that particular round (not *scoring* rules, *playing* rules).

Examples:

- Requiring that the boccie ball must bounce off a specified object before reaching scoring position;

- Throwing the boccie ball with your non-dominant arm;

- Requiring that the boccie ball reach at least a 10' apogee before becoming a legal throw.

Straight-up *Backyard Boccie* can get old, so don't pass up the opportunity to choose some aberrant rules.

Great stuff! I always look forward to a game of knock-your-socks-off *Backyard Boccie* at Adrian's not-so-manicured backyard. Regulation boccie balls are expensive, so try to get hold of a set of croquet balls (someone always seems to be throwing away a mismatched set). But *Backyard Boccie* isn't what I'm telling you about — look at the title above!

More Play

Give each person in your playing group a *Comet Ball* (tennis ball stuck in the end of a knee-high woman's sock) and use a Frisbee of some kind in place of the golf ball above. The rules and scoring are the same as *Backyard Boccie* (that means read what I suggested, then do whatever you want), but the action is wilder and over a greater distance — so don't play in your backyard, unless your backyard is a lot bigger than mine.

If you have never played with *Comet Balls* check out pg. 25 in *Silver Bullets* or pgs. 69–69 in *The Bottomless Bag Again*!?

Try to use colored pantyhose socks for the *Comet Balls* so that players can tell their balls from one another. Vary the playing area and distances, and tweak the rules occasionally to maintain interest (over the shoulder throws without looking, arcing throws over a water hazard, mandatory 360° turns before release, etc.).

Comet-ose (Organized Serendipitous Entropy)

Comet Ball is a new and fascinating experience for most folks.

· ·

Comet Balls are great fun to play with for no reason other than the enjoyment of twirling and throwing. I use them after a program break or after lunch to encourage participants to re-involve themselves with the curriculum in an enjoyable and unstructured way. Twirling and launching a *Comet Ball* is a new and fascinating experience for most folks, and provides an enjoyable something that's hard to identify; perhaps a 20+ years revisitation of spontaneous fun and play.

As people return from lunch break and observe their peers twirling and launching comet-like projectiles, they become playfully and unselfconsciously reinvolved because there's no one to tell them not to. In addition, listen-

ing to the exclamations of surprise and delight, coupled with the highly visual arcing flights of these centrifugally propelled knee-high/tennis ball combos, is enough to attract even those players most saturated with luncheon fare. Before long, everyone is twirling and throwing *Comet Balls* with various degrees of expertise, but an equally high level of enthusiasm.

Someday, I'd like to encourage a group to keep throwing and catching until they didn't want to, but I've always succumbed to the workshop responsibility of moving on; leave 'em laughing is best I guess. Part of that moving on is suggesting programmatic ways to use *Comet Balls* other than just launching them willy-nilly in an open area.

One game, previously outlined, involves splitting up into two teams and throwing the *Comet Balls* en masse back and forth between teams, counting the proper tail catches each time and recording scores if that seems appropriate. Not a bad way to spend a few innings together, also providing a nice lead up to the following spontaneously generated game. (Created about two hours ago as the result of a *it's cold and snowy and I'm bored* conversation with Steve. I wrote this piece last winter.

Play

Divide your group in half again using one of the Category topics (...do you lick your ice cream cone clockwise or counterclockwise?) and give each team *Comet Balls* to equal the number of people on the team. Both teams then meet at the center of a football or soccer pitch. On a signal, one team heads for one goal line, and the other team heads for the opposite goal.

The object is to get as many team members over the goal line as possible in the least amount of time. The only way to make forward progress is to catch a thrown ball.

The final team score is determined by measuring the time it takes all players on a team to cross the goal line, then adding 5 seconds for each ball missed during the various throwing attempts.

Rules

- A ball must be twirled and launched *Comet Ball* style to count as being thrown; a 15-foot minimum apogee is considered acceptably sporting.

- A proper catch involves grabbing ONLY the tail of the ball. Not on the bounce, please!

- A missed ball must be thrown again from the same launching spot, however, catchers (anyone on the team can catch the ball) can stand where ever they like after a miss.

Connect the Dots, and Then...

The Ole Nine Dot problem...

As long as facilitators have been emphasizing the educational and corporate benefits of lateral vs. vertical thinking, the ole Nine Dot problem is regularly dredged up from the files of neat and proper insights. If you don't know the answer to this next problem, you haven't been *facilitating* enough lately. Here's the problem and the solution; hardly profound, but occasionally useful. Considering its well-known solution, the only reason I'm including it here is to pass along an embellishment to the problem that seems worth sharing.

The task is to connect all nine dots with four straight, continuous lines without taking the pen or pencil from the paper, and without retracing a line. The solution is as indicated,

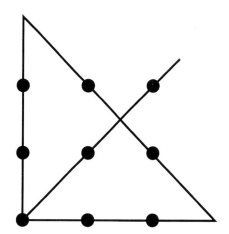

emphasizing that a pre-existing mental set about parameters could inhibit that type of boundary-breaking thought process necessary to solve the problem. People who consider extending the line as cheating are probably those who, as children, always colored within the lines.

Expand the problem by asking a group to connect all nine dots with only three straight lines. The solution is easier to visualize if you make the dots bigger, as below.

Now ask if all nine dots can be connected with one straight line. One solution involves folding the paper so that the three lines of dots align to one another. A single wide pencil line will connect them all.

But the magnum answer that appeals most to me requires that you dip a 4" wide paint brush into some fire-engine-red latex and swipe it fully across all the dots, effectively obliterating and connecting them.

Call this

THE BIG RED LINE

solution.

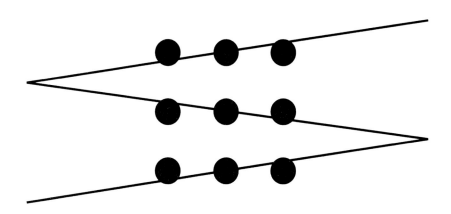

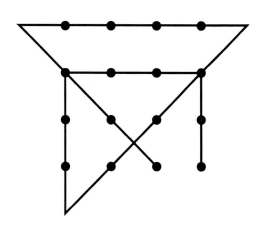

Now add seven more dots to your original nine dot set up for a total of sixteen evenly spaced dots. This time the problem is to connect all sixteen dots with six straight continuous lines.

Does the Big Red Line solution apply here also? Again, generously dip that brush in red, and as Van Gogh so aptly stated, "Dots, what dots?" (Maybe it was Renoir...)

This is another good cerebral activity to include in a *Mastemind Relay.*

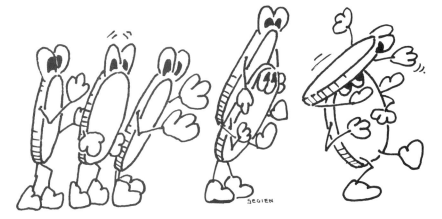

Dimes and Nickels

An old nickel and dime parlor game...

• •

You remember the Initiative problem *2x4*, right? I don't know whether you realize it, but *2x4* came from an old nickel and dime parlor game. I just substituted sexes for denominations and came up with what seemed to be a new people problem. (It's written up in *Silver Bullets*, pg. 123.) Here're two more usable coin-cum-people problems to tickle your initiative and reduce the amount of change in your pocket.

Column Right

Distribute 8 nickels (male participants), and 8 pennies (female participants) as shown in the illustration. The puzzle is to move only two coins (players) so that the resulting coins (participants) will be arranged in columns consisting entirely of pennies (females) or nickels (males); i.e., the first column will be all males, the second column will be all females, etc.

If you don't have enough males or females to fill the columns, ask the participants to hold something obvious that designates them as part of a distinct group of eight. Examples: Rubber ring, rubber chicken, rubber ducky (I'm into rubber products), funny hat, head bands...

King Me!

Arrange ten pennies (people) in a row. If you need an illustration, draw ten little penny-circles in a line — thanks, saves me from having to do it and allows more rhetorical room.

The coinological conundrum is to pick up a penny, jump two adjacent pennies and make a king of that jumped-on penny — two pennies on top of one another; you know, like in checkers. You should have an inkling about what's coming next. Right... substitute people for pennies. So when you make a king, as above, the moving player has to be held off the floor piggy-back style until the problem is completed. (Suggested consequence — if a piggy-back twosome can't maintain their top-to-bottom juxtaposition, the whole group has to begin again.)

You can jump to the right and you can jump to the left. When you jump over a king (piggy-back pair), consider that as jumping two. The jumping and kinging continues until there are 5 kings. Done.

I found the germ for these two coin puzzles in a small book (copyright 1946) that I purchased in Dandenong, Australia. When I asked the store clerk, "How much?" she replied, "10¢." I asked her if she wouldn't mind taking 20¢ (there's no 25¢ Aussie coin), and we both parted happy.

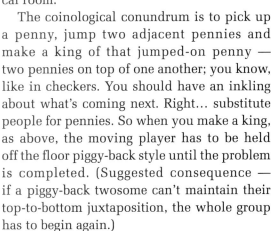

Fractured Aphorisms

Here's a cute word game that I think would be particularly applicable to the elementary grades, and could be presented as either an individual or group challenge.

Did I ever tell you that I used to teach 6th grade? Well, I did (four years), both in the classroom (Avalon Elementary School on Catalina Island, Calif.) and as an outdoor education teacher, also in California. Good, valuable learning years that I think of and occupationally refer to quite often.

What's your favorite aphorism (proverb)? I particularly like, "A king unlettered is a donkey crowned." but that isn't a good proverb to use for this activity, because it should be a maxim that's well worn, almost a cliché. Try, "A bird in the hand is worth two in the bush." You remember that one, right? Type it out like this, Abirdinthehandisworthtwointhebush.

(As an aside — If you have a word processor or typewriter handy, and you use one regularly, try to type the aphorism, as above, without hitting the space bar at least once. Surprisingly difficult, eh?)

Now split that long line of letters up to look like this,

Abir dinthe ha ndis wort htwo int heb ush,

and present this apparently foreign mish-mash of syllables as just what it is, a famous proverb. It's up to the group to try and figure out what the proverb is by correctly reassociating the letters, because they can't start the next one, *Ifit swor thdoi ngi tswor tho verd oing*, until they do.

Note that I used different fonts to highlight the appropriate words. That font's for you, don't make it so easy for your students.

Knee Slap

Our group decided to invite the Soviets to join us.

• •

I'm up at Dartmouth's Mt. Moosilauke Lodge in New Hampshire doing my annual game and Initiative thing for the BIG GREEN. About 15 exchange students from the University of Moscow (right, the old USSR Moscow; kind of dates this activity, eh?) are there doing something else. Just before starting the games workshop, our group decided to invite the Soviets to join us, and they did for the morning session. It proved to be a good decision. They spoke very little English and we spoke even less Russian, but language barriers are easily overcome by play. During that AM games session, one of the Soviet women demonstrated the following knee-slapper activity that I think your students will enjoy as much as we did at the time.

Play

Sit in a circle, close enough to one another so that everyone is literally sitting hip-to-hip — you don't have to announce that particular juxtaposition, just keep skootching toward the center of the circle until everyone's *tight*. Ask playes to extend their arms to the front, palms down, then spread both arms about 12" to the side, right and left, also indicating that it's OK if their arms cross with those of the people next to them; can't help but cross actually.

Without hesitating (don't give the participants a chance to figure out what's going on) ask them to lower their arms, indicating that

all hands should end up on someone else's knee, or some such socially acceptable anatomical area — watch it, there's not much leeway there. (Pay particular heed to the old adage, "Toes to toes, your nose is in it, nose to nose your toes is in it.") As you look at your hands and the hands of the people next to you, it's a bit of a mix-up to tell whose hand is whose, wherein lies the crux, confusion and joy of what's to come.

Because of reduced forward flexibility, you might find that for some individuals, sitting circled as above might vary from painful to impossible. If complaints are reducing the fun or spontaneity of the exercise, ask everyone to stand and assume the hands-on-knees posture. This is certainly not as relaxed a position, and it's kind of hard to see what's going on, but considering what you are attempting, that's not so bad either. One way or the other, you're there, so go for it.

As leader, begin a hand-slap-of-the-knee sequence by simply and compassionately slapping the knee of the person to your right or left. Then, continue the hand-knee slap from person to person, *trying to do so without slapping out of sequence.* Try to go faster and faster. Try not to laugh.

Announce that if anyone to your right makes a sequence mistake, you will immediately restart the sequence to your left, continuing this right/left alternation until either Team A or Team B, WINS.

Start the knee slap in both directions at the same time to see which team returns the slap sequence back to you the fastest. The action can become chaotic — which is as it should be.

Knee Slap is a great example of how you can have some ludicrous fun with head-to-head (knee-to-knee in this case) competition. DO NOT let all this free-wheeling fun turn into a typical win/lose situation. Remember, you are facilitating results, not coaching.

 # Magic

Things like the following numbers trick fascinate me.

• •

I used to have bad dreams about arithmetic, algebra, geometry, etc., when I was in high school, and the dreams were justified because I *always* did badly in classes that had anything to do with numbers. I assume that's why things like the following numbers trick fascinates me. I don't understand how the trick could possibly work, so it's like magic; I'm an easy mark when it comes to numbers and calculations.

Take your house number and double it (my house number is nine, so we're looking at 18) and add five (I can do that: 23).

Multiply that number by half a hundred (50 x 23 = 1150; I had to use a calculator).

Add your age (Wow, this problem is timeless; that's 1150+55 = 1205).

Now add the number of days in a year (1205 + 365 = 1570).

Then subtract 615 (1570 – 615 = 955).

The last two figures of that answer will be your age (55) and the first numeral (9) is your house number. I can't stand it, they're right again.

Numbers Game Variation

If you like this kind of thing, this next one is going to blow you away.

Pick any number from 2 to 9.

Then multiply that number by 9. That will give you a two-digit number. For example, the number three is picked; 3 multiplied by 9 = 27.

Add the two digits of the answer together: 2+7 = 9. The answer will always be 9.

Subtract five from that answer: 9 – 5 = 4. The answer is always 4.

Take the answer 4, and count down that many letters in the alphabet: A-B-C-**D**. D is always the answer. Then think of a European country that starts with that letter. The answer is usually *Denmark*.

Go to the next letter in the alphabet (E). Think of a circus animal that starts with that letter — probably an *elephant*.

Think of the color of that animal: *Gray*.

Final statement by the facilitator: "I would guess that your gray elephant is from Denmark."

This sequence was passed along by Project Adventure workshop participant Lewis Goff.

Mission Impossible

I like this game because it does not fit into a workshop format and is not particularly useful in a school setting; it's just fun to do. Paul Seitz invented the game and was generous enough to share. This is his write-up.

Mission Impossible takes its name from the old TV series, and is simply a game of honor and good-natured daring among friends. The object of the game is to dare friends (includes accepting dares yourself, of course) to practice random acts of kindness, joviality and silliness. The interesting part is that because of the way the game is played, you may never know whether your dare is accepted, and only your own personal sense of honor and integrity and your willingness to rise to a silly challenge will determine whether you choose to accept someone else's dare.

What makes this game unique is that it is played via the space age wonder of answering machines (or voice mail, for you push button hipsters).

Play

First call up a friend's answering machine. Start your message by humming the *Mission Impossible* theme song for a few seconds. Then announce, in your best espionage voice, the following secret message:

"Good day _____ (insert friend's name here). By listening to this message you have just entered the world of *Mission Impossible*. The message that you are about to receive is classified, and is for your ears only (turn off the speaker phone). Your mission _____ (friend's name), should you choose to accept it, is to _____ (fill in the blank with your dare). Unfortunately this message will not self destruct in 15 seconds because of an MCI/ATT optic fiber chiasma."

Then hang up, your dare is done. Dares can be simple or complex, and should be fun and safe.

Examples of good dares:

- Spontaneously hug someone today.

- Go skinny dipping by month's end. (Depending upon the time of year, this dare can be very challenging.)

- Tell the same joke three times to three different strangers.

- Do 1,000 push-ups in the next 30 days.

- Look out one of the windows at your house (your choice) for 10 minutes each day for a week.

- The next time you are driving on a freeway, and there are no cars nearby, scream as loud and as long as you can (Watch the road!).

My Favorite Tangram

Nothing fancy,
just a Tangram I remember
from years ago.

• •

This one baffled me as an adolescent when it appeared in *Boy's Life* magazine. It recently slowed me down again when I rediscovered it in a modern book of puzzles. The object is to make a *perfect* T using all four tangram pieces. Salvador Dali-like *T's* don't count

Photocopy the *Tangram* and snip out the four pieces with a scissors, and without looking at the answer (next page), see how long it takes you to come up with the T. If it takes you less than two minutes, you're not my friend anymore.

Onion Jousting

I learned this game
in central Siberia from
a group of Russian students.

• •

It just goes to show that people love to play all over il mundo. This is a cool stunt because it's bizarre — an odd pair of props, a limited boundary and deceptive action.

Play

Mark off a circular boundary that's about four feet in diameter. Find two participants. Give each person two spoons (soup spoons or large serving spoons may help younger players) and an onion that will rest comfortably in one of the spoons (no onions so large that they topple out at the slightest movement).

Indicate to players that they must place their onion in one spoon then hold that spoon by the handle only; they may not touch the onion. They should hold the empty spoon in their opposite hand. Once both players have the onion positioned and the spoons properly in hand, let the joust begin.

Players attempt to knock their opponent's onion to the ground by smacking the spoon holding it with their empty spoon. Neither player may step outside of the boundary at any time once the contest begins. Players are strongly encouraged to avoid smacking their opponent on the wrist, arm, fingers or any other extremity with their spoon — IT HURTS!

No excessive bodily contact is allowed — no pushing, shoving, tackling, tickling or foot stomping.

Use a rectangular cut section of ethafoam or a crow feather instead of another spoon as the "onion whacker" in order to avoid overzealous attacks and diminished trust.

The well-played joust resembles a dance as players twist, bob, weave, bend, gyrate and contort themselves to avoid the thud of their onion falling to the turf. It's beautiful in an odd way, and quite a bit of fun as well.

To up the ante a wee bit, substitute eggs for the onions. Just kidding... or am I?

Remember Gooney?

Gooney likes the moon but he doesn't like the stars.

Why? Who cares? Well... considering that you *do* care, Gooney likes the moon because there are two identical letters adjacent to one another in the word *moon*. So... Gooney likes the color ye*ll*ow, but doesn't like red, or blue for that matter. And, in a blatant show of egotism, Gooney likes himself.

This can go on and on, and usually does because it takes most people a long time to figure out why Gooney likes this and doesn't like that. Gooney likes... is an interesting "back pocket" activity that subtly indicates how solutions often depend upon a shift from vertical to lateral thinking. If you liked Gooney... you will probably like these variations on a theme.

Variations

Matt likes the color orange but not purple. He likes torches but not chandeliers. He eats berries but not fruits. Following this line of thinking, does Matt like the poet Byron or Keats?

He only likes words that begin with two letter words: orange, torches, berries — Byron.

Betsy likes khaki but not brown; she likes rendezvous but not meetings; she likes mousses but not jellies. Does she like jodhpurs or riding pants?

Betsy likes jodhpurs because she's presumptuous, ostentatiously peppering her English conversation with foreign words.

Kurt likes sequoia trees but not evergreens. He doesn't want either, but would rather suffer from pneumonia than influenza, and he jokes about this facetiously but not humorously. Would he rather buy presents stingily or abstemiously?

Kurt likes any word that has all five vowels in it.

Kali likes knights but not ruffians; she likes writing but not calligraphy; she likes to listen but not to sing. Would she rather read an unknown or famous author?

Definitely the unknown author, because k is a silent letter in that word. Kali likes any word that displays a silent letter.

Answer to *My Favorite Tangram*

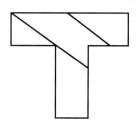

The Spandex Spectacular

ker

If it's good in small quantities, heaps of it must be better.

• •

The only Spandex I ever had direct contact with was the skimpy swimsuit I reluctantly wore in a master's swim meet. As a result of this morphological display (nothing is hidden) I surmised that Spandex (Lycra) was used in small amounts only, but in keeping with the Adventure premise that if it's good in small quantities, heaps of it must be better, we tried fooling around with copious amounts.

Recognizing that we needed larger pieces than a micro swimsuit provided, I made my way down to So-Fro Fabrics (one of those gender stores that males seldom frequent) and asked for some Spandex. I was predictably shown some skimpy pieces by a skeptical, older sales lady, who I'm sure thought I had immoral and/or indecent uses in mind. When I told her that I wanted YARDS of the material, she became a bit more tolerant of my being in her shop, but never curious; at least she didn't let on. Anyway, I found a couple bolts (that's fabric shop talk for lots of material) of neon Spandex — green and pink — that was on sale at half price. I'm sure the sale resulted because of the knock-your-socks-off blazing neon colors, but it was just what I was looking for and at $4.00/yd. — how can you go wrong? Even if I hadn't needed any, at that price I had to buy some. Wouldn't you?

Gloree (my talented wife) sewed the ends together with a double lock stitch (I hope that means something to you), which proved to be a solid connector for the considerable abuse that this fabric was soon to bear.

At the next training workshop, festooned with yards of stretchy, obscenely bright, sexy fabric, I was sartorially resplendent and very conspicuous. More succinctly, I was hard to ignore, a veritable pedagogic curiosity that captured the participant's attention, like it or not. Once the fabric loops were presented for use, anyone with a dollop of play potential knew what to do. Playing with this stuff is definitely *funn* and offbeat enough to attract the most jaded juvenile.

If you get inside the loop with 3–8 other people, and lean back against the encircling fabric, you find that a yurt circle type support band is achieved, as players rely on one another to achieve a literally layed-back balanced position. *A synergistic antipodal balance is achieved and maintained through the paradox of group dependence vs. individual expression.* (Just a bit of BS for those of you who expect or need it.)

Play Ideas

- Ask your large group to fill the interior of a small Spandex loop with themselves and then move somewhere together.

- Half of the group on the outside of the Spandex circle leans in, and half the group on the inside of the circle leans out, producing equilibrium and a balanced standing position for everyone — *you wish!*

- Ask four risk-takers, who also happen to be fleet of foot and don't mind occasional body contact, to locate themselves (north, east, south, west) inside a large Spandex circle and lean back against the material. North and south then rapidly change positions, whilst east and west hold their geography. As soon as N and S change, then E and W change, while N and S maintain position. Sound confusing? Wait until you see it in action. There isn't much time to think, so remember to pass only on the right.

- Try levitating a person who is laying in the folds of the Spandex. Put lots of lifters on the material. Include some swaying and a bit of gentle bouncing.

- Put a large playball inside the loop and holding the other end, spin the ball in a large arc (like a hammer thrower). The object, beyond getting dizzy, is to see if other group members can get in and tag you (*Count Coup!*) without getting slammed by the ball. Folks who like the game *Bombardment* seem to like the action associated with this spinning frolic.

- Stretch the fabric between some people and then thrust your face and hands forcefully against the fabric. Make sure you have some observers on the far side; otherwise, what's the use?

Just for a change of pace...

• •

These tricks and stunts are usable from time-to-time on a rainy day when the group needs a break from "meaningful activities" or just for a change of pace. And if you really need a reason for being tricky, make up a supportive sentence from the following list of positive power words:

- challenge
- self-esteem
- interpersonal relationships
- motivation
- positive self-image
- imagination
- attitude
- expanded satisfaction
- unanimous acceptance
- creativity
- psycho-social objectives
- enhanced self-confidence
- joy

Think of BS in this context as brainstorming and go for it.

Please note the innovative nomenclature system employed for categorizing the following activities.

Trick Question #1

This query is based on fact. An alphabet soup manufacturer would only put the following letters into their product:

AFEIHMLKNVTZWVXY

Why?

Trick Question #2

Lenny always has it before. Paul takes it behind. Bryan has never had it at all. Girls can only have it once. Boys don't need it. Mrs. Mulligan has it twice in succession. Dr. Lowell of Harvard has it twice as bad at the end as at the beginning.

What do these folks have, or not have, in common?

Trick Question #3

There's only one way to drop an egg from a height of six feet without breaking it. How?

Trick Question #4

Where have you seen the letters KOKEN before?

Trick Question #5

What letters logically follow this sequence?

L A K W F _ _ _

If you figure out the sequencing above, completing the following list will offer no problem.

B D J Q P _ _ _

Trick Question #6

You throw away the outside and cook the inside. Then you eat the outside and throw away the inside. What are you eating?

• •

Trick #1

Put a table-cloth on a regular dining table. Rest a champagne glass on top of two nickels so that the circumference of the glass base passes through the center of the two nickels. Before placing the glass on the nickels, place a dime on the table-cloth so that it is located equally spaced between the two nickels and directly under the center of the glass.

Conundrum — How can you get the dime out from beneath the glass without touching the glass or the nickels, and without blowing on the dime? Travesty regulations prevent use of toothpicks, matches or the like for poking the coin out.

Trick #2

Arrange six matches or toothpicks like this: (keep sheet for drawings)

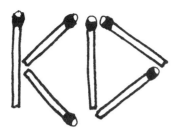

How can you move three of the matches to make eight equilateral triangles?

Trick #3

Place a beer bottle (or the like) upside down on top of a sheet of typing paper. Can you remove the sheet of paper without touching the bottle or knocking it over?

Trick #4

Lay out 15 similar objects in a row (matchsticks, balls, pencils). You may take 1 to 3 objects per turn, and your opponent may do the same. The object is not to get stuck with the last match.

Trick #5

Try to place five pennies in such a way that each coin makes physical contact with the other four coins.

• •

Trick Answers

Trick Question Answers:

Trick Q. #1 — The manufacturer's machine could not make letters with curved lines. All the listed letters have only straight lines.

Trick Q. #2 — The letter **L**

Trick Q. #3 — Drop the egg 6'1"

Trick Q. #4 — The word KOKEN appears in large letters on the foot-rest of most barber chairs.

Trick Q. #5 — a) Any letters that have straight lines. b) Any letters with curved lines.

Trick Q. Ans. #6 — Corn on the Cob

Trick Answers:

Trick Ans. #1 — Scratch the tablecloth with your fingernail just beyond the circumference of the glass and the coin will "dance" its way out.

Trick Ans. #2 —

Trick Ans. #3 — Begin to carefully roll up one end of the piece of paper. When the roll gets to the bottle, it will gently support the bottle while the remainder of the paper is rolled out from underneath.

Trick Ans. #4 — Make sure that you take the 10th item, and you will win every time.

Trick Ans. #5 —

Tricky Triangles

The object of this sit-down Initiative is, with a team of troikas (groups of three), to find the maximum number of small triangles within the larger triangles.

1. The star within a pentagram has 35 separate triangles.
2. The equilaterally stacked triangles represent 47 individual triangles.

Remember, although it's satisfying to come up with a correct answer, the group process (communication, cooperation, sharing, listening, etc.) that occurs along the way, is the *raison d'être*.

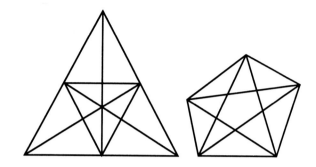

Twirlies

I'm sure these things have a commercial name or two or three, but I call them *Twirlies*, because that's what they are. I've played with them occasionally over the years (they always seem to be available at craft fairs for exorbitant prices), but never paid much attention to their play potential until I bought a few at Victoria Market in Melbourne. I'm not sure why I bought them — the price was probably right — but I'm glad that I did because workshop participants love them.

Timing their use is important, and the right time is right away. When people show up for a workshop and are standing around trying to make small talk and not drink a fourth cup of coffee, bring out the *Twirlies* and launch a couple skyward. Seeing how easy they are to use and how visually gratifying their short flights are, hands-on people can't wait to give them a spin, and even the "We cool" folks that hang on the periphery of participation usually give a *Twirlie* a spin.

Spinning a few of these IFOs (Identified Flying Objects) towards a self-conscious group of workshop participants gives them something attractive to try until the "real" program starts. Spinning a *Twirlie* isn't "all thrill, no skill," but it's close.

A *Twirlie* is simply a small propeller (plastic or wood) fixed to the end of a six-inch long, small-diameter dowel. When you spin the dowel rapidly between your palms, the entire device will helicopter its way up to 25', *IF* you spin the dowel in a counterclockwise direction. Otherwise (clockwise), the spinning propeller will try to eat your knuckles — experiential education at its best.

Using *Twirlies* is kind of like using *Comet Balls*; people like them because they like them, but if you need a game or some goal-setting (sigh), here's an idea or two.

Play Ideas

- Use the *Twirlies* to play a form of Frisbee golf; i.e., spin the *Twirlies* toward an agreed upon goal (tree, garbage can, Rolls Royce) and count the number of turns necessary to hit your target. (NOT turns of the propeller blade; come on, be serious.) Any number of people can play, but have larger groups operate in foursomes (that's golf talk for four consenting players).

- Have two players face one another, each with a *Twirlie*, and about 10 feet apart. See how many double catches can be made by the two players twirling simultaneously. Or use one *Twirlie* between the two, and after a successful twirl-and-catch sequence, ask each player to back up one large step. Continue until one of the players misses catching the approaching *Twirlie*. The measured distance between the two players at maximum is their paired PB (personal best).

- Spin a *Twirlie* between your partner's legs from about 10-15 feet away. Although *Twirlies* are largely innocuous, a rapidly spinning propeller can cause some discomfort if the tip of a blade strikes a sensitive part of your anatomy.

- Spin for height. Who can spin their *Twirlie* the highest? *Twirlie* performance can be altered (improved?) by adjusting the pitch of the blades. Inadvertently stepping on the blade of a *Twirlie* causes profound and irreversible aerodynamic trauma — it don't fly too good after that.

Consideration

DO NOT ALLOW A PLAYER TO SPIN HIS/ HER TWIRLIE DIRECTLY INTO THE FACE OF ANOTHER PLAYER — facial contact with the spinning blade hurts and could cause eye injury. Contact with arms, body, etc., is no big deal. I have only used this toy with adult groups, so you will have to judge its useability with your own participant population.

Twirlies cause people to talk to one another. ("How do you make this thing go?" "Hey, see if you can catch mine." "Where can you buy these?") Don't underestimate their ice-breaking potential. Older folks like them, I suspect young people would too. But don't ask for *Twirlies* at the store because *Twirlies* is a name I made up. Just explain what you want, and if it's a halfway decent store, the clerk will either have them in stock or tell you where to look for them.

Most commercial *Twirlies* break down easily (come apart) after use, facilitating storage in your game bag. I'd suggest having at least one for every two anticipated players.

Up Nelson

Mark Collard taught me this game, so he obviously didn't name it after himself. It's a good game for the right place and the right time.

Set-Up

You need a longish table (the picnic type or the ones used in a school cafeteria) so that at least eight people can sit down facing one another — four on a side. Do you get the feeling that eight people facing one another across a table is going to lead to a competitive confrontation? You're right! Here's how to play.

One team (four people) is given a quarter, or a coin of equal size. With their hands and arms below the level of the table top, they must pass (or not pass) the coin to another team member so that the people on the other side of the table have no idea who has the coin. This mano-a-mano manipulation of the coin is considered preparation time — allow 20 seconds.

Someone on the other side of the table is designated as Captain (this is a temporary title, so don't get upset if you're not the Captain). If someone says, "I want to be Captain," let 'em be Captain; it's obviously important to them.

Play

The team with the coin responds *only* to the Captain's command of, "Up Nelson." When they hear, "Up Nelson" from the Captain, all four players simultaneously bring their clenched fists above the table and slam their elbows onto the table top (don't hurt yourself). Anyone on the other team, including the Captain, can then say, "Down Nelson," at which point the team with the coin attempts to slap their palms down onto the table top as simultaneously as possible, to hide the sound of the coin hitting the wood, Formica, etc.

If anyone on the coin team brings his hands above the level of the table as the result of responding to someone other than the Captain saying, "Up Nelson," the team in possession automatically loses control of the coin to the other team. This rule is obviously included to allow a bit of gamesmanship to hold sway.

As the searching team carefully studies the eight palms-down hands in front of them, they are allowed to ask the hiders to, "move (squiggle) your hands, right, left, away or towards." Then, anyone on the searching team can touch any of the hiding hands, at which juncture the touched hand must go "belly up" (palm up). If the coin is revealed before the last hand is reached, the searching team wins. If the last hand picked has the coin, the hiding team wins — then it's time for another round of *Up Nelson*.

This is basically a role-playing, histrionic, sneaky game. This is not a game to play seriously or take seriously. Get into the action and try to take advantage of the other team — as fairly as possible.

Yurt Rope

ker

A simplistic variation of *The Yurt Circle*...

• •

PA facilitators and many folks who have read *Cowstails & Cobras*, use an activity called *The Yurt Circle* to instigate cooperation without having to verbalize how or why cooperation makes things happen efficiently and in a more satisfying way. This simplistic variation of *The Yurt Circle* can be accomplished in- or outdoors by practically any sized group.

Set-Up

Obtain a length of substantial diameter rope. The length needed depends upon the size of your group. A 110-foot section is a good length for most groups up to 50 participants. The rope diameter should be *at least* 5/8", and be constructed of synthetic fiber. Do not try out a connecting knot that you aren't sure of (a bowline bend is the best), and don't use a section of clothesline, manila or sisal rope.

Play

Simply ask all the members of the group to stand on the outside of the rope circle and pick up the rope. Indicate that all participants should spread their legs to about shoulder width and begin leaning back against the rope, slowly bending their legs until everyone makes posterior contact with the grass at about the same time. After congratulating each other on such a coordinated series of two-point landings, ask the group to try and stand together.

If everyone tries to coordinate their own effort with that of the group, leaning and shifting their weight and pulling force in such a way as to maintain equilibrium, the entire group will stand together and perhaps experience that sense of *team* that comes from jointly accomplishing a feat.

Try sitting, then standing (take one step to the right), then sitting, then standing (take one step to the left).

Have the group count off 1–2, 1–2 and then begin a series of piston-like alternating up and down movements as above.

Closing/Framing

Closings

Here are a few simple closing activities that were recorded by Rudy Pucel after a brainstorming workshop in Wheatridge, CO.

Two Strokes and a Wish — State two positives about yourself and a wish based on something that happened during the workshop.

Key Words — Everyone in the workshop brainstorms a list of key words that describe their experience.

Back Writer — Ask everyone to find a willing someone, then pin a piece of paper to that person's back. Everyone, armed with a felt-tip pen, then walks around and writes a brief message on the backs of those people who impacted them in some *positive* way.

Gift Giving — Provide a different bandana (or some appropriate, inexpensive gift) for everyone in the group. Everyone picks the bandana they like, then gives it to someone else.

Connectedness — Tie a figure eight loop in the belay rope used for the *Pamper Pole* for each individual in the group (or some other activity where *all* of the people participated). Then provide a carabiner for each person, and as they attach their crab to the knot, ask them to state how they feel connected to the other people. (Use locking crabs so the participants feel safe. In case you haven't figured me out yet — that's facetious, son, I say *fa sea chus*.)

Verbal Gift Giving — Pick a person in your group and state a positive characteristic, attribute or trait about that person.

You Fill Me Up — Provide one full, clear-glass water pitcher and one empty pitcher. As participants pour water into the receiving pitcher, they state the ingredient they added to the group and would like the other participants

to take away. After everyone has contributed, stir the water gently and ask everyone to pour a small drink into a provided glass. As leader, provide an appropriate toast, and ask everyone to raise their glasses in good fellowship.

Web of Appreciation — Using a ball of string, construct a web of appreciation. Hang onto the end of the string and toss the ball to someone else in the group. State something you appreciate about that person. The receiving person does the same until everyone in the group has become part of the web. The resulting web symbolizes the connectedness of the group, the available support, the trust factor, the love...

Use a pair of sharp scissors to eventually cut the connecting strings, symbolizing that we must all return to our own lives, but that what was once connected can become so again. Cutting the string can be a very poignant moment, a sad but realistic commentary of our changing lives.

Dull scissors substantially reduce the effectiveness of this exercise.

Creative Heraldry

This exercise has been around for a long time and may be familiar, but if it's new to you give it a try. The format lends itself to creativity, artistic representation, and allows students to indicate positive things about themselves that they ordinarily would not have.

Reproduce the instructional shield as below on one side of a sheet of paper, and a blank shield on the obverse side. Pass out one sheet of paper to each student, then provide enough time so that some thought and creativity can produce a useful sharing tool.

Suggest using a pencil to create the sketches and symbolisms (allows erasing), then encourage emphasizing the verge lines and filling in the outlines with color.

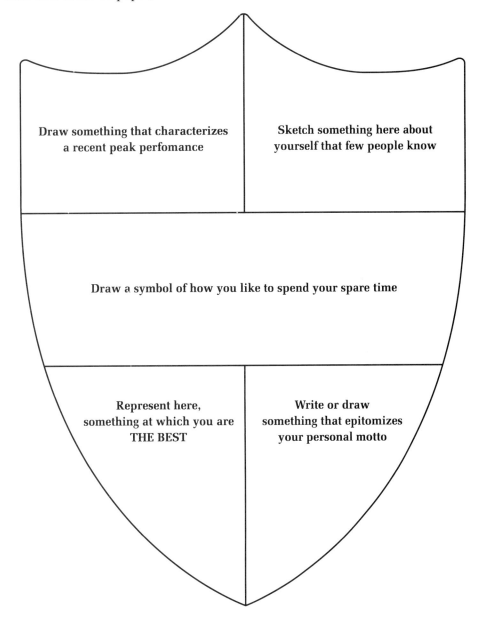

Draw something that characterizes a recent peak perfomance

Sketch something here about yourself that few people know

Draw a symbol of how you like to spend your spare time

Represent here, something at which you are THE BEST

Write or draw something that epitomizes your personal motto

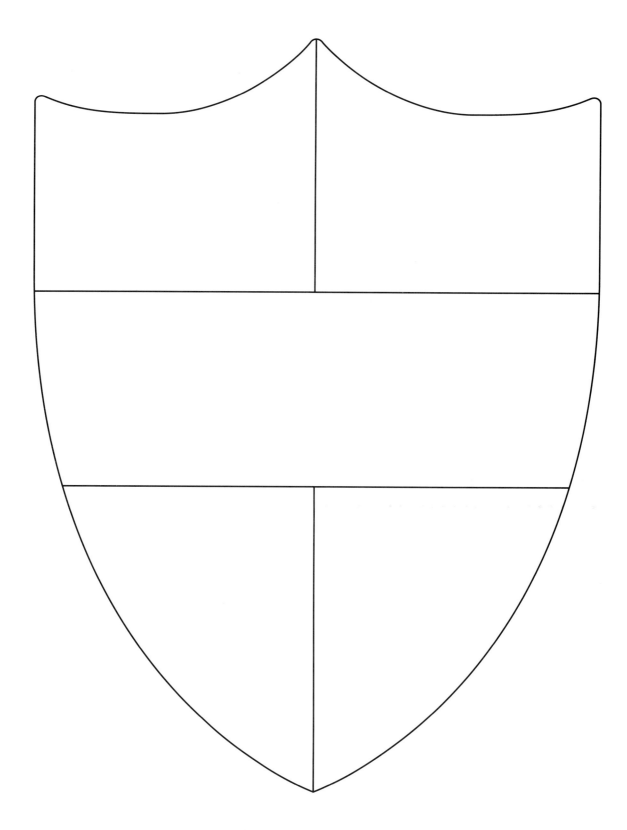

Goal Keeping

Finding new, innovative ways to motivate people is always a challenge.

• •

This idea crossed my desk at some point, and I dutifully recorded the concept because I liked it. Unfortunately, I neglected to remember where it came from. If it's yours, nice job.

There are so many challenges associated with an Adventure curriculum, especially with the low and high ropes course, that finding new, innovative ways to motivate people is always a challenge for us. Not everybody needs this extra push, but techniques like these are useful to know.

Play

At the start of a class or program day, designate a distance scale — for example, 6 inches = 10 miles on a map, or 1 lap = 1/4 inch on a map. Ask the group to attempt an element (*Tension Traverse*, *Wild Woosey*, *Trolleys*) and track how much physical distance they cover doing the event.

So — say Paula travels 16 feet on the *Tension Traverse*; Don goes 17 feet; Song and Lisa both go 14 feet. For the day, they traveled 61 feet. The conversion for the class was 1 foot = 1 inch on a map of the United States. The goal is to see how many trips on the *Tension Traverse* it takes for the group to cross the US by whatever route they map out.

Here's a fun way to track performance, develop positive competition (everyone supports each other), develop and practice recording and math skills, and to establish records and goals that the group can try to surpass in the future. Seems like a winner to me. Lots of good outcomes *and* you're keeping the students occupied with something fun.

For physical educators trying to integrate their curriculum with classroom subjects and vice versa, this is one example of how to create a multi-disciplinary lesson plan. For corporate trainers, this technique might help develop a bottom line to measure performance and determine how the team functioned.

Just remember you saw it here first, I think.

Headband Handle

Encourage role playing and some creative histrionics.

· ·

Thanks to Drew Kaptain of Project Pride in New Haven, CT for this idea.

Set-Up

Hand out headbands to equal half the group. Make the bands from paper, then just slap on a piece of adhesive tape near the back of the head where the ends join together. This doesn't have to be fancy or make a sartorial statement; just a ring of paper maybe 3 inches wide.

Before you tape on the bands, use a felt-tipped pen to print a stereotype on the front of the headband. Examples: Teacher, handsome male, nerd, class clown, leader, someone nice to be with, hoodlum, sexy female, music student, physically disadvantaged (blind, deaf, paraplegic), egg head, jock. Don't let the wearers know what has been printed on their headband.

Play

After the headbands are in place, ask the remainder of the group to mingle with the banded group and treat them as their stereotype indicates. Encourage role playing and some creative histrionics. It gives the group a feeling of walking a mile in another person's shoes.

Don't forget to switch roles and allow the stereotyped group to be the minglers. Make up different stereotypes for the next round. Also, and most importantly, take some time to discuss how both sides felt about representing a stereotype and how they were responded to.

Imaginary Toss

Clear your mind of purposeful, realistic thoughts. Okay, but sometimes I have trouble doing the opposite. *Opposite what?* Thoughts and stuff. *What?* See what I mean?

Think about throwing something really bizarre to another person in your circled or randomly diffused group. Imagine that you have that bizarre thing in your hands (don't worry about whether you can realistically hold or lift the object — we're fantasizing here). Now, histrionically mime how you would have to throw/pass that object to someone else; i.e., actually do it. As you make the pass, announce what it is that you are passing, to reinforce your very excellent job of miming, and also say the person's name whom you designate to receive your gift. The receiving person should also enter into this fantasy role-play by miming how he would physically receive your most

generous mass of mind matter, and also how he would probably emotionally react.

If you need any more instructions you are not in the right frame of mind; come back and read this again later.

Mental Imaging Debrief Topics

Melanie Gray (PA Trainer) sent me the write-ups for these two processing topics. She admitted having lifted the ideas from someone else, but couldn't remember who — join the crowd.

Freeze Frame

Ask the group to relax and perhaps close their eyes if the situation is appropriate (trust level high, appropriate venue, etc.). Ask them to imagine that they are putting a video tape from the day into the VCR, pressing the REWIND button and then PLAY. Encourage them to "see" the day as it plays by, acknowledging that they can press FF or REWIND at any time.

As the day's events stream past, ask the players to mentally press PAUSE at pictures or moments that seem significant or important to them. Ask them to remember those pictures as they continue watching the day play by.

After they are finished with the "tape," ask the group to mentally enlarge (at least 11"x14") one of the pictures, and encourage them to share with the group:

- A verbal representation of the mental picture; include colors, perspective, people, etc.

- With whom would they most easily share the picture?

- If the picture were developed and framed, where would they hang it?

Picture Postcard

Ask participants to mentally choose a picture of themselves from one of the significant experiences that occurred during the day and to transfer that picture onto a regulation-size postcard.

Turn the postcard over and, recognizing how little space is available for a message on a postcard, ask what playeers would write in the limited space and to whom would they send it?

Scoreboard or Score Bored

sb

Get tired of keeping score?

• •

Ever feel that students put so much emphasis on scoring that the fun of the game is lost? Ever think of ways to change that feeling? This idea may offer you a new way to score with a purpose.

Suppose for every point scored in a game of *Moonball*, the group actually earned 3.75 points? Suppose every time a team scores a point in *Striker*, they have to multiply the score by 2/5? Suppose in *Warp Speed* you have to divide your lowest time by seven? Are you get-

ting the idea? Kinda makes you *not* want to keep score, eh?

In any game or activity where a score, time, distance is kept, you can add an additional task by asking the group to track the score and then convert it using another number or fraction. It's a simple idea, but one that either adds challenge and fun to the activity, or makes scoring so onerous that "fun in functional" is all you need to know.

I think you'll enjoy the way this idea can lessen the importance of the score itself and create more of a focus on the process of achieving and understanding the *real* score. Along with *Goal Keeping* in this book, this idea is a way for educators to challenge students on multiple levels with the same activity and to integrate different aspects of problem solving and working together.

Remember, keep it fresh to keep yourself interested, and keep your pocket calculator handy.

Slam Dunk Suggestions

ker

At the end of a workshop day or before the beginning of an evening session that follows an active day, try this scribble-and-scrunch means of providing an anonymous format toward sharing insights and emotions experienced during the day.

Set a stack of blank sheets (all the same color) on a table, and also provide pens for those who don't have one. Ask the workshop participants to take a few sheets and to candidly share on paper something that occurred during the day that was either meaningful, or perhaps could have been improved. No one is to identify a response. Then scrunch up the pieces of paper and shoot/place them (your choice) into a midfloor receptacle (plastic milk carton, clean wastebasket).

Someone then volunteers to shake up the contents, remove a rumpled sheet and read aloud the wrinkly words. Some of the offered ideas and opinions will inevitably lead to discussions about interfacing and earlier occurrences that might have been difficult or inconvenient to bring up at the time. The idea behind this suggestion box format is to provide an anonymous and positive means of sharing sensitive ideas or feelings.

Caveat: If a reader immediately recognizes that a message is inappropriate or offensive, she can reach for another.

Don't use pencils to write the messages. Wrinkled pencil messages are almost indecipherable.

Story-Line Closure Technique

It's useful to have a closure technique on hand.

· ·

Here we are, at the end of a multi-day session, a one-day experience, or even a single activity with a few minutes left in which to gather, process and crystallize the experience(s) into a shared, coherent and meaningful finale. Well sure, I'm asking for a bit much, but if you go for the big banana, maybe a few slices of the right stuff will fall on your multi-grain cereal of life.

Overstated? Certainly! Fun to write? Absolutely! Nonetheless, practically and realistically it's useful to have a closure technique on hand for those times when it seems appropriate.

As the facilitator, begin a factual story (two or three sentences) that relates to what the group has just experienced. Indicate that as your story travels around the circle, that each person in turn should add a sentence or two that either outlines or clarifies something that has occurred. Keep the *Story-Line* going and centered on the shared experience; don't start with *The Mohawk Walk* and end up with which regional pro team is headed for the championships.

Try to establish a *Story-Line* that is ostensibly headed for inclusion in the evening newspaper. Emphasize the facts and remember there is a deadline for publication: Don't let someone start talking and get on a verbal roll. That type of talk is fine for another debrief session, but keep this verbal diorama moving with concise, succinct ideas and sentences.

In keeping with the *Challenge By Choice* credo, allow players at any time to waive their turn. *Waive* does not mean cancel, however, meaning each student should recognize that invoking the CBC deferment does not excuse him from future and continued involvement (physically and emotionally) with the group.

Sundowner

"I had a great time today, but what did we do?"

. . . .

At the end of a workshop , it is predictably beneficial to offer some type of recapping scenario in order to highlight the most significant learning aspects of a very busy and fact-filled day. Either at the end of the afternoon session or at the beginning of an evening session, ask the group to split up into smaller grouplets of participants, super-saturated with new knowledge to share. Their task is to identify those topics experienced during the day that are most important on a need-to-know basis, and then to come up with some mnemonic to help remember the most salient facts.

Each troika or quad, after working together for 20–30 minutes, should reconvene as a large group once again to report and compare what topics they have chosen for scrutiny.

Offering this simple exercise emphasizes the need to occasionally summarize and prioritize what, during an active day, quickly becomes a flood of facts.

"I had a great time today, but what did we do?" "Well, ...first we played *Moon Ball*, and then ...Golly, I can't remember either, but it was fun!"

Foes & Questors

Foes & Questors

A game primarily for older kids.

• •

Foes & Questors (*F&Q*) is a game; an indoor/outdoor, run-around, get-tired, have-fun, sneaky, strategy-filled game with enough rules to confuse and satisfy the most addicted gameophile.

Steve and I developed this fantasy game over twelve years ago, primarily as a means of offering a new gaming situation for *Project Adventure* workshop participants. We were also somewhat selfishly trying to create a rule-heavy activity that adults would enjoy playing and re-playing.

Experience indicates that simple activities are the most usable and most readily accepted by the players in a school curriculum or recreation program, but we aimed to create a highly physical, thinking/strategy game that was primarily for older kids (like us). There was nothing extant to our knowledge, either in books or spoken cultural resources, that provided what we wanted. The on-going complaint amongst our game-playing peers concerned the dearth of physical participation games that are playable for more than five minutes without becoming boring or exhausting.

Steve and I initially inflicted prototype *F&Q* games on unsuspecting participants in PA/NG (Project Adventure/New Games) workshops, and it was their comments and shared reactions, coupled with many hours of brainstorming between the two of us that resulted in the following write-up. Since then, *F&Q* has been expanded considerably to include many different characters and weirdly compelling scenarios. It's true, however, that the basic Ord/Bold/Mage/Omni game is still viable and continues to be the favorite of many players.

The magic of *Foes & Questors* seems to be that adults or youngsters can give themselves up temporarily to their chosen character, briefly living and functioning in a fantasy world that's not encouraged in a pragmatic win-or-what's-the-use society. Considering that, it shouldn't surprise you that *F&Q* is not for everyone.

Some individuals are very control or competition oriented, and an excursion into such an obviously fabricated world (albeit briefly) is a considerable threat to the reality that establishes their security and sense of self. Also, even though *F&Q* is basically a win/lose scenario, the competition is so diffuse and fraught with humor that winning/losing is simply a means of grabbing a breather before the next game begins.

When Steve and I were establishing the playing parameters for *F&Q*, one of the things that we both initially agreed upon was that this was to be a game primarily for older kids; like older than 18. We have occasionally encouraged parents to bring their children with them to play, and for most child/parent combinations the experience has been a good one. But a few very young and/or highly imaginative youngsters have had trouble discerning between reality and fantasy to the extent that some of the game characters have been frightening. The sight of a large adult, brandishing a foam sword and cardboard shield, too easily in the mind of a child crosses over from make-believe to terror. A caveat: Game action, although obviously fabricated, can pose a threat to younger children. Don't expect everyone to like the game just because you do, and if young children are

going to play, tone down the combative situations or warn parents of possible negative situations (nightmares, not trusting adults).

Play

Foes & Questors is basically a combination of Capture the Flag, various tag games, Cowboys and Indians, and Dungeons & Dragons. The format is active, playfully confrontive and given to numerous on-going strategy decisions. Typical games, depending upon the playing venue, take from 15 minutes to over an hour to complete. During this time there is considerable aerobic activity taking place; i.e., running like crazy. Although there have been a couple characters developed over the years for incapacitated or out-of-shape players, most of the game-time is spent in confrontations, sneaking around or running.

No character/player is ever eliminated from a game, suffering only occasional periods of cryogenic suspension (penalty time of one–three minutes spent frozen in position). These down-time penalties, received as the result of coming out on the short end of a confrontation with a swifter, sneaker, luckier, or better armed opponent, allow a breather, a respite for seemingly undaunted combat-oriented players who are actually week-end warriors in serious oxygen debt, and desperately seeking a penalty.

The name of the game, *Foes & Questors*, was chosen primarily because it's fun to say, and upon hearing it the response of a listener is invariably, "What?" which allows the opportunity for further and more detailed confusion. There is not one team of *Foes* and another team of *Questors*. Everyone at some time during a game is either one or the other, depending upon the assumed role at a particular juncture.

After reading through the seemingly endless rules and character definitions, you can't help wondering, "How will I ever be able to remember what character I'm representing or what I'm supposed to do?" True, there are a lot of rules, but you'll find that the detail and colorful panoply soon make the game more enjoyable. Almost everyone who sits through the verbalized rules for the first time suffers a bit of pre-game panic, wondering if they will be able to remember enough to participate without embarrassment.

A hint from one of the game developers who still doesn't have the rules straight: Take on the role of an ORD (the simplest and least powerful character), then follow someone who has played the game before. If a confrontation is imminent, observe, react and let the consequences fall where they may. The worst that can happen is incurring a three-minute time penalty (rest time). Don't worry about the rules, just run around, throw something occasionally, and enjoy the work out.

To win a game, a team must find two of three *hidden objects* and transport them to a defined area. The found objects are joined with a smaller object to establish a whole talisman. The first team to accomplish this task is the winner. Now that wasn't so bad, was it?

The area where you play can be varied to the extreme. Over the years we have quested in the woods, within a beach dune area, in a combination field/woods/building, and entirely within a building structure — all well received venues by the players.

Set-Up

Before I launch into the details of the game, here's a basic how-do-I-play *F&Q* outline to refer to when the rules get in the way of your enjoyment.

- Divide your group into two teams. There's no way around it folks, this is a competitive game. Notice I didn't say, "…split your team into two disparate groups."

- Divvy up the playing paraphernalia. Plan to spend more time doing this than you think is necessary. New players need this time to assimilate the rules and ask unending questions about their personal roles as part of the upcoming action.

- If this is your first time leading or playing *Foes & Questors*, stick with the basic Ord-Bold-Mage-Omni game; i.e., keep the characters and rules to a minimum. You can have a dandy game utilizing only these four basic characters and 10–12 players.

- Assign two players from each team to hide the COSMIC DOUGHNUTS within the playing area that each team now occupies.

Remember that players should "hide" the CD's so that they can be eventually found. No CD's = No Action.

- Each team's DNA rope is placed somewhere within their playing area occupied at the beginning of the game. Place the circular rope where it can be easily defended; don't hide it.

- Answer all questions with an authoritative flair. If the first-time players think you don't know what's going on, all's lost. I've found that, "Yes!" is a functional response to almost any question concerning the rules.

- Encourage talk about strategy and individual roles as they pertain to "winning," then, at the start, watch everyone run around willy-nilly, shouting, questing, completely befuddled by the rules, having a grand time.

- Ready? GO! Look for the CD's; don't get frozen; keep running; put the CD's in the DNA; throw things at people, yell a lot; find your Mage so that the CD's can be united with the Holistics. Done! You win! Do it again.

Now, on to the…

Details

The hidden objects that ultimately determine who wins the game are called **COSMIC DOUGHNUTS (CD's).** [From here-on in the text, *CHARACTERS* will be italicized and **GAME IMPLEMENTS** will be bolded.] In the past we have used round-shaped, cut-out sections of ensolite material for the **CD's**. The cut-out center piece of the "doughnut" is called the **HOLISTIC**. A colorful design is drawn on the **CD** with the **HOLISTIC** in place, so that when the two are separated they need to be reoriented exactly as they were to complete the pattern. In fact, this juxtaposing of design components must occur or the **CD** does not become a power object and the game cannot be finalized (won).

We have recently tried using a rubber deck tennis ring as the **CD**. A deflated balloon represents the **HOLISTIC**, which must be inflated and tied off inside the rubber ring to complete the power package. This inflation/insertion scenario usually takes place while opposing players are attempting to keep it from happening. Truly a confrontation to remember.

At the beginning, the teams separate so that there is an equal number of players on each side. For the sake of those who have never played, try to evenly distribute the veterans.

- Each team decides who on the team is going to take-on each character role.

- All the implements of play are equally divided between the two teams.

- Each team sends two players out into their half of the field-of-play to hide the three **CDs** belonging to the other team, making sure to remove the **HOLISTICS** first. The hiders must remember that the attached, two-foot long length of nylon webbing (color-coded to a particular team) must remain visible. The doughnut portion may be entirely hidden, but the webbing must remain visible. A hidden **CD** may not be placed more than 10 feet above the ground.

- Teams establish where their DNA (Doughnut Area) is to be located, then place the **HOLISTICS** inside this outlined area. The DNA is outlined with a 30'-long length of color-coded rope.

After these preparations are completed, the two teams head for their respective starting positions, which for each team should be in a field position that allows each team to openly view one another, and be about 200–400 meters apart. As the two teams stand looking at one another, one group, in a blatantly combative gesture, raises their arms and weapons overhead, an obvious invitation for the other team to do the same. As each team, amidst whoops and hollers, brandishes their game paraphernalia, players are free to begin running and instituting whatever strategy seems best for their team and themselves. Scenes from *Lawrence of Arabia* best describe this initial shouting, rushing charge.

The game continues without pause until a team places two of their **CDs** into their own **DNA**, so that the *MAGE* can put the **CDs** and **HOLISTICS** together. When this happens, that particular game is over and the winning team gets to blow their own horn as means of celebration (if no horn or bugle is available, jolly shouts of Huzzah!! will suffice) and to reassemble all the scattered players. Begin another game after everyone has had a chance to get together and share some of the inevitable vignettes that colorfully pepper each contest. Then, it's just a matter of redistributing the game paraphernalia, re-hiding the CDs, switching characters (if so desired), adding or subtracting rules, and charging at each other once again.

Knowing the above gives you a glimpse of the barest outline of *Foes & Questors*. To play effectively you will need to know each character, their powers, limitations, and some game vocabulary. Let's get into it...

Power Objects and Characters

(In Alphabetical Order)

▦ BAG OF TRICKS (one per team)

Carried by the *MAGE*, this bag (hip pack) contains several power objects, including the *MAGE*'s **SPELLS**, the **THUNDERBOLT**, the **GOGGLES OF RA**, and the equipment necessary to invoke the *DESPERADO*. The **BAG OF TRICKS** cannot be taken from the *MAGE*, nor can it be picked up off the ground by another character.

▦ BAUBLES OF BANGOR — BOBs (three to five per team)

These are small (smaller than the **CDs**) rubber rings with team color-coded lengths of webbing attached.

- **BOBs** are hidden in much the same way as are the **CDs**, and in the same areas.

- For a team to win, a predetermined number of **BOBs** must be in the **DNA** before the **HOLISTIC** and **CD** can be put together. The larger the teams, the more **BOBs** should be used.

- When found, **BOBs** must be carried in an exposed manner, and whoever first picks up a **BOB** must carry that **BOB** until it is deposited in the **DNA** or until it has been lost in a questing situation.

- If someone takes a **BOB** from someone else as the result of a freezing, that person must keep and carry the **BOB** in obvious sight until the **BOB** has been deposited in the **DNA** or is taken by a subsequent freezing confrontation.

● BOLD (one of more per team)

This character carries the **STINGO SWORD** and two **LUMBARS**. *BOLDs* have a choice of carrying a **SHIELD**. A *BOLD's* power level is one step above an *ORD*.

- If a *BOLD* hits an *ORD* or another *BOLD* below the waist with the **STINGO SWORD**, the struck character looses control of her legs. This loss-of-legs penalty continues until a *MAGE* can touch the afflicted person with the **SPELLBINDER**.

- Fittingly, if a *BOLD* hits an *ORD*, or another *BOLD*, above the waist, the fairly struck character looses control of his arms. The **SPELLBINDER** also relieves this penalty.

- A *BOLD* is susceptible to a **LUMBAR** hit from any character. *BOLDS* are also susceptible to all weapons (and penalties) wielded by characters above the *BOLD's* station.

- A *BOLD's* sword cannot be taken away, unless the *BOLD* drops the sword. Only a *BOLD* can activate the power of the sword for use in combat.

▦ COSMIC DOUGHNUT

This circular object is the source of ultimate power in the game. The make-up and hiding of **CDs** has been previously discussed in the text.

- **CDs** must be carried in plain sight whenever they are moved after the game starts.

- **CDs** can be taken away from a player by freezing that player. Players who take a **CD** away from another player *must keep that* **CD** *in their possession* until it has either: 1) been deposited in the proper **DNA** or, 2) has been taken away by another character

- After a **CD** has been deposited in a team's **DNA**, no one may remove that **CD**.

■ DNA (Doughnut Area)

A vaguely circular area marked off by a 30' length of colored rope. Each team places their **DNA** wherever they think it can best be defended. It is not important to hide the **DNA's** location from the other team.

- **HOLISTICS** start and stay inside the **DNA**.

- Once a **CD** or **BOB** is placed in a team's **DNA**, no one may remove those objects.

● DESPERADO (one player per team — temporary)

This truly awesome character is an *ORD* who has been transformed by his or her *MAGE* into the ultimate power player. Wearing the *DESPERADO* head-band and wielding the specially marked *DESPERADO* **PRO-TON** (both from the *MAGE's* **BAG OF TRICKS**), this invincible warrior is established to defeat all players in the game. (A *DESPERADO's* competition comes only from the *DESPERADO* of the other team). If you see the *DESPERADO* coming, the only thing to do is run.

- A *DESPERADO'S* power lasts for only 5 minutes, and can be invoked only once.

- The *DESPERADO* must wear the distinctive head-band that designates the *DESPERADO'S* awesome status.

- Only an *ORD* can become a *DESPERADO*.

- Time penalty when caught by a *DESPERADO* — 1 frozen minute

■ DRAGON'S FIRE (one per team)

Carried by the *SORCERER*, this large mirror (6" x 6" or larger) freezes players by reflecting sunlight into their eyes — called "the retinal blast." When targeted players recognize that they have been hit (there's no doubt) they should fall dramatically to the ground, indicating that they have been consumed by the fire.

- Time penalty — 2 frozen minutes

● ECRU — [optional]
(Only one character per game — no team affiliation)

The embodiment of all evil, *ECRU* does everything possible to disrupt the winning efforts of both teams.

- *ECRU* has only one special power object, but can steal anything and everything from any player *ECRU* can touch (but only one object per encounter). *ECRU* carries a special power object — a distinctive **LUMBAR** — that is effective only against *VERMILION*.

- *ECRU* cannot be harmed by anyone except *VERMILION* and the *DESPERADO*.

- *ECRU* cannot touch or harass anyone who has a **CD** in his or her possession.

■ GOGGLES OF RA (one set per team)

A player wearing these goggles is immune to the power of both the **THUNDERBOLT** and **DRAGON'S FIRE**.

- The **GOGGLES OF RA** are kept in the *MAGE's* **BAG OF TRICKS** at the start of the game, and can only be obtained by an opposing team by freezing the *MAGE* and demanding the **GOGGLES**. (Use a set of industrial safety goggles.)

- If a player is frozen while wearing the **GOGGLES OF RA**, those Goggles may be taken and used only by the player who accomplished the freezing.

HOLISTIC (One for each Cosmic Doughnut)

A **HOLISTIC** represents the center portion of the **CD**. The joining of the **CD** and the **HOLISTIC** within the **DNA** is one of the necessary final steps toward winning the game.

- If a circle of ensolite is used as a **CD**, the **HOLISTIC** and associated **CD** must be put together so that a colorful pattern or illustration is completed.

- If a **CD** is represented by a rubber deck tennis ring, the **HOLISTIC** should be a deflated balloon of the same color.

HOT TICKET (one per team)

This sturdy pocket-sized card is suitably marked **HOT** to indicate its power as a healing object.

- If this card is given to any frozen player by a teammate, that player is healed and may continue questing, but may not use the **HOT TICKET** again for at least one minute.

- The **HOT TICKET** *cannot* cure a **SPELL**.

- The **HOT TICKET** can be carried by any player, can be transferred freely to other teammates, but cannot be stolen by someone on the other team. If *ECRU* wants it, *ECRU* gets it.

- A player carrying the **HOT TICKET** cannot heal herself. Frozen players cannot transfer the **HOT TICKET** until their penalty is served.

THE (BLACK) HYDRA (one per team)

Usually made up from several pieces of black foam material twisted together, this power object is one of only three weapons that is capable of freezing an *OMNI*. Try to fabricate an object that does not have great accuracy or throwing range. The **BLACK HYDRA** should be thought of as an up-close-and-personal weapon.

- The **HYDRA** will also freeze any other regular player, except the *DESPERADO* and *ECRU*. The **HYDRA** *must be thrown* to be effective.

- If the **HYDRA** is thrown and ends up on the ground, it can be picked up by anyone and immediately used.

- Time penalty when struck by the **HYDRA** — 3 frozen minutes

LUMBAR (two per ORD, one per BOLD)

A **LUMBAR** is the classic weapon of the lowly *ORD*, F&Q's "foot soldiers." In the past, small, color-coded ensolite foam discs were used as **LUMBARS**. More recently fleece balls have been successfully used — your choice.

- An *ORD* can freeze a *BOLD* with a **LUMBAR** and vice versa, but all other players are not affected by this low velocity weapon.

- **LUMBARS** can be picked up and used by any player, but they cannot be taken away from a player.

- Time penalty — 2 frozen minutes.

MAGE (one player per team)

These most important characters wield the most magical forces in the game and must be in control of their full power in order for their team to win.

- *MAGE*s are the only players who can assemble the **CD** and **HOLISTIC** together, and only if they have the **SPELLBINDER** in their possession.

- The *MAGE* carries the **BAG OF TRICKS** and is the only player who can give a **SPELL**. This is done by hitting another player with the **SPELLBINDER** (it must be thrown) and verbally telling that person what the **SPELL** entails. As a result of the **SPELLBINDER** hit, the *MAGE* can either freeze that person for 2 minutes or cast a **SPELL**; however, not the two concurrently.

MAGE (continued)

- The *MAGE* begins the game carrying the **MORTAR**.

- The *MAGE* is the only person who can heal a **SPELL**, and is also the only person who can pick up a **SPELLBINDER**. If a *MAGE* throws his **SPELLBINDER**, it cannot be picked up by anyone (even *ECRU*), but can be kicked by any player.

- The *MAGE* is vulnerable to **BLACK HYDRAs**, **MORTARs** and the *OMNI's* **QUARKS**. *MAGEs* are invulnerable to one another.

▨ MORTAR (one per team)

The **MORTAR** is a thrown weapon made up of a tennis ball in the end of a woman's knee-high sock (a Comet Ball).

- The **MORTAR** must be thrown with a spin and release, no baseball-type throws.

- The **MORTAR** must reach an apogee of at least ten feet to be activated and, to be effective, must hit the ground within ten feet of another player(s).

- If the **MORTAR** hits within ten feet of the thrower, the thrower is also affected by the freeze penalty.

- All players are affected except the *DESPERADO* and *ECRU*.

- Time Penalty — 2 frozen minutes

▨ OM — Object of Movement (one per team)

This healing orb — a tennis ball marked two red crosses — can be used to rejuvenate a frozen teammate from a distance.

- The **OM** must be thrown for it to be effective. It cannot be simply handed to an afflicted player.

- If the **OM** is caught, the frozen player is released from the remainder of their penalty. If the **OM** is missed, the *thrower* also must sit out the remainder of the penalty with the person who made the bad catch. The **OM** (in hand or on the ground) is useless until they are both free.

- The **OM** cannot be taken by the other team. If *ECRU* wants it, *ECRU* gets it.

● OMNI (one player per team)

Wielding two **QUARKS**, the *OMNI* has more fire power than any other regular character.

- So long as the *OMNI* has possession of a least one **QUARK**, an *OMNI* can be frozen by *only* another **QUARK** (used only by the opposing *OMNI*), a **BLACK HYDRA**, or a **MORTAR**. An *OMNI* who looses *both* **QUARKS** is vulnerable to everything, even **LUMBARS.**

- With both **QUARKS** in possession, an *OMNI* may heal frozen players by touching them with both **QUARKS** simultaneously.

- *OMNIs* are not affected by a *MAGE's* power objects.

- Time penalty for a **QUARK** hit — 2 frozen minutes

● ORD (as many per team as desired)

Carrying **LUMBARS** and a **SHIELD**, the *ORD* may not have much power, but strength stems from the masses, and that's what the *ORD* represents — cannon-fodder. Most Questors recognize the uncomplicated role of the *ORD* and pursue it as an escape from the trappings of power and indispensability.

- An *ORD* is the only player who can become a *DESPERADO*. (Yes, even in real fantasy life, the lowest may rise to the pinnacles of power, if only for a brief moment.)

- *ORDs* are vulnerable to everything, and their **LUMBAR** weapons will only vanquish another *ORD* and the *BOLD* character.

▦ POT — Power of Touch

Used primarily by the *THIEF* and *ECRU*.

- Having **POT** means that either of these characters must tag (one hand below the neck) another player in order to acquire that character's power objects.
- Tagging to freeze an opponent may be used by *any* player unfortunate enough to have lost all their power objects. For example, *OMNI* may use **POT** if both QUARKS are lost.

▦ PRO-TON (one per DESPERADO)

A distinctive and brightly colored softish ball used as the ultimate weapon by the *DESPERADO*.

- The **PRO-TON** cannot be picked up or used by any other player.
- Time Penalty — 1 frozen minute

▦ QUARK (two per team)

Carried by the *OMNI*, **QUARKs** (flexible Frisbees) provide their carriers with duo power.

- With two **QUARKs** in hand, the *OMNI* can unfreeze a teammate by touching the afflicted player with the **QUARKS**.
- With one **QUARK** in hand an *OMNI* is still invulnerable to all weapons save the **BLACK HYDRA**, the other *OMNI*'s **QUARKS**, and the *DESPERADO*.
- Although any player may pick up a thrown **QUARK**, only the *OMNI* who is color coded to that **QUARK** may use it.
- An *OMNI* can simply touch a frozen teammate with a **QUARK** to be effective, but the **QUARK** must be *thrown* in order to freeze someone.
- Time Penalty — 2 frozen minutes.

▦ SHIELD (one per ORD; optional for a BOLD)

Shields are cardboard circles approximately 12" in diameter (small pizza size), and have an elasticized strap glued to the back.

- Shields are used as **LUMBAR** deflectors, but can also deflect any other thrown object, except the *DESPERADO*'s special weapon.
- Encourage players to make and decorate their own **SHIELDs**.

● SORCERER (one per team)

This character wields the **DRAGON'S FIRE**, thus controlling large portions of the playing area by choosing a strategic point from which to operate.

- The *SORCERER* is vulnerable to all power objects *except* sunlight reflected from the other *SORCERER*.

● SPELLBINDER (one per team)

This power object (large nerf-type ball) grants the *MAGEs* all their magical abilities.

- A *MAGE* must have a **SPELLBINDER** in his possession to be able to join the **HOLISTIC** and a **COSMIC DOUGHNUT**; i.e., win the game.
- If thrown, the **SPELLBINDER** can either freeze (2 minutes) a player or allow the *MAGE* to cast a **SPELL** on that player, (*MAGE*'s choice).

SPELLBINDER (continued)

- *MAGEs* can remove a **SPELL** from one of their own players by touching that afflicted player with the **SPELLBINDER**.

- The **SPELLBINDER** cannot be picked up by any player, including the *DESPERADO*, but may be kicked away by any player.

▦ SPELLS (an equal number per team)

SPELL cards are carried by the *MAGE* in the **BAG OF TRICKS**.

- **SPELLS** are handed out by the *MAGE* after a thrown hit with the **SPELLBINDER**.

- Some **SPELLS** are permanent (entire game) and some are temporary, (can be healed by the **SPELLBINDER**) — your choice.

- **SPELL** examples:

    1) **ICE CREAM, SPELL** — Afflicted players must scream every word they want to communicate.

    2) **I LOVE YOU, SPELL** — The afflicted player must seek out the first teammate they see, grab them by the arm and say **I LOVE YOU**. Those two bonded players must then seek another teammate, etc., etc.

    3) **SAY IT AIN'T SO, SPELL** — Under this **SPELL**, if a player wants to communicate, they must say the opposite of what they actually mean.

▦ STINGO SWORD (one per BOLD, per team)

STINGOs (ethafoam swords) have a magical, anatomy-specific power. A fair hit suspends either top or bottom movement of a person rather than just freezing the entire organism.

- If a *BOLD* strikes a player above the waist with a **STINGO SWORD**, that player loses the use of her arms until healed by either an *OMNI*, or with an **OM**.

- If a *BOLD* strikes a player below the waist, that player loses the use of his legs until healed as above.

- A **STINGO SWORD** cannot be taken from a *BOLD* unless that player is so unlucky as to drop his sword.

● THIEF (one or two per team)

This player is apt to produce more arguments and confusion than any other character, but what can you expect from a player with a license to steal?

- A *THIEF* begins the game with no power objects, and is vulnerable to all weapons.

- A *THIEF* uses **POT** to immobilize players for one minute, and is allowed to take one power object from the frozen player.

- A *THIEF* may use any power object that they are able to steal, notwithstanding team color coding.

- A *THIEF* must either keep all stolen objects in their possession, or give them to another player. Power objects cannot be abandoned or hidden.

- The following power objects cannot be stolen: **QUARKS, SPELLBINDERS, BAG OF TRICKS, SPELLS, HOT TICKET** and **TNT**.

▦ TNT — Tell No Truth (one per team)

A wallet size card with the letters **TNT** emblazoned on it.

- Players who have this card in their possession are entitled to lie to everyone, even if the other player is using the **TRUTH ORB**.

TNT — Tell No Truth (continued)

- The card does not have to be revealed, nor can it be searched for.
- The **TNT** card may be passed back and forth from teammate to teammate, but cannot be taken or used by the opposition.

▦ THUNDERBOLT (one per team)

Similar to the **DRAGON's FIRE** (mirror), but smaller in size; like a pocket mirror. Carried by the *MAGE*.

- The **THUNDERBOLT** freezes players by reflecting light from the sun onto their retina.
- Players who experience the "retinal flash" must fall dramatically to the ground.
- Freeze time — 2 minutes

▦ TRUTH ORB (one per team)

A mystical shaped object that can be worn on a cord around the neck. The **TRUTH ORB** causes people in its presence to truthfully answer any question posed by a member of the opposition wearing it.

- Wearing the **TRUTH ORB** allows a player, after freezing another player in a regulation way, to ask that frozen player *one* question, which must be answered correctly and distinctly.
- Only the player who is responsible for the freezing throw may ask the question, and that person must be wearing the **ORB** when the freezing takes place.
- Any player may take the **TRUTH ORB** from another player, if they were the one responsible for the freezing throw. A hit from a **STINGO SWORD** does not allow taking the **ORB**.
- When not in use, the **TRUTH ORB** may be hidden under clothing. The **ORB** must be exposed when used.

● VERMILLION
(one per game, no team affiliation at the beginning)

VERMILLION is the arch-rival of *ECRU*.

- *VERMILLION*'s vital function is to control *ECRU*'s depredations, and eliminate her from the action whenever possible.
- In addition to foiling *ECRU*'s plots, *VERMILLION* is a wish-washy caped crusader for good, who tries to help the underdog in every situation. However, whenever *VERMILLION* is frozen by a player, her loyalty immediately switches to that player's team.
- *VERMILLION* carries four **LUMBARS**, and a specially marked **LUMBAR** for combat situations with *ECRU*. *VERMILLION* shouts, "Huzzah!" and, "Well Done Lads!" more times than you want to hear.

▦ WIZBAR (one per team)

A special **LUMBAR** (black) that may be used by any player to freeze a *MAGE*. **WIZBARs** are not effective against any other player.

- Freeze time — 2 minutes

A Few Miscellaneous Considerations

- A player may *not* suffer two penalties at the same time. This is called, no double jeopardy.
- A player from one team may not stand near a frozen player of the other team, waiting for their penalty to expire, with the intention of freezing them again.

- Frozen time is generally estimated. This level of fairness and proper play is entirely up to the conscience of the players.
- Before the game starts, outline the boundaries of play. Eliminate those areas that might cause danger to an enthusiastic player — steep drop-offs, wire fences, rocky fields, etc.
- If there is an abundance of novice players, having a non-playing referee on the field of play during the first game helps considerably.

If you have any questions about *Foes & Questors*, the answer is, "Yes!"

KER — 1/24/94

Project Adventure Services and Publications

Services

Project Adventure, Inc. is a national, non-profit corporation dedicated to helping schools, agencies, and others implement Project Adventure programs. Toward that end, the following services are available:

Project Adventure Workshops. Through a network of national certified trainers, Project Adventure conducts workshops for teachers, counselors, youth workers and other professionals who work with people. These workshops are given in various sections of the country. Separate workshops are given in Challenge Ropes Course Skills, Counseling Skills for Adventure Based Programs, Project Adventure Games and Initiatives, and Interdisciplinary Academic Curriculum.

Challenge Course Design and Installation. Project Adventure has been designing and installing ropes courses (a series of individual and group challenge elements situated indoors in a gymnasium or outdoors in a grove of trees) for over 15 years. PA Staff can travel to your site and design/install a course appropriate for your needs and budget.

Challenge Ropes Course Source Book. A catalog service of hard-to-find materials and tools used in the installation of Challenge Ropes Courses. This catalog also contains climbing rope and a variety of items useful to adventure programs.

Executive Reach. Management workshops for business and professional persons. These workshops are designed for increasing efficiency of team members in the workplace. The trust, communication, and risk-taking ability learned in the executive programs trans-late into a more cohesive and productive team at work.

Program Accreditation. The Accreditation process is an outside review of a program by PA staff. Programs that undertake the accreditation process are seeking outside evaluation with regard to quality and safety. The term accreditation means "formal written confirmation." Programs seeking confirmation are looking to ensure that they are within the current standards of safety and risk management. This assurance may be useful for making changes in program equipment and/or design, and in providing information on program quality to third parties such as administrators, insurance companies and the public.

Publications

If you would like to obtain additional copies of this book, an order form is provided on the next page. Project Adventure also publishes many books and pamphlets in related areas. Described below are some of our best sellers, which can be ordered on the same form. Call or write to Project Adventure for a complete publications list.

Cowstails and Cobras II — Karl Rohnke's classic guide to games, Initiative problems and Adventure activities. Offering a thorough treatment of Project Adventure's philosophy and approach to group activities, *Cowstails II* provides both the experienced practitioner and the novice with a unique and valuable resource.

Silver Bullets — More Initiative problems, Adventure games and trust activities from Karl Rohnke: 165 great games and activities that require few, if any, props. Use this as a companion to *Cowstails and Cobras II* or a stand alone guide to invigorate your program.

Youth Leadership In Action — All too often young people have little access to the resources necessary to improve their skills and develop their leadership potential. *Youth Leadership In Action* addresses this need by providing a guide for youth leaders to implement experiential, cooperative activities and techniques into their programs.

But the most striking and unique feature of this book is that it was written by a group of youth leaders. This group of eight leaders have taken 54 of Project Adventure's most popular Adventure games and activities and rewritten the instructions and rules in the way *they* present and play them. They also give a brief history of Project Adventure, present their own definition of Adventure, and explain some of PA's basic concepts and techniques — Full Value Contract, Challenge By Choice, debriefing, sequencing, etc. They also provide a section on effective leadership and how to start several types of programs.

By combining the magic of Project Adventure activities with the power of young people leading them, *Youth Leadership In Action* provides youth leaders with a valuable tool to help their programs get even better and to *Bring the Adventure Home!*

Islands Of Healing: A Guide to Adventure Based Counseling — Long a standard in the field, *Islands* presents a comprehensive discussion of this rapidly growing counseling approach. Started in 1974, ABC is an innovative, community-based, group counseling model that uses cooperative games, Initiative problem solving, low and high Challenge Ropes Course elements, and other Adventure activities. The book contains extensive "how-to" information on group selection, training, goal setting, sequencing, and leading and debriefing activities. Also included are explorations of model ABC programs at several representative sites — junior and senior high schools, a psychiatric hospital, and court referred programs.

Please send information on the following programs:

❑ Project Adventure Training Workshops
❑ Challenge Course Design & Installation
❑ Ropes Course Equipment Catalog
❑ Executive Reach Programs
❑ Publications List
❑ Program Accreditation
❑ Please add my name to your mailing list

Qty	Title	Price	Total
	QuickSilver	$23.50	
	Cowstails and Cobras II	$18.50	
	Silver Bullets	$18.50	
	Youth Leadership	$10.00	
	Islands of Healing	$20.50	

Subtotal _____

5% tax (Mass. residents only) _____

Shipping (instructions below) _____

Shipping instructions:
Orders up to $25.00 — add $4.00
$25.01 — $60.00 add $6.00
Over $60.00 add 10% of total
(AK, HI, Canada & overseas, add additional $5.00)

Ship To:

Name _____

Street _____

City _____ State _____ Zip _____

Phone (_____) _____

Payment:
❑ Check enclosed ❑ Purchase Order
(For institutions only, over $25.00.)

Charge to: ❑ MasterCard ❑ Visa

Card # _____ Exp. Date _____

Signature _____
(signature required for all credit cards)

Copy or detach this form and return to:

Project Adventure, Inc.
P.O. Box 100
Hamilton, MA 01936
508/468-7981 FAX 580/468-7605
or
P.O. Box 2447
Covington, GA 30209
770/784-9310 FAX 770/787-7764